Panzer Destroyer
Memoirs of a Red Army Tank Commander

Vasiliy Krysov

Translated by
Vladimir Kroupnik

Edited by
Stuart Britton

Pen & Sword
MILITARY

Publication made possible by 'I Remember' (www.iremember.ru) and its director Artem Drabkin

First published in Great Britain in 2010 and reprinted in this format in 2018, 2019, 2020 and 2021 by
Pen & Sword Military
an imprint of
Pen & Sword Books Ltd
47 Church Street
Barnsley
South Yorkshire
S70 2AS

ISBN 978 1 52674 848 5

Typeset in 11/13 Ehrhardt by Concept, Huddersfield, West Yorkshire

Printed and bound in the UK by CPI Group (UK) Ltd, Croydon, CR0 4YY

Pen & Sword Books Ltd incorporates the imprints of Pen & Sword Aviation, Pen & Sword Maritime, Pen & Sword Military, Wharncliffe Local History, Pen & Sword Select, Pen & Sword Military Classics and Leo Cooper, Remember When, Seaforth Publishing and Frontline Publishing.

For a complete list of Pen & Sword titles please contact
PEN & SWORD BOOKS LIMITED
47 Church Street, Barnsley, South Yorkshire, S70 2AS, England
E-mail: enquiries@pen-and-sword.co.uk
Website: www.pen-and-sword.co.uk

Contents

List of Illustrations and Maps

Illustrations

Vasiliy Krysov as a cadet at the Chelyabinsk Tank School in 1941.

Gunner Sergeant Major Mikhail Filippov and loader Sergeant Aleksandr Shadrin.

Major Sergey Fetisov.

A 45-tonne KV-1 heavy tank advances, followed by infantry.

Left to right: unknown, Porshnev, unknown, Polivoda.

Loading shells for the 76mm gun of the KV-1.

Commanders of the 1454th Self-propelled Artillery Regiment, 1944.

Officers of the 1454th Self-propelled Artillery Regiment.

A 30-tonne SU-122 self-propelled howitzer moving forward at speed.

Sergeant Viktor Oleinik, driver and mechanic.

The crew of a KV-1, wearing protective headgear, prepare for action.

Sergeant Major Sergey Amalechkin and Junior Sergeant Mikhail Tvorogov.

Lieutenant Vasiliy Krysov with K. Vaulin in 1944 after hospital treatment.

Residents of Yastrebnya village.

Senior Lieutenant Vasiliy Krysov, 1944.

A group of SU-85 self-propelled guns behind the front.

Red Army infantry aboard an SU-122.

Captain Pavel Golubev, chief of staff.

A typical scene on the Eastern Front: SU-85s on the move in a snow-bound forest.

Officers and crew pose for the camera on an SU-85.

The article 'Valeriy Korolev fights the Stalinist way. In 3 days he destroyed 8 Tigers', as published in *Forward to the West!*, 20 December 1943.

Officers of the 1435th Self-propelled Artillery Regiment.

Maps

Editor's Preface

Published in Russia by Eksmo, Yauza in 2008 under the title *Samokhodki v boyu: Batareya, ogon'!* [Self-propelled Guns in Battle: Battery, Fire!], Vasiliy Krysov's memoirs offer an exceptional look into armoured combat on the Eastern Front in World War II. They are exceptional in part because few Red Army tankers or self-propelled gunners survived the intense combat that Krysov saw. Wounded three times and surviving the irrevocable destruction of four of his own vehicles, Krysov fought from the gates of Stalingrad to the fortress of Königsberg, starting the war in a heavy KV-1S tank and ending it in perhaps the best medium tank of that war, the T-34/85. However, he spent the bulk of his service as a self-propelled gun platoon or battery commander, first in the SU-122 and then in the SU-85. Thus he has the experience to compare the different vehicles, and offers compelling descriptions of combat involving them.

During his three years of service, Krysov saw action on some of the most important battlefields of the Great Patriotic War: Stalingrad and Ponyri Station (Kursk); the liberation of Kiev and the subsequent hard fighting around Fastov and Brusilov in the Ukraine; Siedlce, Poland in July 1944, and the final assault on Königsberg. His regiments, usually operating as an attachment to a rifle division and in conjunction with a tank brigade, clashed with some of the most renowned German panzer divisions of that war: the 1st SS Panzer Division *Leibstandarte Adolf Hitler*, the 3rd SS Panzer Division *Totenkopf*, and the 5th SS Panzer Division *Wiking*. Although Krysov did not know who his opponents were, his combat descriptions make clear that they were tough, determined, well-equipped and dangerous adversaries. As he recounts the constant attrition of vehicles, crewmen and comrades, the reader can see the heavy toll of the war on Red Army tankers. Interestingly, after Kursk 1943, Krysov's battery often operated as part of a division's forward detachment, and Vasiliy describes several eventful forays into the German rear areas.

Krysov began work on these memoirs in the early 1970s as he collected stories and compared recollections with former comrades at veterans' reunions. While he admits to forgetting many of the places and names from his war experience, he was able to identify them and reconstruct his combat path with the assistance of fellow veterans from his regiments. He supplemented this with information collected from research into the Russian Ministry of Defence's Central Archives. The result is a highly accurate account of the operations and combats in which he participated, which often matches available German accounts and records.

It is more than a combat record, however. Krysov addresses many topics in his memoirs, such as the difficult lot of women in the Red Army, the favouritism shown to Communist Party members in official reports and the awarding of decorations and promotions, and his reaction to the German standard of living. Not a Party member himself, he describes the political officers that he knew, and his brush with a counter-intelligence officer. However, he also describes the tight bonds that existed among the fighting men and gives examples of extreme personal bravery that he witnessed.

The translator, Vladimir Kroupnik, helpfully added many bracketed comments to explain potentially unfamiliar terms or concepts. I have inserted additional bracketed comments, but made no effort to distinguish my comments from Mr. Kroupnik's. In addition, I have added end notes to give context to Krysov's account, often by identifying the exact location of the clash or the German corps or division involved in the action he is describing. Other end notes describe pieces of equipment or certain individuals mentioned by Krysov.

In sum, Krysov's memoirs are an important addition to the growing list of Red Army memoirs that have emerged in recent years, after decades of official censorship in the Soviet Union. A great deal of the credit for this welcome development in our understanding of the Red Army soldiers and their contribution to the defeat of Nazi Germany must go to Artem Drabkin, director of the '*Ya pomnyu*' ['I remember'] project, for his long and diligent work to gather Red Army veterans' stories, recollections and memoirs to preserve them for future generations.

Stuart Britton

Chapter 1

My Journey to the Front

The graduation party at our Istobensk Secondary School in Kirov Oblast's Orichev District was held on the eve of the war, on 21 June 1941. Although stubborn rumours had been circulating that a war was about to begin, we didn't even give it a thought. Excited about the graduation, we – cheerful, buoyant and carefree – danced until dawn, and strolled along the high banks of the Vyatka River. No one wanted to leave: everyone felt that this moment would never happen again. Indeed, at noon on the bright Sunday of 22 June we learned that war had begun.

Already on the next day, at 9 o'clock in the morning, all the lads in our class were besieging the doors of the *voenkomat* [military commissariat and enlistment centre]. A group of thirty graduates from the Istobensk and Orichev secondary schools received assignments to the Chelyabinsk Tank School, and I was among them. Proudly and happily, with songs, we travelled to our destination – after all, every one of us, without exception! – was confident that the Red Army was stronger than all others, that our border was under lock and key, and that we would be fighting only on foreign territory! In other words, we were thinking the way the Party and the Government had taught us to think for many years. Who could even imagine that by that time an armada of 170 hand-picked divisions, four panzer groups and four air fleets had already pounced upon our western border; that they were already rolling over our land and striking shattering blows upon the Red Army troops, which, as it turned out, had even been banned from assuming combat readiness.

We arrived at the Chelyabinsk Tank School in the middle of July 1941. The cadet ranks turned out to be very diverse, both in terms of education and age. More than a half of the cadets of our class were people with a higher education: engineers, teachers, school directors, actors and agronomists, as well as sergeants who had already seen action and second-year cadets of the Kazan Tank-Technical School.

The daily routine was quite intense. The three-year training programme was compressed into one year, because the Kirov Works in Chelyabinsk had already begun line production of the KV-1S heavy tank, and there was a shortage of tankers capable of manning them. We studied the equipment and armament of the tank, signalling, topography, tactics, gunnery rules and much else besides.

We, yesterday's schoolboys, and the cadets with higher education studied on equal terms, so during classroom studies and field exercises we had to exert ourselves fully in order to compete with our better-educated peers. Through persistence and our young, reliable memories, we succeeded. However, we all had to study, as the saying goes, by the sweat of our brows.

There were front-line veterans among the teachers. However, they never talked much about their combat experiences, and we were too shy and reluctant to question them about it. At the beginning our platoon commander was Lieutenant Ivan Gurievich Maksimov, our company commander – Gorshkov, who was also a lieutenant. The battalion commander was called Boiko. He was a sensible, fine and exacting man. He had a saying for moments when he saw that we were tired or becoming jaded: 'A soldier might eat straw, but keeps his spirits high!'

However, the company's Sergeant Major Tolkachev didn't make our life easier. He was a very unjust, coarse, dishonourable man. Short, below average height, and freckled, his malicious eyes seemed to burn with hatred. His rudeness bordered on bullying. People like him, using military discipline as a cover, know no limits in humiliating subordinates, but at the least trifle, get all weak at the knees. Indeed, Tolkachev proved this when he refused to come to our graduation celebration, apparently fearing that the ex-cadets would thrash him, and then leave for the front on the next day and search for a scapegoat. Amazingly, this useless character rose in rank with lightning speed: in 1946 I found myself in Chelyabinsk and, of course, I dropped by the school. There, I met this cock sparrow again, who was now a major!

We learned to master the KV heavy tank. At the same time, however, we became lightly acquainted with the T-34. We also had an opportunity to climb into captured Panzer III and early-model Panzer IV tanks. We had only two KV and two T-34 tanks for the whole school and for this reason we mainly used tractors to learn how to drive. There was little actual opportunity to hop into a tank and drive; over a whole year of training, in total, I had no more than a couple of hours of actual driving experience in a tank. We also never had a chance to fire live 76mm shells, but used a Degtyarev machine gun that was inserted into the barrel of the main gun, and practised using the gunnery scale[1] and optical sights that way.

Tactical training was also not very realistic. For example, the platoon would go out for a field exercise. The platoon commander would send signals by flags: 'On foot – as if in tanks!' And off we would go across the field. Why on foot? Each platoon was supposed to have three tanks – but we had no tanks! Therefore, the platoon would split into three crews, the platoon commander would issue orders with flags, and we would deploy into combat formations on foot: 'line', 'right echelon', 'left echelon', 'forward wedge' and 'reverse wedge'.

We were also taught the tactics of combat against the German tanks. The most important thing was to calculate the range accurately and to fire at the side of the hull or at the turret rear. In order to disable an enemy tank more quickly, if we had only high-explosive shells, we were to fire at the tracks, while with armour-piercing shells – at the turret. I must say that I got excellent marks for gunnery and graduated from the school with top scores in every subject.

The more the situation at the front deteriorated, the more diligently we cadets trained. We studied for fourteen to sixteen hours a day, slept little, but in return after six months of drilling we were capable of driving tanks on our own and had learned how to fire from guns and machine guns.

It was incredibly difficult to master the technique of shooting while in motion! Your tank is racing at a high speed over rugged terrain, being jolted by humps and bumps: through your sights you now see earth, then see sky, but you need to locate your target quickly, line it up with the vertical hair of the gunsight, catch the moment when the cross hair centres on the target, and then press the trigger at just that moment!

On 20 June the final examinations on all the subjects began, including the one on formation drill and even bayonet combat. At last the long-awaited graduation day arrived. On the morning of 1 July 1942, immediately after breakfast, the company quartermaster *Gefreitor* [Private First Class] Ryabkov issued us our new officer's uniform: belts, field caps and canvas-topped boots.

At 12.00 we lined up on the parade ground in our brand-new uniforms. The battalion commanders and the entire school leadership, headed by the school commandant Colonel Naumov (he had assumed the post after a disabling wound – he'd lost his right arm at the front) presided over the ceremony. The chief of gunnery Major Kazievsky read out the Order of the People's Commissar of Defence on the conferring of a specific officer's rank to each cadet and his assignment to one of the different *fronts*. As a result of the intense military training, half of the cadets received the rank of lieutenant, 45 per cent became junior lieutenants, and the remainder – senior sergeants. I was conferred the rank of lieutenant and assigned to the Southeastern Front, which later would be renamed as the Stalingrad Front, as a KV-1S heavy tank commander.

Before our departure for the front, we were given a day of leave and issued with 600 roubles each – the first pay packet in advance! Joyful and proud, we headed into town to get photographed and, if there was a chance, to buy something for the graduation party. A loaf of bread cost 200 roubles at the local market, so there was little chance to over-indulge. Then we wrote letters home, to friends and girlfriends ...

At 20.00 we gathered in the mess hall for the farewell party. Of course, we drank a bit, celebrating our graduation and our new officers' ranks, and we offered parting toasts to our classmates – we were all heading to different *fronts*. Then we attended a concert in the club. A day later our group of fifty men departed for Saratov aboard a passenger train.

We immediately encountered problems in Saratov. When we arrived, the Germans were bombing the city and the bridge over the Volga, which linked Saratov and Engels. Panic was spreading throughout the city! People were running in every direction, and taking advantage of the confusion, some saboteur among a crowd fired signal flares towards the bridge, directing the enemy airmen towards the target. The *Luftwaffe* bombers all the same failed to hit the bridge, but they sank a barge near it.

After the bombers left, we went to the garrison mess hall for lunch, and that's when the second problem arose. They refused to feed us, because the senior of our group – a lieutenant from the school staff who was accompanying us – had forgotten to pick up our ration cards before leaving and thus condemned us to go hungry. Some of the guys suggested that we search the lieutenant, saying that he could not have left the cards behind: we remembered very well that back at Chelyabinsk Station, the school commandant who was seeing us off had asked the lieutenant if he had remembered all the necessary documents. Most of us considered a search too undignified, so all the way to Stalingrad we had to make do for ourselves. We sold and bartered whatever we had – soap, new underwear, watches – for bread.

We rode in a freight train to Kamyshin, frequently halting because of bomb-damaged sections of the track. The train stopped for quite some time at Panitskaya Station. Here we were stunned by the criminal barbarism of the local authorities. A huge grain elevator next to the station was on fire, but a guard wouldn't allow the famished locals access to the threatened grain. The authorities had directed to let the fire burn itself out, leaving the locals without anything! As a group, we went over to the burning elevator and gathered a lot of wheat grain into the flaps of our trench coats. The guard wouldn't dare shoot at the officers. En route we had already procured a bucket, so we boiled the wheat we had wrangled, making something like porridge from it. We subsisted on this all the way to Kamyshin itself.

We arrived in Kamyshin, a town on the west bank of the Volga River north of Stalingrad, at night. They began to load wounded men onto our train as soon as we vacated it. We walked through the whole town. We were all shaken by what we saw. The town had been frequently bombed, and it was under attack again. Wounded people were everywhere, while corpses lay scattered in the streets. In the intervals between bomb explosions, we could hear the weak voices of people begging for help. There was a shortage of medical personnel, and the wounded lay on the ground for days without bandaging; there wasn't even anyone to give them water. For the first time, we were seeing the real face of war and it left a very strong impression.

By dawn we had reached the southern outskirts of the town and were moving in the designated direction. Back then there was no Kamyshin–Stalingrad railroad, and we marched on foot through Cossack villages and rural communities of the former Volga German Republic [the local ethnic Germans – Soviet citizens – who had been living here since the time of Catherine the Great, had been deported by Stalin to Kazakhstan and Siberia earlier in 1942]. We were struck by the orderly development, tidiness and rational planning of the agricultural facilities and fields in the area. Our first night was in the village of Gusenbach – we had a good sleep there, undisturbed by bombs.

We were marching very quickly, stopping only at springs to quench our thirst. Enemy fighter planes began to stalk us, so we searched for shelter along our way. We were received in the villages in different ways, but if we asked for a night's lodging, they unswervingly demanded a reference from the local commandant's office, which, as a rule, was always located about 15 kilometres away. Hence we would walk out into the fields and sleep on piles of straw or haystacks.

However, we never had a chance for a proper sleep in the fields, because we were plagued by rats and mice! Apparently they were agitated by the concussions from the bombing raids. All night long we had to knock these pestilent creatures off ourselves, and also had to guard the buckets that contained the rest of our 'wheat porridge', to keep the rodents from sneaking under the plank boards that we used to cover them. The last few days we had been living on sunflower seeds, gathering pocketfuls of the seeds from carts on their way to collecting stations. The Cossack women were very affectionate and didn't curse us, perhaps because some of the officers were quite handsome, or maybe because they felt sorry for us, understanding that we were heading towards mortal combat and many of us were fated not to return. We made our way from Kamyshin to Stalingrad in six days and with no losses, although we were caught under bombing raids and strafing attacks several times a day.

At the personnel department of the Southeastern Front, we quickly received our assignments to our formations and units. Nikolay Davydov, Misha [Russian diminutive for the name Mikhail] Marder and I – we had been in the same training company back in the Chelyabinsk School – wound up in the 158th Separate Heavy Tank Brigade. At the time of our arrival the brigade was stationed at Krivomuzginskaya Station near Kalach-on-the-Don. The brigade had already seen action during the retreat from the Volchansk area, losing forty-one tanks and half its personnel in heavy combat against a panzer corps [the XXXX Panzer Corps].

Misha Marder and I were assigned to the same platoon. The crews received us well. The seasoned veteran Junior Lieutenant Matvey Serov commanded the platoon. At that time there were two officers in a heavy tank crew, and the second officer in my tank was the driver-mechanic, Junior Lieutenant Talash Safin, a Bashkir national. We called him simply Tolya [Russian diminutive for the name Anatoliy]. Tolya had passed through the accelerated one-year training course in the Chelyabinsk Tank School just like I had (they had been commissioned a bit earlier), and thus I could allow myself not to worry about the driver. The gunlayer in my tank was Sergeant Viktor Belov; the loader – Junior Sergeant Mikhail Tvorogov, who could also fill in for the driver. Junior Sergeant Nikolay Orlov was the radio operator and machine-gunner. All the crew members were young and strong guys, but all of them were from the latest batch of replacements and had not seen action yet. The younger sergeants on the crew had only received a three-month course in a training tank regiment back in Chelyabinsk, and manifestly had insufficient experience in driving a tank, as well as in gunnery.

We were issued KV-1S tanks that had undergone major repairs at the Stalingrad Tractor Factory. During the time remaining before entering combat, the crew worked out a system of interchanging roles, thoroughly studied the regulations and maintenance techniques, rehearsed combat tactics while under fire, and practised firing on the move and from a stopped position.

Chapter 2

Stalingrad

In the Bend of the Don River

On 24 July 1942 the tanks were already standing in well-camouflaged positions on the southern outskirts of Kalach-on-the-Don. The Germans were constantly bombing the 28th Tank Corps' area with impunity; the solitary flak battery couldn't cover all the troops and the main crossing over the Don simultaneously. Not a single friendly fighter appeared in the sky in July-August, we saw only U-2s (the soldiers called them 'crop dusters') in the air [the U-2 was an obsolete biplane used mostly for communications and reconnaissance in the daytime]. The Germans were dropping mocking leaflets: 'Yesterday *Obergefreiter* Hans Müller downed a Russian plane with a brick.' We learned from passing units that our forces were retreating across the entire front, that Rostov-on-Don had just been abandoned, and again leaflets with Goebbels' verses were raining down on us from the skies: 'Rostov's on the Don, Saratov's on the Volga, I'm not gonna catch you – you're too long-legged.' The scoundrels were jeering at us, unaware of the retribution lying in wait for them.

So as to prevent the Germans from capturing the main crossing within the great bend of the Don River and thereby create a bridgehead close to Stalingrad, the Red Army High Command decided to strike a powerful counter-blow along the right [west] bank of the Don to the north. In a matter of days, the 1st Tank Army under the command of Major General of Artillery Moskalenko, which included our 158th Tank Brigade as well, had been formed in early July on the basis of the 38th Army.

On the morning of 25 July our troops went on the offensive. Our tank brigade, in full combat-readiness, advanced a kilometre and a half behind the other combat formations of the 28th Tank Corps and didn't enter combat. Small burial details followed us, not having enough time to dig common graves to bury all the dead. The July heat was doing its work – there was the stench of rotting corpses. It was stuffy in the turret even with operating ventilation fans and opened hatch covers; only while moving did the engine fan gently blow through the fighting compartment. The men were tormented with thirst, and at every suitable opportunity the crew would re-fill their canteens with cold water. The nerves of everyone were strained to the limit! For the second day in a row we'd only been watching through binoculars and optical instruments as our comrades fought the enemy on the flat Don steppe! We were all waiting for our turn to engage the foe! After all, none of us had tasted battle yet! In order to give the men more training and somehow keep them occupied, I ordered: 'Search for targets and report to the entire crew over the intercom!'

Our forces suffered heavy losses, but failed to capture the village of Lozhki and the *sovkhoz* [State Farm].[1] On the morning of 27 July we heard the voice of our brigade commander in our earphones: '*Burya* [Storm] 333!' The signal for the attack! A series of green flares soared into the sky! Our engine roared, and our KV moved out towards the enemy. Two tank brigades, a rifle regiment, a mechanized brigade and our own heavy tank brigade, advancing in the centre of the battle formation, were involved in the attack. It hadn't yet grown light – that was why we weren't being bombed, and the tanks were slowly moving to the north, fearing minefields. To the left of us, about 30 metres distant, were the machines of platoon commander Matvey Serov and Misha Marder; Lieutenant Nazarov's tank advanced on the right. We hadn't opened fire yet, trying to surprise the enemy with our attack. The rifle regiment was advancing behind us, the men holding their rifles at the ready. There was still about a kilometre and a half until we reached the enemy positions, it was beginning to grow lighter, and we now could make out the outlines of trees and the buildings of the *sovkhoz*. The Germans hadn't opened fire yet either, apparently conserving ammunition.[2] The crews were anxiously anticipating action. Everyone wanted to strike the enemy more quickly, to end the agonizing uncertainty – for it is true, there is nothing worse than waiting! The guys eagerly pressed themselves against the observation devices, the gunlayer Vitya Belov and the loader Misha Tvorogov lit up 'goat legs' [hand-rolled cigarettes] – how quickly they had learned from the 'old guys' how to roll a cigarette deftly around the little finger. The smell of *makhorka* [cheap and rough tobacco] drifted throughout the machine.

There was now about a kilometre between us and the enemy, and the Germans, having discerned that tanks in large numbers were advancing towards them, opened a storm of fire. The German fire was extremely accurate! One shell exploded about 20 metres ahead of our tank. Almost immediately a second shell glanced off our left side; our 47-ton vehicle rocked and the flame of the explosion illuminated the fighting compartment – it seemed that the tank was ablaze! But the crewmen wouldn't budge from their places; no one wanted to reveal that he'd been scared, and everyone was anxiously waiting for my order. I saw the flash of the gunshot but failed to spot the well-concealed gun and for this reason I ordered the driver: 'Tolya! Forward with zigzags!' Then to the gunlayer and the radio operator: 'Viktor, Nikolay! At the gunners, from the machine guns! Fire!'

Map 1. The attack of Krysov's platoon of KV-1 tanks, 25 July 1942, near the X let Oktyabrya
State Farm.

The tanks accelerated and began to rumble across the field, making sharp manoeuvres and not letting the enemy gunlayers fix their sights on us. Shell strikes continued glancing off the right and left sides, doing no serious damage to the hull – the machine kept rushing towards the enemy guns! All our tanks fired their main guns and machine guns on the move and during short halts. The Germans began to feel not quite comfortable at the sight of the oncoming wave of tanks, and the accuracy of their fire dropped significantly. About 500 metres remained until the village, and I ordered the crews: 'Tolya, stop beyond the hill! Viktor! There's a gun just under the tree! Anti-personnel shell, sight mark 6! Fire!'

'Anti-personnel ready!' the gunlayer replied. The shell exploded a bit in front of the target. I made a correction: 'Sight mark 7! Fire!' The fascist gun fell silent, and, obviously, for good!

'Tolya! With zigzags, at full speed! Forward!'

In order to take a good look around, I quickly spun the periscope. Two tanks were burning to the right. Platoon commander Serov's tank to my left was motionless; I guessed that it had struck a mine, because the commander had thrown open a hatch and tossed a smoke grenade out in front of the tank, to give the appearance that the tank was ablaze. Misha Marder's tank, like our own, was weaving at full speed towards the enemy position. A second gun concealed in a shack was now firing at our tank. The Germans managed to hit us three times before we reached the enemy trenches, but the shells hadn't penetrated the armour. One shell struck the spare 90-litre oil drum, which was clamped onto one side. A flame engulfed the whole left part of the motor-transmission compartment.

'Tolya, crush the gun!' I ordered the driver as I grabbed the fire extinguisher and, leaning out of the hatch, put out the fire. Just 50 metres remained to the shack with the gun! 'Viktor, reverse the turret!' I ordered the gunlayer.

Less than a minute later, the tank heavily rocked, and we could hear the loud sound of grinding metal from beneath the tank. Scattering logs and planks, our tank rammed through the shack.

'Tolya! Reverse!' I ordered the driver. 'Let's give cover to the platoon commander!'

Our infantry was already going into a bayonet assault, shouting 'Urra-a-h!' The Germans faltered and, declining hand-to-hand combat with bayonets, began to pull back to the northern outskirts of the village under covering machine-gun fire through their communication trenches, hurling hand grenades as they went. I will remember for the rest of my life the image of our attacking wave of riflemen as it advanced, their bayonets glittering dully in the rays of the morning sun. There were also submachine-gunners among the attacking infantry; they fired short bursts at the enemy trenches as they approached them. When our infantry reached the enemy position, only three soldiers clambered out of the trench with upraised hands.

Just as the fighting subsided, platoon commander Serov's tank pulled up alongside ours. Indeed they had struck a mine, but had quickly repaired the broken track. Meanwhile, the enemy artillery barrage was intensifying. *Luftwaffe* aircraft also appeared overhead. From a water tower, three enemy machine guns fired directly on our platoon. Serov gave the command to wipe them out. Each of us fired an armour-piercing round and the machine guns fell silent.

Soon the enemy planes ceased their bombing, as our troops had closed upon the enemy defence line. The corps' command, regrouping, directed our brigade towards the *sovkhoz* farm where the main enemy panzer group was positioned, while the 55th Tank Brigade together with a machine-gun battalion began to encircle the *sovkhoz* from the east. The ensuing combat was fierce, but fleeting. The Germans had light Panzer III tanks and medium Panzer IV tanks; we had KV and T-34 tanks, though one-third of all our tanks were light T-70s – the latter could operate only against infantry and artillery.

A Panzer IV tank quickly moved in our direction. 'Armour-piercing! At the tank in line with the chimney! Continuous aim! From a short halt! Fire!' I simultaneously ordered the loader, the gunlayer and the driver.

'Armour-piercing's ready!' Misha reported.

'Lane!' [slang term for a brief halt for firing from level ground] Tolya yelled out and stopped the tank.

'Shot!' the gunlayer reported and pressed the trigger.

The German gunlayer beat us to the punch by just a fraction of a second, and his shell struck the front of our tank. The machine shuddered; a bright flash illuminated the fighting compartment. Fortunately, the tank had 105mm of frontal hull armour – otherwise we would have burned out in a blue flame! However, the German tank blazed up after the hit by our shell! Serov's crew set fire to a tank too. Misha Marder made short work of an armoured personnel carrier. Meanwhile our infantry was sweeping through the *sovkhoz* settlement, taking one building after another. Then, without letting the enemy regain its senses, they captured Lozhki with a resolute attack.

On 28 July savage fighting developed near the village of Lipologovo. A major enemy grouping had concentrated here, which was moreover occupying very advantageous positions on a range of small hillocks divided by deep ravines impassable for tanks. The capture of this line was achieved, but only with heavy losses. About thirty tanks remained operational in the corps; our brigade also lost half its strength. The 28th Tank Corps command took extraordinary measures: a large batch of replacement tanks arrived together with a rifle division and two regiments of *Katyusha* rocket-launchers. The corps' units spent 29 July repulsing several counter-attacks, while preparing to launch a counter-blow.

Two regimental volleys of *Katyusha* rockets signalled the resumption of the advance. Many crews for the first time were seeing the *Katyusha*'s fire, and our admiration for this deadly whirlwind flying towards the enemy knew no limits! Leaving behind all their equipment, the Germans rushed for shelter, which we didn't hesitate to exploit. Rushing forward, we overran a German tank park without any resistance and captured about thirty intact Panzer IV tanks – the machines were standing without any crews and with working engines! We also captured many anti-tank guns, mortars, armoured personnel carriers and other vehicles. We hauled all of this equipment back to Lozhki.

Suddenly pulling themselves back together, the enemy opened strong artillery and mortar fire from the second and the third line of defence. Junker aircraft also joined in: arriving in waves of twenty to thirty aircraft each, they began to pounce on our formations. The fighting on the Lipologovo line continued for another entire week, up until 5 August 1943. On that day the 1st Tank Army was dissolved: it had carried out its task of not allowing the enemy to advance through the bulge of the Don River to Kalach-on-the-Don.

Hoth's Panzer Army is Stopped!

By now, the Red Army was on retreat across the entire front. Throughout the rest of the summer and autumn our brigade, now attached to the 64th Army, remained on the defence on the left flank of the Southeastern Front, which was renamed the Stalingrad Front on 28 September.

We had to repulse the onslaught of enemy panzers time after time, attack after attack from the south and west. On 23 November, our forces closed a ring around the German Sixth Army of General Paulus in Stalingrad. In order to free the trapped Sixth Army, the Germans formed Army Group Don commanded by Field Marshal von Manstein. The Fourth Panzer Army, commanded by General Hoth, which was included in this army group and was reinforced by infantry and artillery units, was operating on our axis.

On 12 December 1943, Hoth's Fourth Panzer Army went on the offensive. Over the course of a day, its LVII Panzer Corps commanded by General Kirchner advanced over 40 kilometres, crossed the Aksay River, a tributary of the Don, and approached the Verkhne-Kumskiy farmstead. Only about 50 kilometres remained before it would reach the Myshkova River. However, near the Verkhne-Kumskiy farmstead, it faced General Trufanov's 51st Army – a motley collection of units and formations gathered together by *Stavka* representative Vasilevsky and Stalingrad Front commander Colonel General Eremenko from various units and formations. The main shock force of this army was represented by General Volsky's 4th Mechanized Corps, which combined the remnants of several tank brigades. The 51st Army, undoubtedly the weak link in the ring of encirclement around Stalingrad, comprised about 100 tanks, 147 guns and mortars, and 34,000 men.

A fierce engagement commenced! We fought for six days to prevent Hoth's panzer army from reaching the Myshkova River. The Verkhne-Kumskiy farmstead changed hands several times. We fought with no sleep and rest, and, it may be said, with no food either.

The 4th Mechanized Corps commander General Vasiliy Timofeevich Volsky distinguished himself as a talented commander. He managed to detach thirty tanks and a rifle regiment from his meagre reserves and sent this force to the opposite bank of the Aksay River, into the German rear, so as to make a show of encirclement and force the foe to take up an all-round defence. This group partially consisted of the tanks of our 158th Brigade; its commander Colonel Egorov led the raid into the enemy rear.

Once across the river, as our first order of business we dug emplacements for the tanks, and the infantry dug foxholes to shelter themselves from bullets, shell splinters and the icy, bone-chilling wind. The Aksay River was not too wide – only 25 metres – which enabled us to keep harassing the enemy with gun and machine-gun fire, and the infantry – with fire from submachine-guns and rifles.

Over six days of action the group destroyed thirty-two enemy tanks, but lost fifteen of its thirty armoured vehicles in return. This was done in spite of the fact that we had to count every shell! We used ammunition as sparingly as we could, knowing that we couldn't rely on our supply lines. The situation was even worse with our rations – we ate dried crust, washing it down with cold water. On 17 December we had used up the last of our ammunition and had nothing left with which to fight. Brigade commander Egorov summoned the officers and made a statement:

> I express my gratitude to all the crews for their performance in combat. Our grouping has fulfilled the assigned task: the enemy advance has been stopped. The enemy didn't dare to advance to the Myshkova, reckoning that we would fall on his rear. Let's pay a tribute to our fallen comrades ...

We all took off our head coverings. Colonel Egorov continued:

> Tonight, we will withdraw back to our lines. We'll cross the Aksay over the enemy's own pontoons. A captured *yazyk* [literally, a 'tongue'; slang for a prisoner taken for interrogation] divulged that the Germans have not removed their crossing, for they expect the arrival of the last battalion of a tank division.

Having waited for the darkness we set off for the crossing. Marder and I were covering the withdrawal with our two tanks. We were the last to reach the pontoon bridge and had already crossed the most exposed part, when strong cannon fire struck us from behind.

I found time to tell Misha over the radio: 'We're on fire!' Then I heard his reply: 'We're on fire, too.'

The Germans had managed to set both of our tanks ablaze by hits on the rear. One shell struck our transmission, and the engine caught fire. At the same moment, flares lit up the crossing and the riverbank. A storm of fire ensued! There was no chance to leap out through the turret hatches – everyone would be mowed down! We slipped out underneath the tank through the emergency floor hatch in the middle of the fighting compartment, having first grabbed the most necessary stuff: submachine-guns, ammunition drums and hand grenades. We also removed a machine gun, first-aid kit, and camouflage cloaks, and then hid in waiting beneath the tank. My entire crew was alive, not even wounded.

But how were things with Mikhail? In the light of the flares, I watched as Marder's crews made their way out of the tank, also via the emergency hatch – it meant that the guys were alive. Remaining concealed, we waited; just when would the Germans get tired of launching flares?!

Soon a group of enemy scouts appeared. We squeezed ourselves into the ground, but the Germans passed us without stopping. At last everything quieted down. We crawled towards Marder's burning tank and met Marder's crew crawling towards us. Misha told us that he had overheard the German scouts saying: 'That's ten Ivans burned up.'

We had to find our way back to our lines. We looked at the map in the light of a pocket torch [flashlight to American readers], determined a route, and headed out. Before dawn we came across a ravine and decided to hide in it for the day. We made a shelter to take cover from the wind and, having concealed ourselves, stiffening from the cold, we spent the entire day in the shelter. When it became dark, we took off again. A north-easterly wind was blowing, kicking up a blizzard from the ground snow. Misha Marder walked out in front so that in case we bumped into any Germans, his knowledge of the language might bail us out. We walked a little behind him, stretching our frozen legs. We had become chilled through over the day of motionless waiting for nightfall, although we all were wearing winter garb: *valenki* [felt boots], quilted pants, quilted jackets underneath greatcoats, and fur-lined tankers' helmets on our heads.

We noticed a column of smoke rising from the ground ahead of us. Having approached it, we discerned a whole row of dugouts, with a sentry strolling about. The German was scared at first, but Marder threw up his arm in the fascist salute: 'Some of your own!'

The guard had just begun to raise his arm in response, when my gunlayer Misha Tvorogov clubbed his head with a submachine-gun, and the German toppled over. We didn't throw hand grenades to avoid raising an alarm.

We walked further and suddenly encountered a security patrol. This time we had no choice – we pelted the enemy with hand grenades and now openly rushed towards our own lines. It took the Germans some minutes to work out what was happening, then they opened machine-gun and later – mortar fire. Some of us were wounded, but we all reached our trenches. Misha Marder was badly wounded in the back, and we immediately sent him to the *medsanbat* [Russian abbreviation for medical-sanitation battalion]. A shell splinter became embedded in my right forearm, but I refused to go to the *medsanbat*.

It had taken us more than a day to get back to our lines, and, one might say, we'd been lucky – we were all alive, though some of us had been wounded. I know nothing of the further fate of Misha Marder. We returned to the farm-stead, to our regiment.

The Germans continued to be hesitant to try to bull their way into Verkhne-Kumskiy: we still had tanks there. However, we had suffered very heavy losses; that whole farmstead was drenched in blood. Just then the corps commander ordered a retreat to the Myshkova River. On the same night that we had returned from beyond the Aksay, our troops began to withdraw to the Myshkova under the cover of tanks, and took up a defence there. We reached the river in the night from 18 to 19 December. On the morning of 19 December the troops of Malinovsky's powerful 2nd Guards Army and the 2nd Mechanized Corps arrived in our deployment area.

Having taken up the defence, Malinovsky's army immediately went into action. Now together with them, we repulsed all the attacks of von Manstein's forces.

From a Tanker to a Self-propelled Gunner

During the heavy fighting near Stalingrad my tank had received many dents and had destroyed a lot of enemy equipment and troops, but then, in December 1942 it had been burned out by a German shell. I refused to go to a hospital and together with other commanders who had been left without tanks I was sent into the reserve and wound up in Sverdlovsk, in the personnel department of the Urals Military District. Here I received a new assignment – to lead a platoon of SU-122 self-propelled howitzers in the 1454th Self-propelled Artillery Regiment.

The regiment consisted of four batteries with five self-propelled guns each, plus the regiment commander's T-34 tank. The regiment also had a company of submachine-gunners, a reconnaissance platoon and a number of auxiliary units, such as supply, repair services, signals, medical services, etc. Being compact in numbers, the self-propelled artillery regiments were very mobile; they could be deployed to areas of an enemy tank penetration within a matter of hours or even minutes, and were capable of destroying the enemy by fire from standing positions. On the offensive, they supported tank attacks. Getting a bit ahead of myself, I can testify that it was difficult or almost impossible for enemy tanks to force their way through our battle lines, where medium or heavy self-propelled guns were standing on the defence.

Personnel from the 5th Reserve Tank Regiment, which was stationed in Sverdlovsk, were used to form the four batteries of self-propelled guns – the mobile unit of the 1454th Self-propelled Artillery Regiment. The headquarters unit was supposed to join the regiment later. I was the last to arrive in my 3rd Battery, which was commanded by Senior Lieutenant Vladimir Shevchenko. Everyone in it had already undergone re-training from a tanker into a *samokhodchik* [self-propelled gunner], and I had to master the equipment and armament of the vehicle in just one week. This was an intricate artillery science: to study the panoramic sight, the rules of firing from covered positions; to be able to prepare all settings for firing using limited data; to plot a parallel fire plane and to adjust the fire given the deviation of explosions from the line of sight.

On the last night before the departure from Sverdlovsk I just couldn't fall asleep. Not because I was anxious or because it was hard to sleep on the tightly-stuffed straw mattresses that butted up against each other on the upper level of the plank bunks. It was simply that the memories of the Chelyabinsk Tank School and the fighting near Stalingrad were sweeping over me, and my wounded arm was troubling me a bit ... 'Reveille!' The command rang out, interrupting my uneasy thoughts.

It took us an hour to have a shave, wash, wolf down a quick breakfast, and to set off on foot by battery towards the Uralmash [Ural Machine Building] Factory still before dawn. The snow produced little squeaks beneath our jackboots. We passed a field, a small copse of trees, and soon found ourselves in the factory yard, where we saw in the pre-dawn twilight our train with the self-propelled guns under tarpaulin covers. Sentries of the special guard dressed in sheep-skin coats and *valenki* stood along both sides of the flat cars. It took no more than half an hour to load the batteries' equipment and gear and to board the personnel onto the *teplushki* [boxcars fitted with plank bunk beds for passengers and a small iron stove for heating], whereupon our train, pulled by two steam engines, rolled out onto the main line and headed westward. We rode at a high speed down the 'green street' [a term for a rail under one-way traffic rules during wartime]. I remember only two stopovers at stations where the engine crews were replaced.

Once aboard the *teplushka*, we stoked the iron stove right away. Through the white shroud of falling snow, we could see station platforms flashing past through a gap in the secured doors; the eyes had no time to make out the names of the stations and we noticed only rare travellers on the platforms. All along the way we sang the then-popular songs – 'The Dark Night', 'In the Dugout', 'For the Holy War', and 'The Spark'. The gunlayer from the battery commander's self-propelled gun, Senior Sergeant Sasha Chekmenov, commonly led the singing in our battery, but when we sang Ukrainian songs, our battery commander himself, Senior Lieutenant Shevchenko, was the song leader.

The train arrived at Pushkino Station near Moscow on the second day of our journey. Here we were met by the regiment's command and the headquarters' staff officers. We unloaded the self-propelled guns by the dim light of the station lanterns and drove them into some woods about 25 kilometres from the railroad. Once billeted in some village dachas, we undertook combat training and breaking-in the crews and units under conditions that approximated actual combat as closely as possible.

The main emphasis in the process of breaking-in the crews was placed on driving the vehicles across difficult obstacles; firing from short halts, especially at moving targets; and on ensuring that each crew member was able to carry out the role of other crew members. Even Private Emelyan Ivanovich Besschetnov (we called him 'old fellow' for he was already over 40), who was the breech operator, could capably drive the self-propelled gun and was a good shot as well, even though he had never served in the tank units before. To tell the truth, however, he was a tractor driver for a collective farm before the war. Our training finished with tactical exercises and gunnery.

On the night before 15 June 1943, the regiment was roused by an alarm and hastily transferred by rail to Kursk. We arrived on the right, northern flank of the Central Front where the 48th Army was defending. The regiment was allocated a sector of the defence in front of Zmievka.

Chapter 3

Kursk 1943

We Prepare a Defence

The crews spent the two days after arrival setting up main firing positions and two reserve positions for each self-propelled gun. We completed this hellish work almost without a rest, anticipating at any moment that the enemy would launch his offensive. Because of the unbearable heat, our combat blouses became soaked with sweat and we were tormented by thirst; a fifth crew member, who was taking his turn for a break – we were short of shovels – didn't have enough time to bring up some drinking water. Having camouflaged the last position and being satisfied, we at last sat to have a rest. Our hands were blistered, but we were now in better spirits – the Germans wouldn't catch us unawares!

The crews spent entire days busily preparing a system of fire and doing drills to implement it. Simultaneously during this time I scrutinized my crew and the platoon, imperceptibly examining the men's reaction to various situations as they came along – now an air-raid, then an artillery barrage – especially when the German *Nebelwefer* rocket-launchers were firing, which were capable of shaking anyone with their howling. Most of all I kept my eye on my gunlayer, on whom much would depend in combat. However, Sergeant Major Valeriy Korolev, who was the youngest crew member, behaved calmly, didn't tremble from the explosions, and didn't take cover needlessly. The rest of the crew had previous combat experience, so I was confident in them.

The night of 4 July 1943 was quiet. Both sides periodically fired machine guns; their tracer rounds would suddenly stitch the darkness with bright, fiery lines. From time to time a shell would fly over us with a hissing howl, and land with a muffled explosion somewhere in the rear. One crew member was on watch in each machine, while the rest slept in bunkers. One of the battery's officers was on watch too; the others were lightly dozing, perched on an earthen bench or lying with the soldiers on the floor, which had been covered with tree branches and tent halves.

The senior headquarters' radio operator ran into the bunker, panting as he reported: 'Comrade battery commander! The regiment commander is urgently summoning you!'

Shevchenko left for the regiment command post, taking his gunloader Sasha Kibizov with him. Kibizov was both the battery commander's messenger and bodyguard at the same time – he had no equal for this role. He was an Ossetian, a tall and physically strong mountaineer who was adept with the dagger. We, of course, quickly guessed why the battery commander had been summoned so urgently in the middle of the night: apparently, *it* was about to begin!

Day One

Shevchenko returned in around fifteen minutes, gathered his subordinate officers next to his self-propelled gun, and gave us our combat task succinctly. The crews began to prepare for battle. In pitch darkness – it was well before dawn – they removed the soft covers from the gun barrels, cleared away any camouflage that might impede firing, and wiped the optical lenses clean. The fighting compartment of the self-propelled gun began to smell of tobacco smoke – the driver Viktor Oleinik and gunloader Vasiliy Plaksin had lit up their *makhorka* cigarettes at almost the same moment. Both of them felt uneasy; they had wives back at home, each of them had two kids, and Viktor also had old parents in his care. Who could foresee what awaited us, and how the battle would end? On the other hand, we all fully understood the strength of the enemy we were about to engage. The gunlayer Valeriy Korolev was silently wiping clean the panoramic sight, and the breech operator Emelyan Ivanovich Besschetnov who had just turned 46 on this day, kept saying again and again as he crossed himself repeatedly: 'Thank God, it'll start up soon; we'll give it to them, this isn't the year '41 for them!'

A deafening rumble burst the silence of the night! The preparatory artillery barrage had begun. I glanced automatically at the luminous dial built into the driver-mechanic's instrument panel: the clock showed 02.20. Through the open hatch and the raised shutters of the panoramic sights, we could clearly see the salvoes of *Katyusha* fire – like fiery serpents they flew towards the enemy with a howl.

Several minutes later at the command of the regiment commander over the radio net we joined the artillery preparation, firing on previously assigned and registered targets. Here, at the Kursk salient, was my first experience with indirect fire from covered positions. Both crews of the platoon fired with pre-established target settings and judging by the comments from the battery's observation post, our shells were falling on target. The artillery barrage on the enemy troops lasted for a good half an hour, then the shelling ceased and a strange, strained silence fell over the battlefield.

By 04.30 the Germans had managed to pull themselves together and began the artillery preparation of their offensive. However, already within five minutes our artillery responded with powerful counter-fire, which again included our regiment as well. It became hot and stuffy in the vehicle; our throats became dry and scratchy from the gunpowder smoke, and our eyes were irritated even though all the hatch covers were open and the ventilation fans were running at full strength. The gunloader and the breech operator were working by the gun in overalls soaked with sweat, now and then taking swigs from a canteen. Both were strong and sturdy, but there was not enough oxygen in the fighting compartment, and the heavy shells – the ammunition carriers had barely been able to bring them up – drained the men's strength.[1] Enemy shells began to burst closer and closer, large splinters were hammering the hatch and the armour, carving out spatters of molten metal. We had to close the hatch covers, and now we could only see through the optical devices the explosions that rocked the 30-ton self-propelled gun as if it was on waves, spattering it with clumps of dirt and engulfing it in flames.

Before the last enemy shells exploded, the dive-bombers came over! In groups of twenty to thirty bombers each, they flew across the front line in waves, kicked over, and plunged towards the ground, dropping their deadly loads onto the defence line before climbing to make a new pass. The bombs were falling with the terrifying howling of sirens, shaking and churning up the earth, collapsing foxholes, trenches, communications trenches and bunkers! However, the most spine-chilling impression was made by the sounds of the aircraft themselves, when in pulling out of their dives they flew just above the vehicle: I was thinking less about a direct hit on the machine, and more about whether the pilot would fail to pull out of the dive and plunge directly into our vehicle.

'Thank God, we were spared, Comrade Lieutenant, that bomb was meant for us, wasn't it?' Emelyan Ivanovich said coolly as if calming the crew down.

'This is their congratulations on your birthday, Emelyan Ivanovich,' Vasya Plaksin joked, before turning to curse and revile the enemy airmen with a cascade of colourful expressions. Then, a moment later, he suddenly opened the upper hatch cover and fired a submachine-gun at a diving Stuka.

At about 06.00 the Germans went on the attack. We could see tanks emerging from behind hillocks through the intervening shell explosions. The German artillery and mortar barrage intensified. They were firing on our battery too, but without a line of sight, because we had very suitable positions on a descending slope leading down to the Neruch River, which was overgrown with shrubs and low-growth forest that offered us additional concealment. Taking advantage of folds and wrinkles in the terrain, the tanks were slowly approaching our defence line, firing on the move and from short halts. The steel tracks gleamed dimly in the rays of the rising sun. We intently scrutinized the outlines of the advancing tanks; I was mentally comparing them with diagrams from our manuals: the vertical sides of hulls, the turret panels, and the long gun barrel with the muzzle brake said that these were Tigers, along with their camouflage paint scheme of yellow, green and brown splotches, which blended into the surroundings quite well. Yes, it was them! Six Tigers were advancing in front of our battery's defence line! Behind them, crawling over the crest of a height in an inverted wedge formation, were lighter armoured vehicles and halftracks with infantry – we could make out medium Panzer IV tanks and assault guns.

The commander of my second self-propelled gun Junior Lieutenant Levanov raised a red flag out of his hatch, to report that he was ready to open fire. I alerted battery commander Shevchenko regarding the platoon's readiness in the same fashion.

Less than a kilometre now remained to the enemy tanks, but there was still no command from the regiment commander to open fire! The Tiger tank had side and frontal armour ranging from 80mm to 120mm thick, and its powerful gun could penetrate 70mm of armour out to a range of 1,500 metres, whereas even the heavy shell of our 122mm howitzer could penetrate the Tiger's armour only out to about 500 metres. We now could clearly see through the periscope and gunsights as the Tigers advanced, slightly weaving as they prowled through the wheat field, their menacing gun muzzles swinging back and forth as they scanned our positions for targets. Having ordered the gunlayer to keep one of the tanks, which had come to the fore and was moving towards our vehicle, in his gunsight, I quickly checked the other guys in my crew: Valeriy Korolev was seemingly composed and had his right hand on the gun's trigger; Plaksin and Emelyan Ivanovich kept their eyes glued to the enemy tanks through their vision slits and were noticeably anxious; the driver-mechanic Vitya Oleinik was agitated, and his hands were idly grabbing and releasing the clutch levers, but at such a tense moment this was natural. As for me – yes, I was also anxious, although I already had experience in battling German tanks, but those had been light Panzer III and medium Panzer IV tanks, while here at Kursk the Germans had Tigers, Panthers, and Ferdinands with very heavy guns![2] In this first unequal engagement with heavy enemy tanks at the Kursk salient I was eager to defeat the enemy at any cost, but also to keep the members of the crews alive! Now, though, as the commander, I had to think about one thing: to ensure that no one let us down in battle!

'Even the devil is not as terrible as he is painted to be,' I kept encouraging my crewmen. 'Let them come closer ...'

The distance was shrinking. There were now 900 metres to the tanks ... 800 ... The Tigers were closing on our outpost line deployed 700 metres in front of the first trench – but still there was no command to open fire!

The tanks were crawling as slowly as turtles. Their tactics were understandable: they were reckoning that our nerves wouldn't hold out, that someone would open fire, and then they could easily, from a safe range, make short work of our tanks, self-propelled guns and artillery. Nevertheless, the regiment commander Major Samyko was showing great self-control. He had acquired excellent combat skills in the 1st Moscow Proletarian Rifle Division fighting for Moscow as an artillery battalion commander, so he had a good understanding of German tactics.

Now the tanks had reached the outpost line. Savage fighting erupted, accompanied by the explosions of grenades, rifle and machine-gun fire, and bright flashes of flame on the German tanks – our infantry was locked in mortal combat, using hand grenades and Molotov cocktails against the tanks. The odds were long, and at last the infantry was ordered to withdraw. Suddenly we heard two powerful explosions, and two of the enemy tanks stopped, but continued to fire from the spot – likely they had struck mines or had been immobilized by anti-tank grenades. The sounds of machine-gun and submachine-gun bursts became increasingly audible – the soldiers, retreating down the communication trenches, were continuing to resist the hard-pressing enemy. My headset was set to receive, and through the crackle of static I could hear snatches of open radio communications in German and Russian – in the latter case with quite audible, elaborate cursing. At last I heard the regiment commander's voice: 'At the tanks! Fire!' I passed the order to my gunlayer: 'Valeriy! At the tanks! Fire!'

Three red flares soared into the sky to signal confirmation of the order, and before the first one had reached its zenith, Korolev, who was waiting for that signal like it was manna from heaven, pressed the trigger. The shot thundered! Levanov's and the battery commander's howitzers roared nearby! Dust and smoke swirled up from the blast wave, concealing the battlefield for several seconds, but nevertheless I made out a flash on the turret of an enemy tank! And then a second flash – a direct hit from the shell fired by Lesha Kuzin – Levanov's gunlayer! To the left, one German tank surged significantly ahead of the others.

'Valeriy! At the second from the left! Fire!' I ordered the gunlayer.

The shell exploded on the upper part of the turret. However, the tank not only kept advancing, but it also continued to fire its main gun and two machine guns. I gave Korolev a new aiming point: 'At the tracks! Fire!' The heavy shell smashed a track! The tank swerved to the left, exposing its right side. Vasiliy Tsybin, the experienced gunlayer on Gorshkov's crew, who hadn't fired prior to this, had been waiting for just such an opportunity – in an instant he sent a shell into the side of the enemy tank and set it ablaze! Korolev also managed to fire, but the German tank had already received its fatal hit a second before.

'A wasted shell!' Valeriy swore sorrowfully.

However, the whole crew was rejoicing at the sight of the first burning enemy tank! The enemy tanks, having lost two machines, halted and began to mill around in place, searching for suitable positions. After having recovered from the initial shock, the heavy tanks resumed their advance, and breached the first line of trenches in some sectors. The fighting on the regiment's sector of defence grew more intense. The battlefield became engulfed with the continous roar of gunshots and exploding shells. Machine-gun bursts could be heard between the explosions. One could see our soldiers in the nearest foxholes and trenches firing from rifles and submachine-guns, but you could no longer hear individual shots – the sounds had merged into the uninterrupted din of combat!

The enemy artillery fire intensified. Tanks of the enemy's second echelon came into sight and had already opened fire. The numbers were now tilting dangerously against us. The enemy was pressing hard against our battery, while the situation for the other batteries was becoming more and more difficult. Heavy shell explosions were tossing rolls of barbed wire into the air, ripping apart the coils. The trench walls and bunkers were collapsing, burying men alive. Those who managed to emerge from the caved-in trenches and shelters were rushing under enemy artillery and machine-gun fire to rescue their comrades. The heavy smoke enveloping the battlefield obscured our view of the advancing enemy through the optics. Taking a quick glance with my naked eye from under the slightly raised hatch cover, I spotted three lines of advancing enemy infantry behind the second wave of German tanks! Oleinik also saw the lines of enemy infantry out of the semi-opened front hatch. He was obviously over-whelmed by the sight – slamming the hatch cover closed, he lit up a cigarette, but said nothing so as not to frighten his mates.

'Valeriy, don't fire without an order!' I said to the gunlayer. 'We have to spare the ammo; there's no chance to bring more up, but we can't let the tanks through. The riflemen will hold the enemy infantry, and we're going to help them do it.'

Then Shevchenko's order rang out in all the headsets: 'Battery! At the lead tank! Aim just below the turret. Concentrate your fire on it. Fire!'

The ensuing salvo blew the Tiger's turret from its hull! Arcing through the air in a semi-circle with its cannon, it fell heavily to the ground. The tank's body was ablaze with crimson-black flame.

Encouraged by this success, the battery commander repeated the order: 'At the third one on the left! Concentrated fire! Fire!'

The forward portion of the second tank's turret lifted a bit along with the gun, and a tongue of blue flame jutted out of the gap that had been formed. Other units switched to concentrated fire following our battery's example. Simultaneously our artillery, deployed to fire over open sights, was pouring fire on the advancing enemy tanks. Around midday, the enemy's advance stalled! Leaving behind more than a few burned tanks, armoured personnel carriers and dead on the battlefield, the Germans began to withdraw, returning fire from guns and machine guns.

As soon as the action died down, we opened the hatches in order to gulp down some fresh air. However, we hadn't yet managed to climb out of our machines when we received an order to shift to reserve positions. Only dummy self-propelled guns were left behind in the entrenchments. Some fifteen minutes later, about fifty dive-bombers with howling sirens came over and began to bomb our main positions, having mistakenly identified the motionless dummies for real combat vehicles. Making several passes over our former positions, they levelled our entrenchments. There were no further attacks on our sector on this day.

After any battle, the first order of business for the crew is to service the equipment. Then I remembered my officer's supplementary ration. This ration was issued once a month: there was a bit of butter, a packet of biscuits, some sugar and a packet of light tobacco in it. Making use of the relative lull in the fighting, I decided to send Plaksin to the provision depot: 'Vasya, ask the stockman to trade us a chocolate bar for the sugar; let's celebrate Emelyan Ivanovich's birthday.'

The crew dined in a celebratory atmosphere. There were two reasons: our successful first battle and the birthday. I presented Emelyan Ivanovich with his gifts – a pocket knife (which I had brought from home) and the candy treat. Touched, our 'old fellow' shed a tear and shook everyone's hand as a sign of his appreciation.

In the evening, at a regimental assembly, Major Samyko expressed his personal gratitude to the entire regiment and conveyed the gratitude and praise from the Central Front commander General Rokossovsky. He then immediately ordered the chief of staff Major Fetisov to draw up award documents for those who had distinguished themselves in combat. At that point, he went into a detailed debriefing and summarized the results of the first day of defence:

> Today the regiment has immobilized and destroyed eight enemy tanks, several armoured vehicles, and dozens of enemy soldiers and officers have been killed. Our losses are five wounded men, two knocked-out self-propelled guns and one irrevocably destroyed vehicle. It's good that we have suffered minor losses and have come off the action against the Tigers with flying colours. We have to give credit to the 3rd Battery commander Senior Lieutenant Shevchenko – he was the first with his battery to apply concentrated fire on one tank.

In conclusion the regiment commander informed us that by the order of the Front commander the regiment would be redeployed to the Ponyri area, where it was anticipated that the Germans' main attack would fall. The chief of staff immediately unfolded a map and showed the line of departure, the routes, the areas for halts and the re-assembly area, indicating when and where the regiment and its rear services were supposed to be during the movement. Then the rank and file dispersed for dinner, while we officers began to plot the situation on our maps in the headquarters' bunker, fixing boundary lines, areas and times.

When we emerged from the bunker, the sun was already setting, its red disc melting into the horizon. The light wind was not carrying the scents of a summer evening through the trenches, but the smell of gunpowder and the stench of burned corpses and matériel. The regiment's chief surgeon Senior Lieutenant of Medical Services Roza Muratova and the senior medic Valya Vorobieva – both quite young and from the Urals – were in a medical tent that had been set up in a deep ravine, treating the wounded. The short, pretty Roza, with eyes as dark as black olives and coal-black hair just as dark, had joined the Red Army in Bashkiria; Valya – a tall, shapely, handsome blonde with blue eyes – joined the *opolchenie* [people's militia] in Sverdlovsk. At the time, Roza was 21 years of age, Valya just 18. By the summer of 1943 they were both pretty well battle-seasoned: Roza had served in a front-line medical battalion, Valya – in a ski battalion on the Kalinin Front.

The young soldiers of the regiment had been eyeing these attractive girls, but tried not to approach them too closely, since Roza was considered the regiment commander Samyko's wife, and Valya – the wife of his deputy, Major Mel'nikov. In reality, these two ladies were 'campaign wives'. Both of these ladies eventually gave birth to a son and gave them the family names of their 'front-line' husbands, who already had families back home, which neither Roza nor Valya suspected. The third girl in the regiment – the beautiful Anya with her hazel eyes – let's call her Ivanova – slept with all the officers indiscriminately. Samyko dismissed her from the regiment in early November 1943 over this very promiscuity.

Freed from the staff duties, I summoned the platoon. My crew was waiting; they hadn't had dinner yet. I expressed my gratitude to all for their excellent conduct in the fighting and firmly shook each man's hand. Strangely, everyone was calm, as if they hadn't just been in action. Vasya Plaksin, on his way from the field kitchen with our mess tins of gruel, was singing joyful songs, and during dinner he bantered with Emelyan Ivanovich: 'Hey, "old fellow", keep your head higher or the mess tin lower, don't get your moustache wet – after all, it's the pride of the whole crew!' We quickly finished our meal and began to prepare ourselves for the march.

The Redeployment

The command 'To your machines!' stirred everyone. Engines roared to life, and the self-propelled guns began to stretch out into a column for the movement. It was already dark; we drove at low speed through clouds of thick dust kicked up by the tracks, and only the glowing red rear lights on all the vehicles prevented collisions with the ones in front. Periodically enemy bombers appeared overhead, but the regiment was safely concealed by the darkness, road dust and treetops. Only once, not far from Lukovets, while crossing a bog over a corduroy road, one of the drivers mistakenly turned on the full lights for just a second, and this prompted an immediate reaction from enemy airmen – they bombed us for half an hour! However, we escaped with no losses.

A forced halt occurred just before dawn: one of the self-propelled guns got stuck in a deep, muddy roadside ditch and blocked the way for the whole column. It was being driven by Mikhail Grechuk – the regiment's most experienced driver. The machine was quickly pulled out by two of the other SU-122s, but the incident became a great sensation in the regiment: 'Grechuk himself got stuck!' – the man who could shift gears without depressing the main clutch pedal. Mikhail was greatly upset and unnerved, and likely it was because of this discomfiture that he avoided contact with his comrades for a whole week. We made a long halt in a forest, having safely concealed the self-propelled guns under the trees and having swept clear our tracks in the dirt with branches.

We emerged from the woods in the afternoon. We moved quickly, but mostly along a cross-country track – through shrubs and copses, avoiding main roads and farm roads. On the approach to Gnilaya Plata, the column was raked by machine-gun fire from a low, heavily vegetated hillock on the opposite bank of a swampy stream. The main forces of the regiment had already passed this place and the fire fell on the rear service units. The Germans didn't know that our battery was bringing up the rear of the column as a rear guard. Shevchenko unhesitatingly ordered: 'Deploy the battery for action! Do not open fire from the guns!'

Several minutes later, three Fritz machine-gunners were killed by submachine-gun fire and hand grenades. We stopped the vehicles and climbed out to have a look. We found two machine guns and boxes with ammunition belts in the emplacement next to the dead Germans; there were also helmets with the swastika on them, cylindrical gas-mask cases made of corrugated iron, and a radio set. Besschetnov addressed me: 'Comrade Lieutenant, let's pick up both machine guns and the ammo boxes, they may be of some use.'

'Emelyan Ivanovich, you grab the machine guns, tell Korolev and Plaksin about the ammo boxes – they'll pick them up.'

I myself most likely wouldn't have thought of picking up the trophies, but thank God the 'old fellow' had suggested we do it. These machine guns would prove quite useful for us very soon!

'I can't figure it out: they were sent here, but why?' Shevchenko said as he examined the radio set lying in the emplacement.

'Perhaps, to report on the movement of our forces,' platoon commander Fomichev pointed out.

'Why did they fire at us then?'

'Maybe they thought that their forces had already broken through our defences, and they'd be here soon,' the deputy for technical services Ishkin suggested.

'Perhaps,' the battery commander agreed, before ordering us to move on.

The Fight for Ponyri

The regiment arrived at its assigned operational sector of the 13th Army at 23.00 on 6 July after a day-long march, instead of the anticipated day and a half. It was the defence sector of General M.A. Enshin's 307th Rifle Division. Here our regiment was placed at the operational disposal of the commander of the 129th Tank Brigade, Colonel Petrushin, even though our regiment was stronger than the latter in terms of firepower, for the brigade was equipped mostly with light T-70 tanks with their 45mm guns.

By the light of the moon, which occasionally emerged from behind some clouds, Colonel Petrushin clarified the location of our positions with the regiment command and battery commanders. The terrain in our sector of defence was almost flat, with a gentle slope downward in the direction of the enemy; a range of hillocks was on the left, and it was here where the regiment commander decided to deploy our battery – in case the Germans managed to penetrate into the depth of our front lines.

Wasting no time we began to dig emplacements, aware that the work would have to be done by dawn. We toiled stripped down to the waist, almost without respite, sometimes ducking from a machine-gun burst or falling flat on the ground from a low-flying shell – we had already learned how to recognize them by their sounds and managed to drop in time. By dawn we were totally worn out, but the emplacements and trenches were ready and carefully camouflaged. We had also policed up the area and brushed away the traces of our tracks. Satisfied with the results of our titanic labour, we took a short break. Overnight, each crew had dug out and moved no less than 40 cubic metres of hard, compact soil in order to build the self-propelled gun emplacements with their ramps and the slit trenches for the personnel. I'm ashamed to say that I thought that the skinny Valeriy and the aging Emelyan Ivanovich wouldn't be able to endure the workload, but it turned out that it was Plaksin who first became exhausted. Oleinik kept poking fun at him: 'Now you know, Vasya, to dig trenches under enemy fire isn't like singing love songs on Malaya Bronnaya Street [a street in the centre of Moscow with several theatres and entertainment halls].'

On the morning of 7 July, enemy bombers appeared, and in their wake an artillery barrage began. The crewmen were in their positions, the hatch covers were battened down, but sometimes the explosions were so close that we could see nothing but flames through the optical devices – it seemed that the self-propelled gun was on fire! The ensuing terrible drumbeat of rocks and dirt clods falling on the armour from the geysers of earth blown high into the sky by the explosions nearly deafened us. As the dirt and dust settled, they covered the machine with a thick, impenetrable layer of soil, and it was becoming as dark as night in the fighting compartment. Fearing that we'd miss the start of the enemy attack, we frequently opened the upper hatch cover briefly to have a better look around and to wipe clean the optical lenses. Once when looking out of the hatch, I saw a terrible scene: three nearby villages were burning, enveloped in thick clouds of black smoke, and just in front of us one could see the infantry positions – there men were frantically trying to dig out comrades who'd been buried under piles of dirt and logs, collapsed trench walls and bunkers.

'Comrade Lieutenant, get back into the machine.' Fearing for my life, Emelyan Ivanovich was pulling me down by my belt.

Through the semi-opened hatch cover, we were hearing the artillery cannonade that had erupted in our rear – hundreds of our guns and mortars had opened return fire at the enemy! Then we heard the buzz of low-flying aircraft and we rejoiced to see squadrons of our Il-2s flying towards the enemy lines in waves.

Half an hour later everything grew quiet. Only the distinct tapping of rapid-firing cannons and machine guns could be heard from high in the sky – up there our airmen were engaged in fierce aerial combat.

The minute of calm was replaced by another enemy artillery barrage. Rockets streaked towards our lines with their characteristic howling – the enemy artillery was covering their troops as they moved out. The attack had begun! I was examining the brigade's front through the commander's panoramic sight – and I saw enemy vehicles everywhere. In the first echelon, crawling out from behind shrubs fringing the headwaters of the Oka and Neruch Rivers, tanks were slowly advancing; moving out behind them were assault guns and armoured personnel carriers.[3] They were moving in a wedge formation, led by Ferdinands, judging from all indications, with their 200mm of armour protection. I thought to myself: 'It's going to be harder for us today; it won't be easy to repulse such a powerful attack.'

Silence reigned inside the vehicle; obviously no words were appropriate. Valeriy Korolev was frozen at the gunsight, moving only to wipe the fogged lens of the eye-piece from time to time. The rest of the guys were also stuck to their vision slits, silently observing the menacing enemy advance. Perhaps everyone was thinking about the same thing: would we stand our ground or not? After all, today there were several times more tanks and assault guns on the attack than there had been the day before at Zmievka. Nevertheless, I felt that this time the men were less anxious than they had been before the first engagement.

I spoke up, trying to embolden my crew: 'The Fritz advances impudently, until he gets punched in the snout. We'll let the lead tank come to within about 500 metres, set it ablaze, and then proceed with the others.'

At the same time I was thinking agonizingly: what if a Ferdinand forces its way through directly? This was the most powerful heavy assault gun – it could after all just crash through the battle lines.

Across the entire front of the attack, black plumes of smoke appeared in front of the tanks of the first echelon, and there were bright flashes where shells were striking the tanks – it was our artillery's defensive fire. Some of the shells were ricocheting off the armour, sometimes skipping more deeply into the enemy's combat formation. However, not a single tank had caught fire so far! The steel armada kept approaching our defence lines. Over the radio I warned Levanov, the commander of my second self-propelled gun, not to open fire before our first shot. Then suddenly I decided to check on his crew. Ducking to avoid the whizzing bullets and howling shells, I ran towards Junior Lieutenant Levanov's machine, rapped on the hatch and climbed inside once it opened. The crew met me with astonishment, but I immediately sensed doubt and ambivalence in the men's mood, which vexed me:

> Why are you so gloomy?! Your howitzer will penetrate both a Tiger and a Panther from 500 metres! You have good cover; we're properly entrenched! We'll fight to the death! The main thing is self-control, no hasty actions! Fire only with dead certainty! That's both a request and an order too!

Having done my bit to encourage the depressed crew, I rushed back to my vehicle and was already climbing into the hatch when I saw the machine of Fomichev – the 1st Platoon commander – back out of its emplacement, and using the concealment of the thick smoke blanketing the area, bound at high speed into a heavily overgrown ravine about 200 metres away from the battery's position. This manoeuvre was apparently made at the battery commander's decision with a tactical aim: to gain flank shots against the advancing enemy and to strike unexpectedly at a key moment.

The range to the Nazi tanks was still distant, so the crews of the 129th Tank Brigade's light tanks were not shooting yet. Our self-propelled guns stood silent too, but the gunlayers, including our Korolev, kept the leading enemy vehicles centred squarely in their gunsights. The tension was rising with every minute. We could clearly discern in the rays of the morning sun the rectangular hulls and vertical armour plates of the Tigers among the various enemy tanks, and their characteristic brown-yellow camouflage. A turret-less monster with an equally large gun kitted with a muzzle brake was moving towards our platoon, and we understood that it must be a Ferdinand. I broke into a cold sweat – just what I'd feared was happening! How to cope with it?! What to do?! I had no time to reflect – the order to fire was just about to ring out! Stop! Stop! There was a solution! I quickly issued my commands to the platoon gunlayers: 'Korolev! When I give the command, fire at the right track! Kuzin, you'll fire at the left one!'

The Germans had already opened fire, but they were firing randomly, and their shells were hitting the trench parapet or glancing off our armour. The enemy was obviously trying to provoke us to fire, in order to pinpoint and to suppress our firing emplacements. Apparently their command was unaware of the arrival of a regiment of self-propelled guns in the 307th Rifle Division's sector, and the Germans were advancing confidently in a head-on assault designed to demoralize the defenders.

'That's all very well for them; their rate of fire is twice that of ours!' Korolev declared indignantly, as if having read my own thoughts.

'Be strong, Valeriy, cool-headedness is the guarantor of victory,' I said to calm down the gunlayer, who was beginning to become nervous.

There were now about 600 metres to the enemy tanks, when at long last the order arrived from the command post. The gun was already loaded and Valeriy, having checked his aim, pressed the trigger, yelling as he was supposed to do: 'Shot!'

Everyone intensely watched for the strike – where would the shell hit?! The shell exploded on the right side of the frontal armour. Well done, but the Ferdinand kept advancing as if nothing had happened!

'Valeriy! Hit it lower, on the track as it is moving up the slope!'

Korolev fired twice more before managing to break the track. The Ferdinand slowed and swerved to the left, but it hadn't even managed to cover several dozen metres before Lesha Kuzin from the second crew smashed its second track! Both crews then fired three more times at the now immobilized Ferdinand! Five shells out of six struck the superstructure, stunning the crew so badly that the Germans abandoned the vehicle, gripping their heads with both hands. Meanwhile, the battery commander's and Gorshkov's self-propelled guns were still firing on the slowly advancing German tanks. Fomichev's self-propelled gun remained silent. Since the moment of opening fire, the crews had been allowed to use plain speech over the radio. I got in touch with Levanov, and he reported: 'There's been a ricochet hit by an armour-piercing shell, but there are no casualties.'

At the very same moment I overheard communications between the battery commander and Fomichev: 'Petr, why aren't you shooting?!'

'Vladimir Stepanovich, still too early.'

'My hopes are on you! Watch out, and don't miss the right moment!'

In the meantime the enemy tanks of the first two lines had merged into a single battle formation, and the tanks of the third line were already approaching them. Judging from the thin guns on some of them and the stubby howitzers of the others, these were light Panzer III tanks with 50mm guns and assault guns armed with 105mm howitzers. The latter were not a great threat to us, but due to them the German tank avalanche grew considerably in numbers and fire-power – they were badly harassing the infantrymen in the trenches with their plunging fire. Korolev fiercely sent three shells at the nearest tank. The tank brewed up, and no one emerged! (When action ended on this sector, we learned that it had been a Panzer IV tank, but with attached extra armour.) However, we hadn't had time to celebrate Korolev's success, when almost simultaneously several armour-piercing shells smashed onto our emplacement! The left and the right parapet were swept away as if by a broom, and the gunloader's periscope was knocked off. The lower part of the periscope rattled on the floor of the fighting compartment after bouncing off Besschetnov.

'Thank God, we got off lightly; the periscope only hit my leg,' Besschetnov muttered, wincing in pain as he was already opening the breech for another round.

Suddenly one of the Ferdinands advancing in the centre of the combat formation stopped and began to pivot in place. We guessed that it had struck an anti-tank mine. Two more tanks were immobilized by mines, but the rest maintained their relentless advance. The crews of the enemy tanks were firing furiously from machine guns and main guns at the trenches and foxholes of the infantry. The raking fire was so heavy that our soldiers couldn't even raise their heads above the parapet to fire back! Several lines of enemy infantry advancing behind the tanks were also spraying our trenches with long bursts of fire from submachine-guns and machine guns.

The more closely the enemy approached, the more heavy was the enemy shelling on our positions. The ground was being churned up and quaking from heavy shell explosions. We could feel our vehicle bouncing a bit into the air, before being inundated with dirt. As a result, we could no longer see each other, nor see to shoot – we had to climb out of the vehicle under fire and wipe the optics clean. One shell, which exploded very near the vehicle, lit it up in such a way that we came to the conclusion: 'That's it! We're on fire!' The crew responded calmly, however. Plaksin and Besschetnov grabbed fire extinguishers, and then saw that Levanov's guys and the battery commander's crew had each set an enemy tank ablaze – and the face of my lads literally brightened up! Crewmen were leaping out of the two burning German tanks – two from one, three from the other, all in black uniforms and black berets, but they immediately came under machine-gun fire from our tanks.

Oleinik, who was watching through his vision slit as the Germans leaped from their turrets, suddenly asked, 'Comrade Lieutenant, are they allowed to leave a tank that simply has some battle damage?'

'I don't know, Vitya, but if they abandon it, that must mean it's permitted.'

His curiosity was understandable – we could leave a tank only if it was on fire or damaged so badly that it couldn't shoot or move; otherwise we could be charged with cowardice. A lot of factors were at work in such cases. Some crewmen, being so patriotic, utterly refused to abandon their machine and remained with it until the end, while others wouldn't leave because they feared the consequences for doing so. However, it was common for us to stay with a tank as long as it wasn't on fire and could still shoot. The equipment was valued higher than the men inside – that was the way we were taught.

Although our troops were on the defence and well dug-in, all of them – the 129th Tank Brigade and our regiment, let alone the 307th Rifle Division, were suffering losses. A T-70 tank started to burn in front of the battery and to my right, two more tanks and a self-propelled gun were blazing.

Amid the thunder of battle, I didn't hear it, but I saw it: a large flash of fire spurting out of the barrel of the gun hidden in the ravine! Moments later, the German tank on the extreme right burst into flames. Fomichev had sprung the ambush when the enemy tank had moved to within about 300 metres of his self-propelled gun. Literally within a second his machine disappeared – it had backed down into the ravine to re-emerge quickly in another place: staying concealed in the bushes, but constantly shifting position, it kept firing.

A warning came from the regiment headquarters:

> Be prepared to destroy tracked anti-tank mines.[4] They look like tankettes, but are packed with explosives and are meant to destroy tanks and self-propelled guns. They may be destroyed only by a shell or by an anti-tank grenade.

This message didn't cheer us up: we had only F-1 hand grenades[5] in our ammunition allowance – no anti-tank grenades. It meant all our hope was pinned on Korolev and his howitzer.

'Valeriy, you will fire fragmentation shells at these damned machines,' I warned Korolev. 'If there's no direct hit, the blast might still flip it over or onto its side.'

'Got it, Comrade Lieutenant! I won't miss the mark by any means!'

'By any means' – that was his favourite expression. However, we needn't worry about the tankettes at the moment. Having lost a lot of tanks and men the Germans began to withdraw.

Having fallen back to suitable positions, the enemy began to prepare a new attack. About sixty aircraft bombed our defence lines for half an hour. Then the artillery and mortars began to plough the whole front line! Wire entanglements were uprooted and blown apart, infantry foxholes, trenches and communication trenches were collapsed, and the artillery positioned for firing over open sights suffered badly too. Our own emplacements didn't escape some damage.

As soon as the enemy barrage subsided and the shells had stopped falling, the tank and self-propelled gun crews leaped out of their machines, trying to bring their machines back to combat-readiness as quickly as possible. The moans and cries for help were heard from the collapsed infantry entrenchments – over there, those who had survived the bombing and shelling were feverishly shovelling away the debris and obstructions to recover the living and the dead from under the earth and logs. As if rising from out of the ground, three young female medics also appeared and tended to the wounded men. During these tense minutes of the short lull I tried not to think about the tankettes, but alarming thoughts were persistently coming to my mind: how to cope with them?

In the meantime some crewmen were learning how to handle the German machine guns we had picked up, the MG-34 and MG-42. Both fired 7.92mm calibre bullets, the cartridge belts were the same, and both were air-cooled and light enough. I had always felt sorry for our poor machine-gun devils with their 64-kilogram Maksim [the Russian spelling for Maxim] heavy machine guns, which they had to carry on their shoulders across the country in heat and frost, through deep snow and knee-deep mud ... We always tried to help them, and gave them lifts on our self-propelled guns whenever we were going in the same direction.

The short lull eventually led to a new enemy attack. Now their tanks and assault guns advanced behind a smokescreen, which forced us to fire almost blindly. On top of everything else, one of the accursed tankettes appeared from out of the smoke and was moving directly towards us! The black, squat, tracked unit, less than a metre high, was deftly manoeuvring over the surface irregularities, and by the way it was going around obstacles we guessed that it was being steered by an operator, but we didn't know yet how it was being done – whether through a cable connection or radio remote control. Two more of them appeared on either side of the first one. We immediately opened fire on all three tankettes; Korolev and Kuzin were shooting at the one that was advancing towards Levanov's machine. At this moment I heard Fomichev contact Shevchenko over the radio from his ravine: 'We need the help of submachine-gunners! The Fritzes are pressing hard, and my track's jammed! I need maintenance guys with a steel cutter!'

Soon the deputy commander of technical services Ishkin made his way to us – he'd been assigned to lead the rescue team and decided to take along one of our captured machine guns just in case. Having quickly shown him how to operate it, we gave him the MG-42 with two cartridge belts, each with 250 rounds of ammunition. A minute later I watched as a company of submachine-gunners and the repair team crept off towards the ravine.

While most of the crews were busy firing on the tankettes, the Germans set ablaze three more light tanks of the brigade and one T-34, and one of the regiment's self-propelled guns as well. In return, three enemy tanks had halted and were smoking. Now the Ferdinands were advancing at the head of the wedge. Despite the direct impact of our shells on the front of their armour, they kept advancing, relentlessly approaching the front line. Just a little bit ahead of them the tankettes were crawling with their deadly load – tracer rounds were spraying off their hulls, causing them no damage, and their controllers were saving them from direct hits from guns, mortars and anti-tank rifles by skilfully manoeuvring over the terrain. Nearby rapid-fire flak guns also opened fire on the demolition tankettes, yet also with no result. Their seeming invulnerability began to frighten the crews, for everyone knew that within a matter of minutes, our self-propelled guns would be blown sky-high. At long last, to everyone's joy, one of the frightening tankettes closer to our line than the others, vanished in a deafening blast; likely, the anti-aircraft guns had gotten it. However, the two other tankettes, bypassing burning tanks, maintained their terrifying advance. One of them was still advancing towards Levanov's machine, the other – towards the vehicle crewed by Ural guys under the direction of Sergeant Major Minin.

Having directed the gunlayer to fire at a Tiger, which was firing from behind a hillock, I tried to contact Levanov over the radio. As always, the airwaves were full of an unimaginable chaos; snatches of German phrases were mixing with the brusque language and orders of our commanders. With great difficulty I managed to make contact and, having ordered a switch to a back-up wave-length, I issued Levanov a short instruction: 'Ivan, fire only on the tankette! Also, check your machine's readiness in case you need to pull out of the emplacement!'

'Understood. Carrying it out!'

His gunlayer had already expended three shells on the tankette, but had failed to hit it, and the infernal thing was coming closer and closer! Continuing our duel with the Tiger, we were unable to offer him any sort of help. The Tiger had selected us as his target and in this one-on-one fight, the odds were against us: we were fighting in different weight categories, and at any moment it could set us ablaze, even if we had some concealment from smoke grenades. With his next shot, Korolev finally planted a shell right under the turret of the

Tiger and jammed it – the enemy tank had lost its ability to turn its gun. Taking concealment behind a cloud of smoke from a smoke pot, the Tiger turned around and began to withdraw. Right at that moment Valeriy fired a parting shot – and hit it! The crew began to clamber out of the burning tank and fell in flames to the ground. A long burst from the captured MG-34 fired by the gunloader Plaksin passed over the turret and the men in black uniforms. Our Vasya had missed! Stung, Vasya began to curse the Fritzes and their Führer until he was slowed down by Oleinik: 'Vasya, although you're a seasoned machine-gunner, you don't know how to shoot at jumping Fritzes – you aimed at their heads and hit nothing but air. Had you aimed at their bums you would have hit their heads exactly.'

'You're the instructor, aren't you?' Vasiliy retorted. 'Don't you understand that it's not our machine gun? It needs to be zeroed in.'

'Exactly!' Valeriy joined the conversation. 'It doesn't want to hit its own men!'

'Valeriy! The nearest tank is the target!' I ordered Korolev, interrupting the squabble. At that same moment, the self-propelled gun strongly rocked and the engine compartment was instantly engulfed in flame. The crew became anxious – no one wanted to be burned alive!

'Viktor, try to put out the fire with the engine!' I ordered Oleinik. The driver stepped on the accelerator to rev the engine. The engine roared, spinning the powerful ventilator fan with a shriek, and the flame began to dwindle. However, as soon as Oleinik let off the accelerator, first a trace of smoke reappeared, and then the flames flickered into life again. Grabbing a fire extinguisher, I leaped out onto the grate of the engine compartment. The foamy spray from the nozzle stubbornly battled the blue-white flame of the burning oil and at last extinguished it.

As I climbed back into the vehicle, I took a glance over the battlefield, and I was shocked to see that the recently departed company of submachine-gunners and the repair team were beating off a fascist attack at a point only halfway between our position and the ravine, and that Germans were standing on top of Fomichev's self-propelled gun! Without a doubt, Fomichev's crew was in terrible trouble!

'Plaksin! At the fascists up on Fomichev's vehicle! From the machine gun! Fire!' I ordered the gunloader.

Under the long bursts fired by the experienced machine-gunner, the Germans began to topple, as if they'd been cut down, some onto the armour, others onto the ground. I quickly reported on the situation in the ravine to the battery commander. The strain of battle on the main axis of the German attack was growing. The Ferdinands were applying particularly heavy pressure, and the impregnability of these monsters began to cause us to waver. At long last, Sergeant Major Zavyalov's crew managed to smash a track on the lead Ferdinand, and then to set it ablaze with a hit on its flank. This seemed to cool the combat ardour of the other enemy crews and the pace of their advance declined noticeably. However, the powerful avalanche of enemy tanks continued to press on our defence with its wedge, stretching our defences to the breaking point, and the Germans were continuing to send more and more armoured vehicles from the second and third echelon to replace their knocked-out and destroyed machines.

Then several shells struck the self-propelled gun of Porfiriy Gorshkov, which was about 50 metres from Levanov's, almost simultaneously. The machine rocked violently and burst into flames. No one emerged from it! Levanov with his breech operator Khalilov rushed to save the crew under heavy artillery and machine-gun fire. They tried to open the hatches, but both of them – the commander's and the driver's – were warped and jammed. They shouted to the trapped men to open the emergency hatch, but obviously amid the roar of explosions they couldn't be heard, though they caught the sound of some hammering from within the burning vehicle. With lumps in their throats, the two men crawled back to their self-propelled gun, bitterly suffering the death of the crew and their own inability to help the comrades.

Meanwhile, the two tankettes that remained unscathed had stubbornly kept advancing, although apparently the thick smoke from the burning tanks had affected their guidance – now they were moving forward in a straight line, no longer manoeuvring. However, the menacing one that had been directed at Levanov's self-propelled gun was now just several dozen metres from its target – in a couple of minutes, either its operator would press a button or the collision would generate an explosion!

'Levanov! Toss a smoke grenade and get away from there!' I ordered at the last moment.

'Understood, carrying it out!' Levanov replied.

A cloud of sooty smoke instantly formed in front of the self-propelled gun, and with a snort of its engine, the vehicle seemed to leap out of the emplacement. At nearly that same moment, the tankette clambered up over the front parapet, rolled down inside the emplacement, and exploded in the empty pit with such a force that it created a huge crater on the spot. Still, fragments from this 'walking bomb' struck Levanov's machine, damaging the howitzer's armour. However, the machine and the men survived!

With a near-miss, gunlayer Pavlov managed to overturn the final tankette moving towards Minin's self-propelled gun. Its tracks were still turning when a second shell slightly lifted the tankette from the ground, and at the very same moment it blew up with a powerful, fiery explosion. The blast violently rocked and immobilized a passing enemy tank, which had been damaged by fragments from the explosion.

At this, perhaps, most difficult and critical moment of the action we watched as a large German shepherd dog with a pack and a pintle on its back ran past us towards the enemy tanks, and ran directly under a Tiger moving at the head of the advancing formation. A deafening explosion followed as a tongue of flame shot into the air, and the 55-ton steel monster broke apart into two burning pieces of wreckage. To our left and right, we heard several more explosions of similar power. After the engagement we learned that ten dogs specially trained to blow up tanks had been unleashed in our sector, and they had performed well. Several enemy tanks were destroyed.

The destruction of the tanks by the dogs slowed the German advance still further, but they refused to abandon the attack and kept fighting resolutely and aggressively. The fierce battle continued for another half-hour before the Germans finally acknowledged their failure and withdrew to their start line.

That is when we discovered that by some miracle, Porfiriy Gorshkov's crew were still alive! Once the action ended, we rushed over to his self-propelled gun, where we found other men of the battery bunched around Gorshkov's lads, who were vying with each other to tell the story of their survival. The men had been suffocating, trapped inside the machine, and the fire was spreading from the engine compartment into the fighting compartment. All the hatch covers turned out to be tightly jammed, so the men tried the emergency exit in the bottom of the machine, but found it was jammed, too. However, its hatch was more convenient to pound with a hammer. Gasping and choking from the fumes, taking turns, the crews kept pounding the distorted emergency hatch cover with a heavy sledgehammer. However, their strength was failing, so the men were silently bidding farewell to life.

Vasya Tsybin, the gunlayer, who looked like a stoker that had just crawled out of a factory furnace, chimed in:

> However, our Lieutenant turned out to be the strongest. He struck the hatch so well that with his second go, its hinges began to buckle. The hatch cover yielded a little bit, he gave it a couple of more whacks, and then the hatch cover was hanging vertically! Our commander was the last to crawl out, his overalls already on fire but with two fire extinguishers, and immediately rushed to smother the flames – first through the grill, then through the hatch of the engine compartment. We also began to extinguish the fire, some with dirt, and others with pieces of tarpaulin. Then we managed to open the upper hatch cover and prevented the ammunition from catching fire, and thus we saved the vehicle.

The sledgehammer with which they had broken their way out of the 'crematorium' was lying on the armour, and the entire crew were still coughing and panting, trying to get as much oxygen as possible into their lungs. We cheerfully looked at their blackened faces. What a wonder was this crew, an international one! The commander Porfiriy Gorshkov was an Udmurt; the gun-layer Vasya Tsybin – a Russian, the driver-mechanic Kachkun Mukubaev – a Kazakh, the gunloader Nazar Kushubekov – an Uzbek, breech operator Egor Gordienko – a Ukrainian.

Here I have to say that apart from the Russians, Ukrainians and Belorussians, only men of other nationalities who were well-educated and highly proficient in the Russian language were drafted into the armoured forces, because all orders given in combat had to be understood instantly and correctly. Thus, all tankers had to think in Russian, so as not to lose time while interpreting Russian into their own language. Such were the capabilities of this crew.

Judging from the way things were going, we couldn't expect any long respite. On top of other matters, it was already past noon, the sun was high and the heat was extreme; sweat was pouring down our faces in streams, and we were very thirsty. However, both of our canteens had been emptied long ago, and we would have to put up with this situation till late evening when the action would stop. There was a temptation to get water from the engine's cooling system, but we didn't go for it, because we had to take care of our machine as the top priority.

About 16.00 up to 100 bombers struck our positions again, which was followed by forty minutes of shelling on the 307th Rifle Division's front lines from artillery and mortars. The restored fortifications were once again destroyed and rubbled. The target of these bombardments was some distance from our battery, but we also swayed due to the shaking ground for more than an hour.

Then a new German attack began, once again by large forces! Three enemy tanks moved towards our battery, supported by assault guns and infantry. Battery commander Shevchenko skilfully directed the battery's fire, concentrating it on the tanks advancing in front. Our battery managed to set one tank ablaze and to immobilize another, and the remaining tanks and assault guns had to fall back to the centre of their combat formation. However, this time the enemy managed to penetrate our defences, although not on our sector. We understood this from the intense sounds of fighting to the right of us. Having turned the commander's panoramic sight in that direction, I suddenly saw our battery commander leap from his self-propelled gun with the dexterity of a cat and disappear into a trench. A couple of minutes later, I spotted him belly-crawling in our direction. Leaping up onto our vehicle and taking cover behind the superstructure, the battery commander first showed me the lines and some villages on the map through the celluloid cover of his map case, and then gestured through the smoke and haze at them with his hand:

> Vasya, you with your platoon will counter-attack; we must dislodge the enemy from our lines on the north-eastern outskirts of Ponyri. One platoon from each battery of the regiment, a company of T-34s from the 129th Tank Brigade, and a rifle regiment will take part in the counter-attack. The jumping-off area will be the grove north-west of the 1st of May State Farm. Start immediately!

Having signalled the order 'Follow me' [literally, *'Delay, kak ya!'* or 'Do whatever I do!'] to Levanov by flags, I instructed the driver: 'Viktor! Head for the grove at full speed!'

Fifteen minutes later the platoon was in its jumping-off positions. The other units had arrived there too. Deputy regiment commander Mel'nikov laid out the task for the crews on the edge of the grove:

> We are to drive through the Germans' combat formations and link up with a tank regiment advancing from the west. In the course of the attack we'll be joined by infantry whose positions we'll be passing through. The immediate task: Cross the open country as quickly as possible and engage the enemy in street fighting at close range. The signal to attack: three red flares.

The commanders quickly returned to their vehicles. Then the flares soared into the sky. I ordered my driver-mechanic Oleinik, 'Full speed, with zigzags!' The self-propelled gun leaped forward.

The Germans promptly opened fire on us. Although I was confident in my crews, I kept glancing intermittently at the concentrated faces on the guys in my vehicle. The engine was howling from strain, the self-propelled gun was bouncing over shell holes, and everyone was tightly gripping the arms of the seats to keep from being thrown around and bruised, though we all had helmets on our heads. Shells were sometimes bursting several dozen metres on either side of the machine, sometimes ricocheting off the ground in front of us, their trajectory indicated by barely visible traces. We also received several glancing hits on the hull and superstructure, which sometimes were followed by shell explosions with flames that almost blinded the crews; a couple of times it seemed that the self-propelled gun was on fire. The Germans obviously believed so, for they would suddenly switch to a different target for several minutes, but then would resume firing at us with renewed strength. The 129th Tank Brigade's T-34s were also closing on the enemy at top speed, trying to make use of folds in the terrain and firing on the move from their main guns and machine guns. The attack turned out to be well coordinated, resolute and

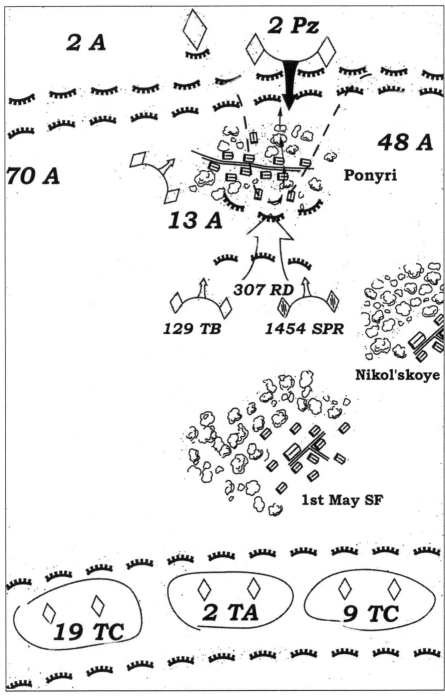

Map 2. The counter-attack at Ponyri during the Battle of Kursk, 7 July 1943.

unexpected for the Germans, but it was very hard to counter-attack across open terrain under such fire! The tankers and the assault gun used smoke grenades to give a decent imitation that their machines were on fire, but the Germans nevertheless managed to set ablaze two tanks somewhere in the middle of no-man's-land. One enemy tank hidden in a garden was firing at a T-34 moving in front of us.

'Viktor, stop behind the hillock!' I ordered Oleinik. Then I immediately told the gunlayer, 'Valeriy! At the tank in line with the chimney! Continuous aim! Fire!'

A shot thundered. The ground erupted just in front of the target.

'Aim at the centre!' I said, to adjust the aim. 'Fire!'

From the second shot, a bright burst of sparks appeared on the tank's frontal armour, and the target backed up and disappeared into the depths of the garden.

Turning the commander's panoramic sight, I quickly examined the battlefield. All around me, the unharvested rye was burning. Levanov's self-propelled gun was firing from a position within a bomb crater. Now three of our tanks and one self-propelled gun were burning, but the attack continued at the same high pace. The infantry was advancing together with the self-propelled guns, sheltering from enemy fire behind the armour of our combat vehicles. The infantry commanders were sparing their fighters for the decisive battle in the trenches. A platoon of thirty men was advancing behind our self-propelled gun, led by a junior lieutenant whose name, unfortunately, I don't remember – before the attack we had only managed to exchange a few words. He was a Russian Hercules from Siberia, who had fought from the first day of the war with the exception of two months in a hospital, and another three months on a course for junior lieutenants in Ryazan. It was a brief front-line acquaintance, but at that time one didn't need a longer one to get a feeling about a man, to understand that you could rely on such a commander in any battle. For some reason I remember his huge pigskin boots, with puttees that wrapped his legs almost up to the knees, which didn't seem fitting for his handsome, manly face and impressive height.

After dealing with the enemy tank in the garden, our vehicle moved forward again. Just in front and to the left of us, another of the brigade's tanks erupted in flames, and only two men got out of the turret. Now dozens of houses were burning in Ponyri, obscuring the Germans' vision with a curtain of smoke. Their tanks and assault guns now had to fire almost blindly, and glancing hits on our armour began to happen more rarely. Now, however, we were in danger from the fire of our own artillery, as we were entering its zone of fire. In such situations we liked to say, 'Hit your own to scare the enemy,' – such things happened when we rapidly advanced into sectors, which the Germans had just abandoned, and our artillerymen didn't know this and kept firing. This time, thank God, Mel'nikov, who was in the commander's tank behind the battery, managed to get in touch with the artillerymen and warn them of the need to shift their fire into the German rear.

The battle had reached its culminating point. Now everything depended on the speed and resolve of both sides in the fighting. The Germans launched counter-attacks on some sectors, deadly hand-to-hand clashes of unprecedented brutality were breaking out, and submachine-guns, hand grenades and bayonets were being put to use!

'Viktor, head towards that partially demolished building and break into the village!' I ordered Oleinik.

'Understood! I'm heading for the trenches!'

The Germans were spilling out of their trenches on our sector too, rushing into a counter-attack. As we reached their trench line, I managed to toss two hand grenades into the trench while the self-propelled gun was crossing over it, crushing several enemy soldiers under its tracks in the process. Just as we moved up to a large brick building, an armour-piercing shot flew past us from behind with its characteristic hissing sound – it had just missed us!

'Get this machine to the right of that house!' I ordered Oleinik immediately.

Now there was only 50 metres between us and a German tank – to put it more simply, two houses. This close proximity promised nothing good. I waved my helmet over my head towards Levanov's vehicle, which meant 'radio contact'.

'Ivan, a tank is sitting behind the second house from us. Turn your self-propelled gun around and keep both corners of the house in your gunsight! Don't let it withdraw!'

We quietly waited for when the German tank would begin to move; in the meantime, we prepared to defend ourselves from German tank-hunting teams. I stood in the hatch with hand grenades; Vasya Plaksin was next to me with a machine gun. Something caused me to turn around, and suddenly I became a witness to the assault of our infantrymen on an enemy trench: a savage hand-to-hand action broke out instantaneously. My platoon leader acquaintance from Siberia, having grasped the rifle of a falling soldier, within the blink of an eye bayoneted two German soldiers who were trying to fire submachine-guns, and then leaped into the trench with lightning speed and began to work with bayonet and rifle butt in the middle of a stunned group of Fritzes! Plaksin and I held our breath as we watched the scene unfold, and exhaled only when the work had been done.

I only turned my attention back to our quarry when I heard Besschetnov's pleading voice: 'Comrade Lieutenant, let me sneak up on the tank and treat them to a grenade bundle.'

'No, Emelyan Ivanovich, you can't, they have submachine-gunners over there for sure. We have to bide our time, the Fritzes will get antsy soon; they'll begin to withdraw for the initiative is in our hands.'

Two or three more minutes of agonizing waiting had elapsed, but the Germans behind the house remained ominously silent, even though intense fighting was going on nearby. How long should we wait?! I resolved to send Plaksin to reconnoitre, to find out what the Germans were doing – whether they were preparing an attack or maybe they were making repairs on the tank?

Vasiliy got out through the emergency hatch and crawled through the bushes towards a corner of the house. Soon we heard a loud explosion. Vasiliy ran back immediately and climbed into the fighting compartment, groaning and clamping his hands over his ears. He began to tell us loudly:

> I had just reached the trench and wanted to drop down into it, when suddenly a hand holding a bundle of grenades reached up out of it. There was no time to think or shoot, so I instinctively whacked it with the barrel of my submachine-gun! The blow knocked the grenade bundle out of the hand and it exploded in their trench! The blast hurled me 5 metres away! My head is still ringing! Comrade Lieutenant, that Fritz was definitely planning to throw that grenade bundle under our vehicle!

Suddenly we heard the enemy tank's engine start up, and judging from its rising rumble, the German tank was beginning to move. Several seconds later from the direction of Levanov's machine, a howitzer shot thundered. I leaped out of my machine and peeked around the corner of the brick building in the direction of the German tank. It was standing motionless. Its left track had been knocked off, and I could see none of the crew. Hence, the Germans had abandoned their tank!

My order followed over the radio: 'Well done, Levanov and crew! Resume the advance!' Together with the remaining tanks and the infantry that had come up, we began to advance slowly from one line to another, firing from short halts.

The Germans ferociously returned fire, but kept retreating to prevent being caught in a pocket. They were concealing their combat formations with some powerful smoke device. Glimpsing through the curtain of smoke a silhouette of a tank moving towards us, I ordered the gunlayer: 'Valeriy! At the tank, continuous aim! Fire!'

While the gunlayer was searching through the smoke for the target, I looked out of the hatch and saw with my naked eye that it was a ... T-34 moving towards us! 'Belay that order!' I yelled, and having fired a green recognition flare, I wiped the cold sweat from my brow with my sleeve.

Thus we had linked up with the tanks advancing from the west, and the enemy had been driven from Ponyri. Later we learned that these were tanks from the 27th Guards Heavy Tank Regiment.

The sun was just beginning to set, but the Germans ceased their attacks and returned to their jumping-off line, having left behind destroyed equipment and dead soldiers on the battlefield. With this, the long day of enemy attacks ended.

Rifle units moved into the positions captured from the enemy. Medics, sweating from the heat and physical exertion, quickly carried our wounded men to field ambulances, as well as wounded Germans left behind by their troops during the retreat. At the same time, they were collecting corpses and loading them onto the backs of trucks. Among the dead were those who had been killed during the preceding fighting – they were found in no-man's-land. The corpses had already begun to decay because of the unbearable heat.

We returned to our main positions by the same route we had taken in our advance that day, so as to avoid any German or friendly anti-tank mines. Having moved our self-propelled guns back into their emplacements, the crews rushed for the cistern of cold water that had just been brought up by the quartermasters. Eagerly, they gulped down the life-giving fluid, quenching their many hours of thirst! Then, having serviced and camouflaged the self-propelled guns, we spent a half-hour beating the dust out of everything – our pores, our helmets, overalls, uniforms and even canvas-topped boots. We washed our grubby faces and necks with difficulty, sparingly pouring a tiny amount of water onto each other's hands from the tank's canteens.

We returned right at the appointed time for the officers to assemble. Regiment commander Samyko summed up:

> The regiment's units have destroyed five and damaged six enemy tanks. Over 100 enemy troops have been killed or wounded. Our losses: seven men killed and twenty wounded. Two self-propelled guns irrevocably destroyed, five more knocked out. The most important result: we have held our sector of defence! Moreover, we've dislodged the enemy from Ponyri, for which the Central Front commander, Army General Konstantin Konstantinovich Rokossovsky, expresses his gratitude to us. My congratulations to all the men! It's a great honour to meet with the approval of such a military leader!

The intense day of action was coming to a close; a warm wind was stirring the treetops and waving the tall rye that had somehow survived the fighting and fire in places. The crimson-red sunset seemed to be a reminder of the hellish bloody action of the elapsing day, but also finalizing it, driving it into the past ...

We were engaged in hard defensive fighting at the Kursk salient for a few long days and nights, continuing to repulse several mass attacks daily. On 12 July, by the order of the Central Front commander, we pulled out of our positions near Ponyri, which were stained with the blood of our comrades. On that day the regiment passed to the control of Lieutenant General Bogdanov's 9th Tank Corps, and became attached to the 95th Tank Brigade.

The second, offensive stage of the Kursk battle, known as Operation Kutuzov, was about to begin.

Chapter 4

Operation Kutuzov

The Battle for Glazunovka

For two days our 1454th Self-propelled Artillery Regiment, engaging in short clashes, advanced to the north-west in the first echelon of the 9th Tank Corps. In order to carry out our main task – to capture the settlement and railway station of Glazunovka, we assembled in a forest near the settlement of Kunach' on the western bank of the Neruch River.

Approximately at noon the Il-2 *Shturmoviks* flew over our forest in the direction of the Germans and plastered their defences with bombs. Then the artillery shelled the enemy with mass concentrated fire for a quarter of an hour. With its final salvo, our tanks, self-propelled guns and infantry rushed into the attack. Pushing through the enemy artillery's strong barrier fire, we approached the Kursk–Orel railroad and here we came under heavy fire from tanks and self-propelled guns. Two of our tanks were set ablaze and the attack stalled. The source of fire was a grove adjacent to the railway station, and the majority of our tanks and assault guns on the left flank concentrated their fire on this grove. The open terrain put our troops in a very unfavourable situation, and they were on the verge of retreating in order to avoid further losses. Suddenly two of our self-propelled guns launched a flank attack at high speed, charging through a field. They raced towards the southern edge of the grove from where the enemy tanks were firing. We watched transfixed as we continued our slow advance. The armour of the two self-propelled guns was literally enveloped with the black plumes of explosions and lit by sparks from glancing hits, but they continued to advance through the storm of deadly shells, as if charmed! Soon, however, the expected happened to dash our enthusiasm: one of the self-propelled guns erupted in flames just before reaching the grove, and as far as we could see only one man managed to escape the burning machine.

Nonetheless, the second self-propelled gun plunged into the grove, and the enemy's fire in our direction noticeably weakened. Taking advantage, the tanks and self-propelled guns rushed towards the enemy defence line at full speed, firing their main guns and machine guns ceaselessly, and from the march seized the eastern outskirts of Glazunovka. Hand-to-hand fighting between our riflemen and the enemy infantry broke out in the first trench, and house-to-house combat began. Some of the houses changed hands several times. The Germans counter-attacked time and again. The stubborn fighting had continued already for more than an hour, when an enemy counter-attack struck the right flank of our advancing forces with tanks and infantry.

In this complicated situation our command urgently formed a combined detachment from a tank company, two batteries of our regiment, a platoon of flame-throwing tanks, and two companies of motorized infantry in order to launch a sudden attack on the enemy's flank and rear. Major Fetisov, the regiment's chief of staff, was put in charge of the special detachment. The operation began with a heavy barrage on the enemy. Under that covering fire, the detachment moved out, in a combat-ready array, prepared to repulse attacks from left and right, and advanced into the enemy's rear. Major Fetisov followed the self-propelled guns within the platoon of flame-throwing tanks, which consisted of two heavy KV-1 tanks equipped with the ATO-41 automatic flame-thrower, which could throw burning fuel for a distance of 200 metres. Apart from the flame-throwers, each tank had a 76mm gun and two 7.62mm calibre Degtyarev tank machine guns.

Due to the impetuous and resolute attack of our detachment, which could not be called either a forward unit or a reconnaissance unit, we managed to break into the enemy's rear. The Germans became disorganized and attempted to re-form, which is just what we exploited! We knocked out four assault guns and a tank. Our detachment lost one T-34, and Lieutenant Miroshnikov's self-propelled howitzer was badly damaged. Its commander was badly wounded but refused to leave the battlefield, and wasn't evacuated until he collapsed unconscious.

The enemy managed to reorganize its fire and turned it against the detachment. Our advance immediately slowed. All the tanks and self-propelled guns took cover wherever they could find it – behind houses, in farmhouse gardens, behind the parapets of the captured trenches – and returned fire. Soon Fetisov brought up the artillery, which opened fire on the second German position, and our advance resumed, though at a slow, slogging pace. Immediately in front of our detachment's advance, there was a badly damaged red brick building with no roof. No one could imagine that the Germans would be capable of turning it into an anti-tank nest so quickly. Several guns fired a volley from it. The leading tank immediately burst into flames. Another tank and two self-propelled guns were knocked out.

'Viktor! Get this machine into the shrubs!' The self-propelled gun jolted into motion, and just then an enemy shell whizzed right past us. Seconds decide everything in combat and we might have burned alive had I delayed with the order for just an instant …

I saw with joy that Levanov's machine had managed to escape the initial volley too, but now a Hornisse tank destroyer [later renamed the Nashorn] caught them in its gunsight. The Hornisse was heavily concealed in some bushes, and it was impossible to target it. Just at this moment, however, the self-propelled gun of the commander of the 4th Battery Vasya Porshnev raced past Levanov's vehicle! It was recognizable by the three stars on the left side of its superstructure, which signified three destroyed tanks. It was hard to surmise the commander's intentions, but Porshnev was, perhaps, the most experienced officer in the regiment, and his driver-mechanic Afanasiy Zakharov, a man with an iron character, was one of the best. I couldn't take my eyes off the racing self-propelled gun, and it rammed directly into the Hornisse at top speed, the impact driving it backwards for several metres. One track of the 'beast' fell into a trench, and now it was immobilized and couldn't fire – that had been Porshnev's calculation! The commander emerged as the victor! It was the 1454th Self-propelled Artillery Regiment's first case of deliberate ramming. However, Porshnev's feat somehow didn't receive sufficient acclaim, apparently due to the modesty of the hero. Yet I remember thinking back then that it had been a good thing that our self-propelled guns were equipped with short-barrelled howitzers. Had the gun barrel struck the armour of the enemy machine during the collision, the whole howitzer would have been driven back into the fighting compartment.

The detachment's subsequent advance was still being impeded by the German position in the brick building. Our shells were not doing any considerable damage to its sturdy masonry, creating only small impact marks, whereas the fascists were firing from the ground floor windows, which had been turned into embrasures, so intensely that any further advance was out of the question. At this moment chief of staff Fetisov advanced the menacing flame-throwing KV tanks towards the enemy citadel. They followed the tracks of Porshnev's self-propelled gun, and, having stopped about 150 metres from the building, they gave it a long squirt. Two torrents of flame fell on the enemy gun crews, which had no overhead protection. The second squirt blazed into the embrasures from which the anti-tank gun barrels protruded. The firing stopped immediately. The bloodcurdling screams of burning gunners and the muffled explosions of shells spewing flames and black smoke carried from the building.

Moving past the ill-fated building, the tanks and self-propelled guns broke into the enemy defence line and began to grind the infantry positions beneath their tracks. Our battery burst suddenly into the enemy's artillery positions. We were unexpected! The gunners began to rush around the guns; many of them immediately took to their heels in flight. However, the crew manning the gun towards which our self-propelled gun was moving was by no means among them. These guys were dedicated – they stuck with their gun, intending to fire at point-blank range, and were already turning the gun in our direction.

'Viktor! Overrun the gun!' I ordered the driver.

Viktor stepped on the gas and released the main clutch. The moment of truth had arrived: *Kto kogo?* [Who will destroy whom?] Seconds would decide the fate of our crew and the gun crew! They were going to set us ablaze or we were going to crush them. We couldn't let the enemy fire a shot! The self-propelled gun raced towards the enemy at such a speed that we had no time to register our surroundings, felt no jolts, and I understood that if I interfered with a command, it would inevitably slow down the actions of the driver and for this reason I fully relied on his skills.

Just before reaching the gun's position, our vehicle struck a tall, thin tree, which knocked it into the gun just as its crew managed to get off their shot. The falling tree struck the gun barrel, causing the shell to miss us. The front of our machine rose into the air, then we felt a metallic thump on the bottom, there was a scraping sound, a strong lurch, one more jolt – and then the vehicle leaped out of the revetment! Without any orders and before the enemy could recover from their surprise, Oleinik turned and immediately knocked over a second gun that had been abandoned by its crew. Then, dashingly turning away, he stopped the self-propelled gun in an orchard beside a house – we had to position ourselves.

Opening the hatch cover, I took a look around. The battery commander's and platoon commander's vehicles were wiping out the enemy infantry and guns amidst smoke and dense clouds of dust kicked up by their tracks. Levanov's and Gorshkov's self-propelled guns set ablaze an assault gun by almost simultaneously fired shots. Our foot soldiers were moving in behind the tanks and self-propelled guns, going down the German trenches and shooting from rifles and submachine-guns at the enemy infantry, which had already begun to retreat. When the Germans tried to counter-attack, our men made use of bayonets and rifle butts – most of our foot soldiers back then were still armed with Mosin-Nagant 1891/30 rifles equipped with triangular (three-edge) bayonets.

The two hours of fighting had heated up the gun barrels, and it was hot and stuffy in the fighting compartment, even though we opened our hatch covers from time to time and the ventilation fans were working at full power. Now, however, we were being forced to fire less frequently, as we'd nearly run out of ammunition. We still had about a quarter of the allotted combat load, which we could not expend without permission of the regiment commander, and we had little hope that it would be replenished any time soon.

Having switched to external radio communications I was just about to report to the battery commander about the ammunition shortage, when I heard

Fetisov's voice in the clear – he was asking the regiment commander in plain speech to bring up the 'cucumbers', which was our code word for shells. Just then we heard the sound of an engine approaching from behind – it was a Lend-Lease Studebaker, with crates of shells in the back. Boris Pushkov – a driver from the ammunition supply platoon – was behind the steering wheel; Senior Medic Valya Vorobieva was sitting next to him. They'd sneaked through to us literally right under the guns of the German tanks at the moment of our great need. Jumping from the vehicle, Valya immediately rushed to the wounded men. We had to recognize the courage of these two – an 18-year-old lad from Verkhniy Volochek and a 19-year-old girl from Sverdlovsk: what they'd just done was practically a death order! Their vehicle was riddled with dozens of bullet holes and shell splinter holes. Both would rightly be awarded the medal 'For Combat Merit' for this exploit.

After a 15-minute long barrage from our artillery, and having replenished our stocks of ammunition, the detachment resumed the advance, now together with the main forces. Failing to withstand the resolute attack from the front and from the flank, the enemy abandoned Glazunovka.

Men hugged each other! They congratulated each other! It was our first significant victory of Operation Kutuzov. We all were so grubby that we could recognize each other only by our eyes and mannerisms.

As always after an action, we first took care of our vehicle, looking after it like it was a new bride. It was our law – to refuel it on time, to tune it up, to clean components and weapons, and to check all electrical contacts. The engine was supposed to be clean, with no stains, dust or dirt. We regularly checked the oil level. If there were any leaks, they had to be cleaned up, but we would certainly try to find the source of the leak, or make sure that it wasn't just a spill during refuelling.

We took care of the gun as well. It was unfailingly cleaned after each action. We used a special, durable wooden pole, its end wrapped in rags, to swab the gun barrel of powder residue. It was a tough job, and the entire crew would work together to clean the tube and polish the interior to a mirror-like lustre. Once clean, we would then cover the muzzle without fail. God forbid a bit of sand or some pebble found its way into the barrel – we had to guard against a 'lily', when a shell's premature explosion in the barrel would tear the gun apart and cause the barrel to 'bloom' with sharp, lacerated petals, looking like the flower.

The trophy machine gun had to be in operational condition at all times. This was the gunloader's realm, and the machine gun had to be maintained and oiled. We never forgot to scrounge ammunition for our faithful combat helper that we had obtained from the Germans. I may add that two PPSh submachine-guns were among the self-propelled gun's armament, and all crewmen had their personal sidearms: I always had my pistol, others had Nagant revolvers, and I made sure the guys didn't forget to clean and check them.

After ensuring that the machine was combat-ready, we brought ourselves to a fair condition – for quite some time we were shaking out dark-brown dust from our clothes and helmets, and washing off the dirt and sweat.

Between Battles

Continuing the advance, the 9th Tank Corps' troops liberated hundreds of settlements in Orel, Bryansk and Kursk Oblasts, and on 19 August we were concentrated in a forest 3 kilometres south-west of the Ivanovskoye settlement, where we had a long rest and prepared for forthcoming battles. First of all, we dug ourselves well into the ground and thoroughly concealed our presence. Then we would do whatever we could to take care of hygiene and personal grooming. On the second day we washed in a tent *banya* [bath].

The quick scrub was bliss. There had been constant fighting for two months – we had no time for a *banya*. It was summer, though, and hot! The lice were here and there. Unlike with the infantry, lice were not that widespread among us – assault gun crews and tankers – but sometimes, not very often, such things happened. Then we would take certain measures, discard our underwear and put on stuff we got from the Germans. The Germans, though, had French silk underwear with mesh in it: a louse would be on the outside, it would roll down the silk, grasp the mesh and bite through it. Even now it is disgusting to think of it. So we preferred our underwear.

Whenever we halted, if we were to remain for several days, the quartermasters would try to organize a *banya* for us. More often they would set up a tent for it, but if some kind of shack was available, they would drag some rocks inside it, make a stone stove, build a fire, heat some water (if only a bit) – and the men would wash. The underwear would be replaced too, thank God. Of course, the quartermasters distributed army-issue, because they didn't have any captured material.

Compared to the other military arms, the tank and self-propelled gun crews lived in luxury. Why? Because they always had captured goods and matériel! The poor foot soldier, though, had his puttees, trench coat, rifle, helmet, gas mask, ammunition pouch – with all that on him, he could barely walk, much less carry extra items. We, on the other hand, had a steel stove on the rear armour plate between the exhaust pipes, attached by four screw-bolts. It was quite sizeable and had a door, which could be tightly closed. We used this stove to store things we couldn't fit inside the vehicle.

On that August night of 1943, after the first day of rest and cleaning up, the men slept soundly. Only sentries were vigilantly carrying out their security duties, while with sweating brows officers were at work in the regiment head-quarters, taking turns to rest.

Already at daybreak, walking past Levanov's machine, I saw that for some reason the commander himself was on watch. I decided not to say anything. Then around noon the officers were summoned to headquarters for a meeting in regard to combat preparations. As I was on my way to the meeting, I watched as Levanov stumbled on level ground and almost fell over – the commander was practically sleepwalking.

'Ivan Petrovich, didn't you get any sleep last night?' I asked.

'No, I didn't.'

'Why not?'

'I was guarding the self-propelled gun.'

'Why? You have four men in your crew, why were you on duty?'

'They all say they have night-blindness.'

'Have they been to the medical unit?'

'They have, but there's nothing to treat it, not even brewer's yeast.'

'I'll cure them today!' – and with that, I ended the conversation.

We went to the headquarters and attended the meeting. Once it became completely dark, I woke up Plaksin: 'Vasya, go and see Levanov's guys, tell the men quietly that they've delivered some seized German honey to our machine, so let them come around with mess tins.'

Plaksin left, and I took a glance at the luminous face on my watch – its hands were indicating that it was just after midnight. A warm drizzle was falling, the sky was heavily overcast, and it was so dark that it seemed that I'd been left alone in the whole world. A wave of grief for my fallen comrades came over me.

The rapidly approaching sound of cracking twigs and rattling mess tins snapped me out of my distressing thoughts – aha, they were coming at a run! In the inky darkness of the night, you couldn't see your fingers in front of your face, much less the tangled deadfalls lying in their path, but they were rushing head over heels, nimbly leaping over fallen trunks and snags in the path. They ran up to the assault gun and suddenly caught sight of me! They were taken aback and stopped in their tracks, disheartened.

'This is what you're going to get, instead of honey!' I growled as I shook my fist at them. 'I'll show you honey and night-blindness. You'll be telling your grandchildren, so they'll never have it!'

They hung their heads. I added harshly: 'Get out of here and go do your duty.'

That's how I cured them of their night-blindness! With that, the incident was over. Later I spoke to Levanov privately about the extra ration of honey, and he began to share it with his crew.

The extra ration was issued to officers as compensation for the large demands placed on them. A front-line commander bears a double, even a triple load: night watch, checking on the sentries, going around the positions to check on the men, and reconnoitring, which was often connected with crawling out to observation posts. All this was in addition to the routine concerns and burdens that officers shared equally with the non-commissioned officers and the soldiers.

However, at the front where all of us – the rank and file and the officers – together had to endure cold, hunger, fear, wounds and death – here all the qualities of a man were ruthlessly stripped bare for all to see, regardless of rank, and just as pitiliessly, without exception, assessed. Including one's stinginess, and Levanov was a miser, a miser by nature. He ate his ration on the sly and wouldn't share it with his crew. I never saw my own officer's supplemental ration. My crew got it and ate it together. There was not much in it anyway; they'd have a mug of tea – and that extra ration would be gone.

The question asks itself: Were the crew's expectations fair? Was a commander obliged to share what he was entitled to receive? Seemingly, it was unjust, and he shouldn't have had to do it. However, I repeat – the front line had its own rules. Here, military hierarchy doesn't reign, but a human hierarchy, which meant that the crew's attitude was perfectly legitimate. Ironically in the future Levanov's crew would become one of the most cohesive in the entire regiment.

Today they talk about a 'front-line fraternity'. Essentially, this kind of fraternity was to arise after the war: whenever former comrades from the same unit come together after the war – there's your front-line fraternity. At the front they were combat buddies. What does this mean? It means that one has to save another in combat, to protect each other, and not hide behind a comrade's back, but to defeat the enemy together. In our arm – in the armoured units – if a machine was on fire, we ran to it and worked to help the crewmen escape it until the shells it was carrying began to explode. We didn't talk about this mutual assistance aloud, nobody discussed it, but in the regiment each man knew that the others would fight for his life to the very end.

In addition, everyone knew who was who. There was one assault gun commander from Ivanovo Oblast among us – a former teacher, but a bit of a coward. He came up with a certain peculiar way of acting when in combat: his hatch cover would be raised, yet he'd not be standing in the hatch, but instead crouched behind the armoured superstructure, giving directions to his driver by prodding him with a long stick. If he smacked the driver on the head, that meant 'stop'; if he poked him in the back – 'forward'; tapped him on the left shoulder – 'turn left'; on the right shoulder – 'turn right'. His surname was Abramov. Of course, not everyone knew about this – when the action starts, who's going to keep an eye on him? However, those directly around him knew, and guys like him were shunned by the rest.

We remained in the forest near Ivanovskoye for about two weeks, meticulously preparing for upcoming clashes. Special attention was given to night attacks. On three occasions, we rehearsed cooperation between the armour and infantry during night-time exercises. During our leisure time we sang and danced. We also watched several films.

Chapter 5

To the Dnieper River, August–September 1943

The Death of Battery Commander Shevchenko

We hadn't managed to fall asleep one night after one of these exercises, when a combat alert sounded. In no more than a quarter of an hour, the assault guns were formed into a column that stretched along the forest edge, and raising dense clouds of dust, we headed in a south-west direction.

The march was going to be difficult. It was almost impossible to discern through the darkness of the night and the dense clouds of dust the two red tail-lights on the machine ahead of you, and hence the drivers and the commanders constantly had to be vigilant. By dawn the regiment had assembled in an offensive combat formation in a forest near the settlement of Starshyeye Melnichishe. We were to attack towards the village of Posadka, which was located at the boundary junction of Kursk, Bryansk and Sumy Oblasts, and thus the enemy was defending the place with large forces.

Having gathered the commanders on the forest edge, the regiment commander Samyko had issued combat orders. The artillery began to rumble as the commander finished his instructions – the attack's artillery preparation had commenced. Now in my vehicle's hatch, I was anxiously comparing my map to the locale. Almost 2 kilometres of wide, flat wheatfields spread in front of us, half-harvested and dotted with sheafs. To the left, there were six German-held villages. Beyond Posadka there was the village of Sal'noye, which was situated on a dominating height. The enemy artillery could place direct fire on our left flank, and my platoon would be occupying the left flank of the regiment's advance. In other words, the situation was most unfavourable for us in terms of fire and tactics.

The normally self-restrained Korolev spoke up: 'Comrade Lieutenant, why is it that for two weeks we've been drilling under night conditions, and today we're going to attack in broad daylight across wide open terrain? This isn't good at all.'

'It means, Valeriy, that's the way it must be,' I replied briefly. An order is an order. I was impotent to change anything.

'Emelyan Ivanovich, Vasiliy, hurry over to the supply unit!' I ordered the breech operator and gunloader. 'Bring back around fifty smoke hand grenades, twenty-five for each crew.'

Then the offensive began! The tanks of the 95th Tank Brigade led the attack, our self-propelled guns and the infantry followed. It must have been a terrifying spectacle for the defending enemy. About 100 tanks and self-propelled guns and about a dozen armoured cars were attacking on a narrow sector of the front. In addition, no less than 1,000 soldiers were running behind us, filling the battlefield with thunderous and continuous shouts: 'Urra-a-a-h! Urra-a-a-h!'

Nevertheless, the briefly stunned enemy came to his senses. We had managed to cross only about half of the field, but the enemy artillery was already firing on the attackers. Guns were firing from the village of Posadka itself. They were also firing from Sal'noye – over the heads of their own troops. Heavy fire coming from Taborishche and Bereznyak on the left worried me most of all – their fire on the assault guns' weaker side armour threatened heavy equipment losses. The infantry advancing across the huge open field, though, had the hardest time. There was not a single hillock or shrub – not the least bit of cover, other than our combat vehicles. Dozens of machine guns and hundreds of submachine-guns were firing on them, forcing them to crowd behind the tanks and self-propelled guns moving in front of them. Without any commands, the tanks and assault guns abruptly accelerated and began to weave, trying to throw off the aim of the enemy gunlayers. Shells were exploding closer and closer, enveloping the armoured vehicles with clouds of smoke. Several tanks had already been struck and were burning. It bitterly echoed in our souls: everyone could all too easily picture how it was for their crews – to burn alive while being wounded, or to leap out of the vehicle with your overalls on fire. However, we couldn't help those who had come to grief, for to halt your machine during an attack meant ruin for both yourself and the whole cause. A motionless target inevitably becomes the enemy's prey!

Shells were bursting in front and behind us, and frequently ricocheting off the armour. When two tanks on our flank exploded, I ordered Levanov 'Follow me!' At full speed we climbed a low hill and turned towards Taborishche, from where the enemy anti-tank guns were firing point-blank on our attacking armour. Shrubs gave us some concealment and the crews, having quickly determined the target settings, opened fire right away. Gunlayers Korolev and Kuzin fired five shots each, and the enemy guns in Taborishche ceased firing!

My platoon returned to the main axis of the advance. The enemy artillery was still firing intensely from the villages of Sal'noye and Dobroye Pole, and now five of our tanks and one of our self-propelled guns were burning on the battlefield. Five more damaged vehicles had been immobilized. However,

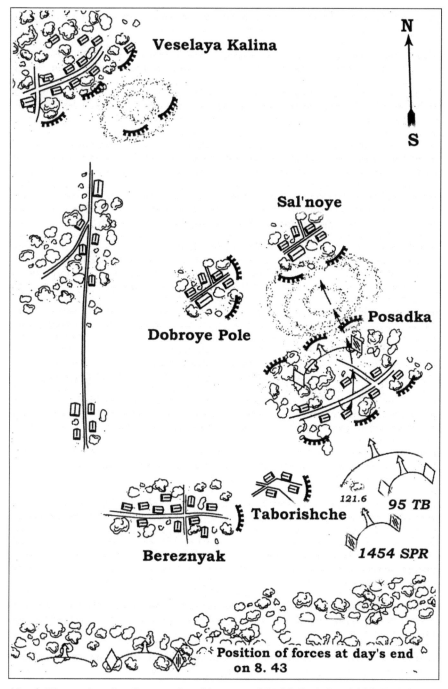

Map 3. The attack on Posadka as conducted by troops of the 9th Tank Corps' 95th Tank Brigade and the 1454th Self-propelled Artillery Regiment during Operation Kutuzov, 27 August 1943.

the most advanced units had already gained a solid foothold in the orchards on the eastern outskirts of Posadka. Stukas at low altitude dropped small bomblets – apparently anti-tank – on us and strafed us with their automatic guns, displaying their sinister black crosses. Vasya Plaksin shot at several of the planes from our captured machine gun, registering hits on one or two, which caused the pilots to pull out of their dives. The Stukas began to avoid our assault gun and the other vehicles of our battery as well.

Making extensive use of smoke to conceal the assault guns, Levanov's crew had already expended all of their smoke grenades, and when we began to overrun the German trenches on the outskirts of the village, an enemy shell struck the left side of Levanov's assault gun. The machine burst into flames. The commander was the first to exit through an upper hatch, and having managed to issue the order to abandon the machine, dropped unconscious on the spot. With long machine-gun bursts, my crew tried to provide cover for Levanov's guys, who were already under pressure from enemy submachine-gunners attacking through the orchard. Levanov's gunlayer and gunloader rushed to rescue the commander, while the driver and the breech operator battled the fire that had already engulfed the fighting compartment. Following a track imprint in the dirt, the medics Aleksey Volobuyev and Nikolay Petrov crawled up under a hail of bullets, picked Ivan [Levanov] up and carried him down into a trench, where they began to apply a tourniquet to stop the bleeding from his mutilated leg. The leg appeared to be completely torn off and was being held in place only by the commander's overalls. Having clambered out of my vehicle, also under the fire of submachine-gunners, I jumped down into the trench to say goodbye to my battle comrade. Vanya was fading in and out of consciousness, but he lightly gripped my hand, and I thought at that moment how it would be for him to return home, where his wife and three kids were waiting for him, without a leg . . .

It was time to get back, but then the battery commander's assault gun pulled up: he wanted to say farewell to Levanov too. The hatch cover opened, and Shevchenko began to emerge, but then he suddenly staggered and collapsed – a bullet had struck him directly in the eye. Now we had to send two of our comrades back to an army hospital in Fomichev's self-propelled gun, which had just arrived.

To our great sorrow, our battery commander Senior Lieutenant Vladimir Stepanovich Shevchenko died two hours later without regaining consciousness. Junior Lieutenant Ivan Petrovich Levanov was evacuated to the rear. Unfortunately, I know nothing about his subsequent fate.

All of Levanov's crewmen had been wounded by splinters from their own armour, which had sprayed the interior of their vehicle after the hit by the same shell that had removed their commander's leg. However, none of them abandoned the machine – as soon as Fomichev's vehicle departed, disappearing into a cloud of dust, we continued the fierce combat against the enemy tanks and artillery. The infantry and the submachine-gunners were now locked in hand-to-hand fighting in the German trenches: machine guns and submachine-guns were chattering everywhere in foxholes, trenches, communication trenches and weapon emplacements. The battlefield turned into a hellish cauldron! The ground was heaving with explosions, and covered with clouds of choking smoke and soot. Gunshots rumbled. Hand grenades and shells burst. Thousands of shell fragments were zipping through the air. During brief intervals in the nearly ceaseless din of battle, you could instantly hear the heart-rending screams of wounded men and the crackle of burning vehicles.

The tanks and assault guns finally managed to break through to the artillery positions. Levanov's crew was one of the first to begin crushing the enemy guns – fiercely and mercilessly! Nothing and no one was spared. The self-propelled gun of Lieutenant Khludov from the 2nd Battery surged ahead of us on the right and overran a gun straight off. However, one track of his vehicle slid into a trench and it became immobilized, leaving his assault gun a sitting duck. We had to get the guys out of trouble: the German crews manning the two surviving anti-tank guns were already turning their barrels towards the tilted self-propelled gun! At this moment the enemy infantry, which had allowed us to pass through their ranks, rose to counter-attack the following infantry with fixed bayonets. On this sector they were opposed by young recruits, who were experiencing combat for the first time – they began to retreat, pausing and turning to return fire. Encirclement and the loss of the captured gun emplacements were being threatened. First of all, though, we had to get rid of the guns.

'Valeriy! Fragmentation shell! At the gun! Fire!' I ordered the gunlayer instantly.

The shell hit the target, having just managed to beat the fascists' own shot. I immediately tossed a smoke grenade, for we had time neither to shoot nor to retreat before another one could fire at us from point-blank range! We were in a desperate situation. Just at this moment, however, a 'saving angel' T-34 turned up out of nowhere and destroyed the second gun with a well-placed shot and burst of machine-gun fire. The thought flashed through my mind: 'Thanks, comrade, although I don't know who you are, you've saved me!'

'Vasya! At the infantry, from the machine gun! Fire!' I ordered the gunlayer, and the fascist infantry hit the deck.

Behind the curtain of a smokescreen, we managed to tow Khludov's vehicle out of the trench, and together we kept advancing. The tank clash in the centre of our combat formation began to subside. Enemy tanks were retreating towards Sal'noye, returning fire, and the infantry was following their withdrawal. When we emerged on the western outskirts of the village, the Germans had already passed over the low ridge between Sal'noye and Posadka. That evening, we learned that the assault guns of Porshnev's 4th Battery and Polivoda's 1st Battery had smashed the German rear in the centre of the village, destroying many vehicles, six guns and fourteen carts, and killing several dozen of the enemy's resisting troops.

In the twilight hour, a skinny, grubby boy about 12 years of age crawled up to our battery from the direction of Sal'noye. Having introduced himself as Vanya, he told us in childish haste that the Germans had killed his family three weeks ago. The tears in his eyes had dried long ago, and now his eyes were burning with hatred – it was obvious that during these three long weeks after the death of his family, he'd been looking for a chance to take vengeance. The crews quickly gave the lad something to eat, and then together with him they crawled up the height, from where Vanya pointed out the large buildings where the Germans were storing ammunition. Senior Lieutenant Stepanov, who had taken over the command of our battery after Shevchenko's mortal wounding, immediately reported on this to the regiment commander and received the order to wipe the depots out. The battery crews stealthily pulled the self-propelled guns up to the crest of the height, and having switched on the gunsight's internal illumination, they fired two well-aimed shots. Then they quickly returned to their original positions. The enemy depots burned all night long. We could hear the muffled explosions of mines and shells, the popping of grenades, and see jumping tongues of fire. A whole colour spectrum of different flares soared above the low ridge, producing a brilliant display of fireworks.

In revenge, German howitzers and mortars shelled our positions with indirect fire from behind the height, and at about 02.00, the Germans counter-attacked from two directions: with infantry and medium tanks from Sal'noye, and with heavy tanks and infantry from Pozdnyakovka. Nevertheless, both of the attacking groups ran into a beaten zone of defensive artillery fire, several tanks struck our minefields, and the enemy counter-attack quickly faltered.

Vanya lived with us for almost a week. We fed him to let him gain strength before sending him to the rear.

A Flank Attack

The night was dark and uneasy. German scouts were prowling everywhere along the front, probing for weaknesses in our defence lines. Our scouts were on the alert too. Soldatov together with the best scouts of the regiment – Senior Sergeant Egorov and Sergeant Potemkin – managed to sneak into the enemy positions and drag back a prisoner. Based on the prisoner's interrogation, the command decided to continue the advance by outflanking Sal'noye on the north.

All night long the regiment's sapper platoon, led by Sergeant Major Vorontsov, and the 95th Tank Brigade's sapper company were busy clearing gaps in the minefield and simultaneously beating back German forays. On the morning of 28 August, after a short artillery preparation, the combined forces of the 95th Tank Brigade, the 1454th Self-propelled Artillery Regiment, and the infantry went on the advance. They managed to break through the single enemy defence line almost immediately with a sudden attack, and our troops headed towards Veselaya Kalina. As we approached the village, we were counter-attacked by tanks and infantry, which fell on us from behind the height. A fierce and close-range clash broke out on a narrow sector of the front. In the first minutes of the battle, tanks and self-propelled guns on both sides began to brew up. The battlefield was covered by dense clouds of smoke and soot, and only from time to time would glimpses of the extremely brutal engagement – a frontal collision of two battle groups – appear in the intervals between strong explosions. Having overtaken us, a T-34 smashed into a Panther! Both crews fired simultaneously and both burned up together with their tanks. A Panzer IV tank appeared out of the smoke right in front of us, our gun was loaded, and Valeriy immediately pressed the trigger. The enemy tank erupted in flames that rose above its turret. None of the crew scrambled out. We heard Plaksin's gloating remark: 'You deserved that crematorium, you bastards! It will save us the ammunition!'

Shots were thundering from every direction, but because of the heavy smoke, the enemy tanks weren't visible. From the receding sounds of firing, we guessed that the Germans had begun to withdraw. The heat of the battle gradually subsided, and when the command committed the second echelon of infantry regiments and a tank battalion into the battle, the enemy, having no reserves, began to retreat across the entire front. However, it was too early to rejoice. When breaking through, we had bypassed two villages – Polyanka and Dobroye Pole – and we now found ourselves in the enemy rear, encircled by enemy formations. We could clearly see in the bright August sunlight as fascist tanks and several waves of infantry descended the western slopes of the dominating height near Sal'noye like an avalanche. Another wave of enemy tanks and infantry were moving down the western slopes of some hillocks near Polyanka, while a third group was emerging from some shacks on the north-western outskirts of Dobroye Pole. Simultaneously, the units that had been retreating to the south stopped and turned back to the north, thereby starting to close the ring of encirclement. It was clear that the enemy had not submitted to the loss of Veselaya Kalina, which had an important tactical value, and now was preparing for counter-attack to restore the situation.

Veselaya Kalina was proving to be not too *happy* for us [a play on words – *veselaya* means cheerful, happy or joyful in Russian]. Our units hastily took up an all-round defence.

For a full hour, groups of fifty to sixty enemy aircraft hammered our troops with bombs. Then, supported by artillery, the enemy attacked Veselaya Kalina simultaneously from three directions. Our battery held the eastern side of the defence line together with the infantry. Our vehicles were deployed on the edge of a garden and orchard. Fifteen tanks and waves of infantry supported by massive artillery and mortar fire were advancing on us, coming down from a hill in the direction of Dobroye Pole. The battery fired at individual tanks with concentrated salvoes. We managed to knock out two of the enemy tanks. The others immediately slowed their advance. Suddenly three deafening explosions thundered behind the battery, one after another. Three huge tongues of flame soared high into the sky, and burning fluid began to rain in every direction from them. The Germans' fuel depots had blown up! The explosions certainly gave us a moral boost, but at the same time it was a signal for the southern enemy group to counter-attack from the direction of Sorokovye Bal'chiki. The regiment commander immediately ordered the battery to pull out of its positions and to take up a defence line on the southern outskirts.

We had barely managed to move into the new line when about a dozen fascist tanks supported by infantry advanced to the edge of the forest in front of us and quickly deployed into a battle line. A fire-fight began. However, the German tankers didn't venture to attack across the broad clearing that separated Veselaya Kalina from the forest.

Behind and to the right of us, we could hear the sound of approaching engines ... and then we saw our tanks. Units of the 9th Tank Corps' second echelon were coming up!

The enemy counter-attack faltered on each axis, and the Germans began to pull back. As a result of the action near Veselaya Kalina, several hundred enemy troops had been annihilated, together with ten tanks, eighteen guns and fifteen mortars. We also captured a lot of ammunition.

Before sunset, the main forces departed Veselaya Kalina covered by a strong vanguard. We headed southward through a virgin forest as dense as taiga wilderness.

With decisive combat actions over the night and with numerous short, sharp battles the next day, the 95th Tank Brigade captured Krasnaya Polyana, Sorokovye Bal'chiki, Vol'naya Sloboda and Esaman' from the march.

I remember the latter most of all. The railroad station and the town shared the same name. We captured plenty of equipment, vehicles and supplies there and even a still-operational large dairy factory. The Germans had not managed to burn or to blow up anything in their panicked flight. Our self-propelled guns stopped by the dairy factory and waited there for quite some time for fuel to be delivered. We went inside the plant to take a look around. There were several workers there, the equipment was operating, and the overall sterile cleanliness was amazing. The workers happily treated us to some sour cream, cottage cheese and butter, and so as to assure us that nothing was poisoned, they tasted all the products in front of us. The crews ate their fill of the long-forgotten dairy products, and filled their mess tins with sour cream and cream for a reserve supply.

By the end of the day, the division had assembled in a forest near Orlov Yar. The town of Glukhov was in front of us. We were now right on the Ukrainian border, and all night long with no rest or sleep we prepared for the advance.

The Capture of Glukhov

At dawn tanks and assault guns supported by infantry and submachine-gunners began to advance on Radionovka, a suburb of Glukhov. Only a hemp field separated it from the town. From the left and in front of us, we could hear the sounds of intense fighting. We knew that Colonel Demidov's 23rd Tank Brigade and Colonel Gusev's 70th Guards Rifle Division were already locked in combat there, fighting to liberate the town. The 95th Tank Brigade managed to dislodge the enemy from Radionovka by a sudden and decisive attack. Without losing momentum, our units continued the advance towards Glukhov. However, we suddenly came under such a heavy air-raid of dive-bombers using anti-tank bombs that we had to hide in the saving hemp field. Fortunately, the hemp was tall and similar in colour to our armoured vehicles, although the Germans succeeded in setting ablaze one tank which had not managed to hide.

As soon as the bombers left, we immediately resumed the advance. Now, however, the enemy unleashed a storm of artillery, tank gun and automatic weapons fire at us. They were shooting from windows and garrets, having converted every house into a pillbox. An assault gun, positioned in a garden located between two brick houses, was obstructing the advance of our battery and a tank company here with its fire. How, though, to get at it and destroy it? On the left there was a shallow ravine – or rather a narrow gully with a creek at the bottom of it. I reckoned if I could sneak through the fire zone along the gully and penetrate the German defence, I'd be able to approach the gun from the rear. I sent a command via signal flag to Aleksey Kuzin, who had taken over command of Levanov's assault gun after Levanov's wounding: 'Follow me!' Then I transmitted to my driver-mechanic Oleinik over the vehicle's intercom: 'Keep left and move forward along the ravine!'

Both self-propelled guns moved slowly down the swampy creek bed, preparing to make a rapid dash once we reached a point right in front of the enemy defence line. Three or four enemy machine guns were sweeping the gully with fire, preventing our infantry from assembling in it. Two tanks from the 95th Tank Brigade rolled down into the creek bed to assist us, apparently having noticed our manoeuvre by spotting our antennas.

Having closely approached the enemy line, the tanks and assault guns literally leaped out of the gully at high speed, unexpectedly emerging right in front of the enemy's gun positions. Our surprise appearance startled the crews, who quickly tried to turn their guns. It wasn't going to do them any good! We immediately scattered and mowed down the greater part of the crews, while the rest took off in every direction at the sight of our armoured vehicles. My assault gun had reached the first trench-line of the enemy defence when we felt two strong blows to the machine. The vehicle pitched downward and stopped abruptly. The engine was turning over at full speed, but the vehicle was motionless. It was clear: we were positioned over a trench and our tracks had been smashed. Slightly raising the hatch cover, I rejoiced: our two tanks and Kuzin's assault gun were crushing the German guns. Glancing to the right along the trench-line, I went momentarily numb: the Germans were setting up an anti-tank rifle aimed right at us – I knew these rifles well.[1] We had even fired one once, having picked it up somewhere as a war spoil.

'Vasya! Three grenades, at the trench to the right of us, now!' I yelled to the gunloader, not even having had time yet to grasp the horror that was coming over me.

All the enemy soldiers hit the dirt after the first grenade. After the second one, they disappeared around a bend in the trench, leaving behind one man dead and the anti-tank rifle lying nearby. However, repairing the self-propelled gun was simply out of the question. At least three machine guns were firing at us from the ground floor windows of the nearest house and one more, seemingly a large-calibre one, was hammering our vehicle from the attic. I ordered the breech operator to open the emergency hatch cover, and I took a look around through the commander's panoramic sight. A T-34 was burning in the garden, and the other tank and Kuzin's assault gun, having turned around, were firing on the German assault gun. Again I looked to the right and even gasped: now two soldiers with incendiaries were running towards us along the trench!

'Vasya! To the right of us in the trench, two grenades, now!' I ordered Plaksin, and it flashed through my mind: if these hefty burning 'kugels' [German for 'ball', but also possibly a reference to the Jewish baked side dishes and desserts] reached us, we'd blaze up like a torch over this damned trench. These guys were quite good at setting fires: when retreating they lit everything that could burn and these two were from a special incendiary detachment.

I heard the muffled sound of a shot to my left, felt a metallic hit on the left side of our assault gun and, having glanced in that direction, I again saw enemy tank hunters with an anti-tank rifle. Instantly, I grabbed one of the hand grenades that Valeriy had laid out within easy reach, pulled the safety pin, and threw it at the enemy to my left.

At last, everything calmed down in the trench on both sides of the assault gun; only the two incendiary devices were still burning on the trench floor to the right. The crew had calmed down a bit, though they were still somewhat unfit for action, seeing as how we were still literally in a suspended condition. We could see from the emergency hatch both of the thrown tracks lying across the trench, but the heavy machine-gun fire along the length of the trench and from the machine gun in that attic kept us trapped inside the vehicle. There was no chance to get to the drive sprocket.

'Valeriy, fire on the attic! Fragmentation! Fire!' I ordered the gunlayer.

'The gun angle's not high enough, Comrade Lieutenant!' Korolev reported.

'Fire on the ceiling joists! Delayed fuse! Fire!'

With that, the enemy machine gun fell silent. Suddenly we heard through the semi-opened hatch: 'Ur-r-a-h! Ur-r-a-h!' ... It was the rifle units of Gusev's 70th Guards Rifle Division on the attack. Soon hand-to-hand fighting broke out in the trenches, accompanied by submachine-gun bursts and grenade explosions. Motorized riflemen and submachine-gunners drove the enemy out of the first two trenches with a resolute and rapid attack, and the fighting shifted into the town.

The fighting became house-to-house. The Nazis had turned each building into a genuine bastion, protected by thick, ancient walls of brick, and using the window openings as embrasures. However, our tanks and assault guns methodically targeted these fire emplacements, eliminating them and thus paving the way for the rifle units. Three tanks and two self-propelled guns – Stepanov's and Fomichev's – were on their way to our immobilized SU-122, followed by scouts and almost the whole command platoon led by its commander Lieutenant Matveev.

Fighting for the houses nearest to us was still going on when Ishkin's emergency repair team rolled up to the self-propelled gun and we immediately began the repairs.

'Lucky you, Vasiliy Semenovich!' Ishkin said cheerfully.

'Lucky, but not that much, Vasiliy Vasilyevich – we've been hanging over this trench already for about an hour, and took almost no part in the action.'

A tank recovery vehicle came up and pulled our self-propelled gun off the trench. Shells were still exploding around us with distressing frequency, making us drop flat on the ground, but in an hour the vehicle was repaired through the combined effort of the mechanics and the crew. Happily, we headed off to catch up with the battery. Ishkin, who always preferred to be in the thick of the action, sat perched behind the superstructure with the captured machine gun. We rejoined the combat formation just as our troops were repulsing a counter-attack. Several more tanks and self-propelled guns came up and the enemy counter-attack collapsed. The enemy began an overall retreat.

By midday the town of Glukhov had been liberated. Although the troops of the rifle division and the tank brigade crews were the main liberators, flowers were thrown upon all of us from windows and balconies. Bouquets were falling onto the armour and into open hatches. We felt ebullient. An ancient Russian town had been liberated! By night, having dug in on the north-western outskirts of the town, we set up solid defence lines in case of an enemy counter-attack.

The night was quiet. However, from dawn the next day until midday we had to beat off three large counter-attacks by enemy tanks and infantry, which were conducted with the active support of artillery and the *Luftwaffe*. All the counter-attacks were thrown back, and the Germans suffered heavy losses in men and matériel.

That same afternoon, our troops resumed the offensive. It was unleashed so rapidly that the enemy had no time to organize a defence, even on terrain favourable to them. Within five hours, the settlements of Poloshki and Yaroslavets (here our machine was knocked out and we stayed with it) were liberated, and our troops continued their advance, later liberating Salomashin and Dmitrievka. By the end of the day, they had crossed the Ret' River and destroyed a large enemy combat group, liberated the town of Krolevets, and cut the Mikhailovskiy–Konotop railroad.

For more than a day, the crew under the direction of Ishkin worked to repair our machine with no rest or sleep, so we could catch up with the regiment as soon as possible. We were immobilized between a house and a large pond. The mistress of the house cooked for us, using our dried rations and her own vegetables. Her name was Hanna; she was 30 years of age: tall, slender, and with a beautiful, dark-complexioned face. In 1941 the Germans had nearly shot her, having taken her for a gypsy. For long hours, with tears in her eyes she had been forced to try to prove to the Nazi commandant that she was Ukrainian, until he tore open the top of her dress and saw that she was wearing an Orthodox cross – only then did he let her go. When talking to us, Hanna expressed her surprise: 'Our guys are so young and short, but they are driving back such burly Germans!'

This was true. A large replenishment of 17-year-old lads from the liberated areas had joined the rifle regiments after the Battle of Kursk – skinny, shortish, a half-bayonet lower than their own rifles, they could barely drag their personal weapon during foot marches. Tankers and assault gun crews tried to give them a lift on their armour during advances, but each time they did so with concern: the riflemen would often fall asleep quickly and tumble onto the ground, and might wind up beneath the tracks. There was such a case. We were moving through a forest at night. I was sitting on the driver's hatch cover, and noticing that the tree branches ahead of us would brush against the superstructure, I yelled: 'Hold on!' Then I looked back and saw no one on the armour! They had already been swept off to the ground as if by a huge broom. Fortunately, the driver who was following us noticed the accident and stopped his vehicle in time.

We arrived at Krolevets in the night. Having found our battery, we parked our SU-122 in a firing position.

In the Vanguard: The Liberation of Konotop

Our troops held the southern outskirts of Krolevets for several days, repelling several German counter-attacks; in between fighting, we spent the time doing routine maintenance on our vehicles that they hadn't seen for almost ten days, and worked to repair damaged tanks and self-propelled guns. Only on the evening of 5 September did the enemy attacks end, giving us a chance to look around this ancient Ukrainian city. During the time of Bogdan Khmel'nitsky[2] Krolevets was the garrison town of the Nezhinskiy Regiment. We toured with interest a baguette bakery and a textile mill that had been damaged by air-raids and the recent fighting.

On 6 September our troops resumed the offensive. The forward detachment of the 95th Tank Brigade, consisting of a motorized rifle battalion, a tank company and our battery, which had four self-propelled guns, reached the Seim River 3 kilometres east of the Krolevets–Konotop railroad. We immediately began to search for a crossing, and came across a German road sign: 'Bridge for tanks and tractors. 800 metres.' We sent some scouts ahead, in case enemy vehicles were concealed in the brush along the river. Returning, the scouts reported to the forward detachment commander: 'Indeed, there is a bridge – a pontoon bridge, solid, with several layers of thick logs. The enemy is concealed on the opposite bank; the crossing is being covered by infantry and artillery.'

The captain summoned the officers and announced his decision: 'We will cross the Seim over this bridge. The tanks will lead the way, followed by the assault guns and motorized infantry.'

Our battery commander Senior Lieutenant Stepanov immediately suggested: 'Let's put German crosses on the lead tank in order to fool them.'

So it was done. Within ten minutes, we had fashioned crosses: two white circles cut out of an undershirt, with black crosses of bearing grease painted on them.

The forced crossing began. The impostor tank rolled down the road openly, while the other vehicles advanced to one side through the scrub. When the tank reached the middle of the bridge, the Germans figured out the ruse – they took alarm, opened machine-gun fire, and the crews rushed to their guns. However, we blanketed them with gun and machine-gun fire from the near bank, and in the meantime the lead tank clambered up the left bank and overran the enemy weapons emplacements and flak guns. While our main forces were on their way to the bridge, the forward detachment had to repulse two enemy attempts to recapture the tactically important crossing.

By nightfall, we had taken from the march the settlement of Podlipnoye near Konotop, thus securing the combat deployment of not only the main forces of the brigade, but also of the entire 9th Tank Corps, for the assault on Konotop. A fierce, two-hour long struggle for the city conducted together with other units of the 60th Army concluded with the capture of Konotop. The Germans left the city in such panic that they did not even manage to blow up the communications centre and railway station, let alone the pump-house and the city's other infrastructure. However, everything turned out to be not that simple – we discovered that all these installations had been rigged with demolition charges in quite an unusual way. Half an hour after the capture of the city, three German prisoners were brought to brigade headquarters. They insisted on seeing the commander. The soldiers then revealed that they had been under orders to blow up the mined objects, but hadn't done it. Our sappers were immediately put to work to remove all the demolition charges.

We began to set up fire positions on the north-western outskirts of the city. Our battery was positioned on the edge of a park, with the task to cover the Konotop–Krasnoye road. We found a German military cemetery in this ancient park. I went to see it. The wooden crosses were standing in precise rows: every soldier had an individual grave, marked by a cross bearing the name and surname of the interred man. His helmet was perched on top of the cross. The deputy for technical services of the 2nd Battery Kezen spat angrily:

> The German even uses a straight edge to bury his dead! But the Führer really cheated them: instead of the promised Russian estate, they received just two metres of dirt, and won't even have that for eternal usage.
>
> That's the way it is for them … but what about us?! Common graves … twenty or even thirty men thrown into it, and even their names aren't recorded!

On Night Watch

We remained on the defence for three days in Konotop, a most important rail and road junction. On the third day the regiment commander summoned the officers to his command post, which was located in the roomy cellar of a brick building. When we entered it the regiment's command staff was already there, and regiment commander Samyko was giving the rear services commander Tumakov a real dressing down for the failure to supply the personnel with food during our march between Krolevets and Konotop: 'So you're scared of air-raids and shelling?! What, you reckon the regiment was strolling down Nevskiy Prospekt [the main street of St. Petersburg, formerly Leningrad]? I see that it's been too long since you've done any belly-crawling . . .'

Major Samyko abruptly terminated his angry reprimand, but fixed the face of the commander of the rear services with such an icy stare from his hazel eyes that even we started to feel uneasy, while cold sweat beaded on Tumakov's forehead, and he seemed to shrink in size. We understood the reference to belly-crawling. Back near Ponyri, Major Samyko had ordered Tumakov to deliver food to the front line by himself, under enemy fire.

Now that the commanders had all assembled, Samyko briefly announced:

> Comrades officers, there are eight assault guns and my tank left in the 1454th Regiment. Only fifteen tanks are operational in the 95th Tank Brigade. Under the existing circumstances we will be active only at night; during the daytime – only in extreme situations. Tonight we must take the points Belovezhi-1, Grigorovka, Gaivoron. We'll be setting out at 22.00. I will detail the combat orders on the jumping-off line.

During the night we dislodged the enemy from all three settlements by a resolute attack. Afterward, we assembled, now with the 108th Tank Brigade, in a forest near Gaivoron, thoroughly concealing ourselves under cover of the forest. We spent the next day quietly.

Once it had become dark, a reconnaissance patrol took off towards the settlement of Golenki, led by the chief of scouts Soldatov. It consisted of scouts, the regiment commander's tank, my self-propelled gun and Sergeant Major Martynenko's armoured car. Upon emerging from the forest, we had to cross a low-lying meadow, where Martynenko's BA-64 started to bog down, and began to make very slow headway, though its engine was straining. The tank and my self-propelled gun proceeded ahead and stopped in some bushes about 500 metres from Golenki. Soldatov, Lieutenant Shishkov – the commander of Samyko's tank – and I immediately climbed out of our vehicles and headed around the village on foot, followed by the scouts. We crept through the shadows of the trees, stopping at times to wait for the moon to pass behind some clouds before resuming our movement. To the left of the road we saw a low hill on the far side of the village, and Soldatov ordered us to follow him on our bellies. From atop the knoll, the sleeping village spread before us. We could see that a significant concentration of enemy troops was inside the village. We could discern dozens of guns and a large quantity of tractors and vehicles. There were also many tanks scattered in the orchards and gardens. Soldatov ordered the scouts:

We have to count the tanks. Private Chugunov will do it. Sergeant Kochetkov and Private Tyulenev are to cover his foray. I'll give you an hour to carry it out. Sergeant Potemkin and Lance Corporal Rassokha are to return to our vehicles and set up an ambush position beside the road there.

The slender Rema Chugunov – the 'son' of the regiment [a common wartime nickname for a teenager adopted by a military unit during a campaign] – was the first to crawl off, followed by Kochetkov and Tyulenev. Potemkin and Rassokha crawled away in the other direction, then minutes later flashed us a signal with the green light of a torch that everything was quiet near the vehicles.

Time passed agonizingly slowly. We lay in silence. We could hear every rustle distinctly, night birds called, and a gentle breeze from time to time carried the sound of distant dogs barking in neighbouring villages. The group returned in about forty minutes.

'There are thirty-two tanks in the village,' Rema proudly reported to the chief of scouts, and even identified the types. Soldatov expressed his gratitude on the spot and congratulated the lad on his first successful reconnaissance.

The scouts returned to the waiting armour of the 108th Tank Brigade and our regiment without incident. Soon we could hear the quiet rumble of engines and then saw the dark silhouettes of tanks and assault guns emerging from the forest. They slowly deployed into a combat formation on the western slopes of the hill separating us from Golenki. Our preparations were quiet and stealthy, as we were counting upon a surprise attack, and judging from what we had seen during the reconnaissance, the enemy was not expecting a night attack, moreover one from the west.

The Night Massacre in Golenki

The radio sets of all the crews were set to receive, and when the signal 'Storm 333' came over the radios, we moved out towards Golenki. The motorized riflemen and submachine-gunners followed the armoured vehicles, but no one had opened fire yet. Able to see nothing through my commander's periscope, I was standing in the open hatch. I watched as the faint outlines of houses appeared as we approached the village. As we drew closer, I began to discern the silhouettes of tanks, vehicles and guns. The assault guns bounced over a ditch with a light jolt and crashed through a fence, when suddenly an enemy tank came into sight! Against the background of a white hut, its dark hulk stood out as clearly as if on a cinema screen. There was no time to think about movies, though: we had to make use of the precious minutes of surprise until the crews woke up!

'Viktor, turn left by 30 and stop!' I ordered Oleinik.

On both sides of us, the main guns of our other vehicles were already shattering the silence of the summer night with thunder and bright flashes.

'Valeriy! Fire at the tank!'

Korolev had barely finished his shout 'Shot!', when the enemy tank burst into bright bluish flames, illuminating the fruit trees and vegetable gardens and the German tankers running towards it. We watched the burning tank as if we were spellbound. It was a medium Panzer IV tank and the flames now revealed its every detail to us. The barrel of its long 75mm gun was pointed directly at us!

'Comrade Lieutenant, it's good that we were the first to fire on them, otherwise that gun would have shot a round right through us!' Korolev yelled cheerfully.

'You're right, Valeriy! But now we have to search for another target before the German regains his senses.'

Two more German tanks were burning to the left and right of us – the crews of Kuzin and Polivoda had fired point-blank shots at just-discovered targets. The machine guns and submachine-guns of our infantrymen had also already begun to chatter, and hand grenades were bursting here and there. Red Army tanks had already reached the centre of the village – the 108th Tank Brigade's tankers and Shishkov's tank were rolling over light vehicles, carts and wagons. In the glow of the burning houses, we could clearly see Germans tumbling out of buildings in their underwear. Near the exit from the village their artillerymen were trying to start tractors in order to tow the guns away. Korolev immediately demolished the lead tractor with an accurate shot.

Nevertheless the Germans were quickly coming to their senses: their remaining tanks had already opened return fire and were falling back to an unlit part of the village. However, one panzer didn't manage to sneak through the illuminated area and exposed its flank to a well-aimed shot from Shishkov's tank. Everything happened instantaneously, right before our eyes: Shishkov's tank had bounded past our assault guns, halted briefly, turned its gun and fired at the side of the withdrawing enemy tank!

I ordered Oleinik, 'Viktor, cross the street at full speed!'

'Understood. Under way!'

The SU-122, having raced through the exposed and illuminated area, entered a garden. While we were choosing a suitable position, two shells whizzed right over my head. The next shell struck Kuzin's vehicle. It didn't catch fire, but in the glare of the flames in the burning village, I could see a stream of smoke drifting from his vehicle across the ground. At my query, Kuzin replied: 'The entire crew is wounded and the machine's damaged.'

I ordered Kuzin: 'The entire crew is to evacuate the vehicle through the emergency and front hatches!' Then I immediately instructed Vasya Plaksin to cover the crew with machine-gun fire.

Almost as soon as the last man had left the assault gun, a second shell struck it and it burst into flames. A minute later, its stock of shells began to explode. Kuzin and his crew headed to my self-propelled gun, and reached it almost simultaneously with the medics Valya Vorobieva and Aleksey Volobuyev. The medics escorted the wounded men into a cellar for initial treatment, and we and some submachine-gunners returned to action.

The Germans kept firing heavily, but randomly, and the storm of shells and streams of tracers in the dark was so dense that any further advance became impossible. To the left of us the assault gun of the commander of the 1st Battery Polivoda was advancing by bounds from one piece of cover to the next; to our right there was the vehicle of our battery commander Stepanov. We caught up with Shishkov's tank in a garden – it had halted and was firing from its main gun and machine guns at enemy anti-tank guns, but his fire was not too accurate – the darkness and the trees impeded it. Suddenly, as if by prior agreement, all of our vehicles raced forward! 'Crush 'em!' I managed to order Viktor.

Skilfully manoeuvring in the darkness between trees and buildings, Oleinik threw the vehicle this way and that, constantly overruning enemy guns! The assault gun would climb with a grinding sound; then it would tilt so that it seemed as if it was just about to topple over onto its side; after all that, having raised its nose high above the gun limber, it would flop down back onto the ground. Then it would rush to another target – and onto another enemy gun. The driver acted in the heat of the battle at his own discretion, for it would have been useless to give him orders. I only had enough time to keep watch lest the machine came too close to another self-propelled gun or tank, or saw glimpses of the enemy artillerymen fleeing in panic in every direction under the light of flares. Yet this didn't help them either – most of them fell under the submachine-gun fire of the infantry advancing right behind us. In this crazy onslaught, we were tossed to and fro, and could barely keep our seats! I estimated by the jolts and sounds that Viktor had already smashed four guns.

Our brother crews were also crushing guns and machine guns, and all the battery's assault guns emerged on the north-eastern outskirts of the village almost simultaneously. Here, however, on the outskirts of the village, the enemy greeted us with the most powerful artillery and machine-gun fire. As a result of the retreat, approximately twenty enemy tanks and assault guns, together with infantry, had concentrated within a narrow sector here on the edge of the village, and all this gathered mass fell upon our approaching battery simultaneously! Our crews, hastily manoeuvring, searched for more suitable firing positions from which to continue the engagement. Thank God, our submachine-gunners managed to find some cover in a nearby ditch, and were already firing.

Cannon shots rumbled on both sides of us. Long flashes of flame were leaping out of gun barrels, ripping apart the darkness of the night and momentarily illuminating the steel monsters which were producing this hellish fire. The chatter of machine-gun and submachine-gun fire could be heard between the cannonade rumble of guns. Then suddenly the thunder of combat which we had been hearing behind our group since the beginning of the attack began to subside. It tremendously worried me and to my chagrin I couldn't help but wonder whether our attack, which had started promisingly with our advantages of surprise and darkness, had failed? There was no more than an hour left before dawn, while we could still exploit these advantages.

As if to confirm my fears, German infantry began to approach in short rushes, attempting to bypass an area illuminated by the fire of a burning house. The enemy tanks and assault guns intensified their fire – so strongly that it seemed that they were on the verge of attacking! Although shells and bullets were flying overhead, I nevertheless decided to open the hatch in an effort to get a better view of what was going on. I had barely unlatched the hatch cover, when I saw dozens of multi-coloured flares overhead, fading as they fell on the eastern side of the village. Immediately, such a powerful artillery cannonade resounded from that direction that it seemed the ground was shaking! We joyfully realized that the brigade's main forces had entered the battle, falling upon the enemy flank! Within several minutes, the momentum of combat began to change. We could hear the approaching 'Ur-r-a-a-hs!' of our infantry through the solid rumbling of gunshots and explosions. The enemy fire on our group began to weaken noticeably, and then ceased completely. We moved out onto the attack again, pursuing and striking the enemy. Using the last minutes of the dark September night, the Germans were hastily abandoning the village. The enemy had only one way to retreat – northward, towards Bakhmach. In chess language, they were in *zugzwang* – they had to move, but they had no safe move available to them. Pulling out, they entered their own minefields, incurring additional heavy losses in men and equipment.

Ordinarily, I wouldn't want to report the figures for the enemy's losses in the night action for Golenki, based upon the after-action combat report of the 108th Tank Brigade – back then, there was a tendency to overestimate enemy losses in all reports. However, this time the enemy's losses were indeed very heavy! Plenty of tanks, guns, motor vehicles, tractors, mortars and machine guns, radio equipment, ammunition and other combat matériel was captured and destroyed. The action itself was succinctly and laconically written up in the report:

> The 108th Tank Brigade, having completed a 40-kilometre march together with the 1454th Self-propelled Artillery Regiment, advanced into the rear of the [German] 183rd Infantry Division. The night action for Golenki was typical of a successful surprise attack. A lot of enemy equipment and troops were destroyed.[3]

For the next several days, we repulsed fierce enemy counter-attacks from the line Grigorovka–Malyi Gambur. However, the Nazis failed to gain revenge for the night massacre in Golenki. They were forced to retreat in a south-west direction, which we were dictating with the pressure we were placing on them.

Ten tanks were now left in the 108th Tank Brigade; four self-propelled guns and the regiment commander's tank remained in the 1454th Self-propelled Artillery Regiment. We advanced for an additional 60 kilometres through bold night attacks with this small force, in the process liberating dozens of settlements in Chernigov Oblast, including Verder, Fastovtsy, Ivangorod, Krupichpol, Vishnevka, Svarichevka, Volodko-Odevitsa, and by the end of 20 September we were assembled in Bezuglovka, 18 kilometres south of Nezhin.

The regiment remained here for two days. We had a chance to shave, wash and grab a bit of a sleep after many sleepless nights, and a chance to reflect upon past battles, including the most recent one. Although we were fewer in numbers in that action, we continued to hold the tactical initiative – we had been the attacking side. However, two more SU-122 assault vehicles had been destroyed in this engagement – ours and Samoilov's, but both crews survived ...

On 22 September, the 1454th Self-propelled Artillery Regiment received the order of the Central Front commander to move by train to Mytishi Station near Moscow without our vehicles, to be placed at the disposal of the *Stavka* [Supreme Headquarters] of the Supreme Commander.

Chapter 6

Reorganization near Moscow, September–October 1943

On the late night of 24 September 1943, the regiment arrived at the already familiar Pushkino Station, instead of the originally designated Mytishi Station. We disembarked under full lights, and couldn't even believe that we need not fear air-raids. We were lodged in the same pine-tree forest in the same People's Commissariat dachas where we had been billeted before moving to Kursk. On the very first day after a long interval in time, we bathed in a real *banya* and fell soundly asleep in the dachas.

The next morning, right after breakfast we were already receiving our new SU-85 self-propelled guns, which like the SU-122, were built on the chassis of the T-34 tank. We were first interested in the performance characteristics of the new machine compared to the SU-122. It wasn't much different in size, weight, manoeuvrability, ground pressure per square inch, speed or armour protection, but there was a lot of difference in the main armament. Its high velocity D-5T 85mm anti-tank gun as opposed to the SU-122's M-30S 122mm howitzer had an initial muzzle velocity equal to 792 m/sec versus 515 m/sec. The gun had an effective direct fire range of 800–900 metres at a tank, and 600 metres at guns, i.e., at a lower target. The rate of fire of the new gun, which used rapid-firing fixed rounds, was three times faster than that of the howitzer, which used separate loading, and the ammunition allowance increased from forty to forty-eight shells. The outward appearance of the self-propelled gun had changed too: the new machine looked more imposing due to its longer gun barrel.

The crews received replacements. Losing no time, the regiment headquarters expeditiously redistributed the crew members to ensure that each crew had seasoned front-line veterans. Our battery had to replace almost half its personnel, and three new officers arrived. Senior Lieutenant Pogorel'chenko took over command of the 3rd Battery to replace the fallen Shevchenko.

Familiarization with the newcomers occurred quickly, in the front-line manner. The new battery commander Pogorel'chenko was a year older than me. He was a brown-haired man with dark hazel eyes, a penetrating gaze, and a determined face with regular features. He was rangy, above average in height and slightly stooping. Platoon commander Rusakov – a fair-haired man with blue eyes and an aquiline nose, made a good first impression: he was tall, with a still slightly gangly physique and perhaps the youngest officer in the regiment – he had just turned 18. Makarov – the commander of the second self-propelled gun in my platoon – was ten years older than me. Before the war he'd been a horticulturist. He had no military bearing, but he was solidly-built and a bit below average height, which with his classical nose, red hair and mirthful, hazel eyes, combined with his simple-natured character, impressed all the men of the battery.

The crew of the new tank destroyers consisted of four men. Due to this and the reshuffling of crews, our 'old fellow' Emelyan Ivanovich Besschetnov was taken from my crew and transferred to Khludov's crew as the gunloader. Junior Sergeant Schetnikov, a 19-year-old soldier from Saratov Oblast, replaced Oleinik in my crew as the driver-mechanic. He had undergone three months of study in a training tank regiment. The breaking-in of the newly-formed crews took three weeks and concluded with tactical manoeuvres and gunnery practice in both difficult terrain conditions and complex combat situations. After this the 1454th Self-propelled Artillery Regiment embarked on two trains and again sped westward along a 'green street' to the front. Each train was being pulled by two engines.

Along the way there were no special incidents, with the exception of what happened at the L'gov-2 Station, when a very young and very cute medic named Valya, who had wandered away from her medical train, joined our first train, which was carrying our vehicles, together with their crews and our commanders. Apparently she was being motivated by feelings of patriotism and romanticism, and a desire to participate in combat directly. So, she stayed with our regiment.

Chapter 7

The Liberation of Kiev, November 1943

Crossing the Dnieper

The train with the vehicles and commanders disembarked at Bobrik Station; the second train carrying the regiment's rear units – at Lebezhki Station, near Darnitsa – at the time a left-bank suburb across the river from Kiev. Marshal Rybalko's 3rd Guards Tank Army, to which our 1454th Self-propelled Artillery Regiment had been assigned, was then just in the process of completing a secret redeployment of forces from the Bukrin bridgehead situated south of Kiev, to the Lyutezh bridgehead north of the city. This movement to the north was done only at night, with the tanks, self-propelled guns and vehicles driving with darkened lights, while tractors with burning lights moved southward, in order to give the enemy the impression that the offensive was being prepared in the south. As had been intended by Rybalko, this lengthy lateral troop movement deceived the enemy intelligence, which concluded that the Russians were building up within the Bukrin bridgehead.

The 1454th Self-propelled Artillery Regiment made the night march to the north together with the tank army, reassembling in a pine forest between the villages of Lebedovka and Novoselka. Already on the following night, we began to cross to the right [western] bank of the Dnieper aboard 30-ton ferries. The crossing was conducted under the fire of heavy enemy artillery, while the *Luftwaffe* struck with bombs, and kept the bank under the constant illumination of flares suspended from small parachutes. At a radio signal from the deputy for technical services Vasilyev another tank destroyer would emerge from the forest and with darkened lights move to the riverbank, following only the green light of torches flashed by the guides. With their motors straining, the experienced driver-mechanics Oleinik, Grechuk, Grechin, Amelechkin, Zelenskiy, Borisovskiy, Zakharov, Tvorogov and Mukumbayev hurried their tank destroyers across the sandy ground of the riverbank, their bottoms ploughing the soil, and dexterously drove them onto the ferry before clambering out of the machines. During the period of the crossing, they would be under the temporary control of the tugboat commander.

Back on the eastern bank, we experienced each vehicle's crossing with a pounding heart, for we could clearly see under the light of the flares that the river was boiling with whirlpools and soaring fountains of water – the tugboats were towing the ferries through a solid wall of shell and bomb explosions. The ferries were being tossed about by close bursts, at times precariously listing, and the tank destroyers aboard them were sliding around the deck, although each vehicle was tightly fastened with cables and clamps.

Our battery was being towed by a boat commanded by a stocky, red-bearded sergeant major, who was wearing a weatherproof jacket – a real 'sea wolf' judging from his appearance and decisive actions. Taking advantage of intervals of darkness appearing over the water, time after time he would bravely and resolutely tow the barge at top speed across the black abyss of boiling water, which was being lashed by a strong wind and a storm of artillery fire. Everything went well, although we had to suffer a lot of concern over our machines. Indeed, just before dawn about 10 metres from the right bank, the ferry was so badly rocked by a nearby explosion, that having snapped its lines, Vasya Rusakov's SU-85 plunged into the water together with its happy-go-lucky driver Shalaginov. Only the tip of the vehicle's antenna remained above the water. However, the rescue team went to work exceptionally well. At an order from Senior Technician-Lieutenant Sapko, the mechanics Dronov and Shimraenko immediately dived into the dark, icy water and strictly by feel managed to attach cables to the front tow shackles on the sunken tank destroyer. Sitting in his seat up to his waist in water, Shalaginov was on the verge of abandoning the vehicle, but having heard banging on the armour, understood that it was being hitched and restrained his impulse to leave it. A prime mover quickly pulled the armoured vehicle out of its watery grave.

The SU-85 emerged on the bank, with water cascading from it. The upper hatch opened and Pet'ka Shalaginov climbed out of the turret in his soaked overalls. From the light of the flares, we could see that he was shivering; his face was pale from the cold and, most likely, fright. The deputy of technical services Vasilyev was the first to approach him and gave the violater a thorough scolding: remaining in the vehicle during the crossing was not permitted! Quickly, however, he tempered his wrath with mercy, pulled out a flask, poured a tumbler of vodka (he always had a glass tumbler in his pocket) and offered it to the guilty party: 'Have a drink or you'll get sick!'

A dry uniform, pair of underwear and a quilted jacket were quickly brought up. Shalaginov, his teeth still chattering, hurriedly changed into the dry clothing, and then went with his crew to bail the water out of his vehicle and put it back into order. Already at dawn, the ferry landed on the right bank for the last time, and the last of our tank destroyers, having deftly climbed the steep bank, snuck into the bushes.

The 1454th Self-propelled Artillery Regiment, which had been subordinated to General Malygin's 9th Mechanized Corps of the 3rd Guards Tank Army, deployed in a virgin coniferous forest, well-camouflaged under the tree crowns from air-raids. Occasionally, a heavy shell from long-range artillery would come crashing into the trees and explode with a muffled blast. Large shell splinters, flying in every direction, were whizzing over our heads and falling onto the battery's position. The crews were meticulously preparing themselves for the oncoming action, knowing that the enemy would do his best to hold Kiev.

The Offensive Begins

At dawn on 3 November 1943 thousands of guns and mortars opened a concentrated fire on the enemy's defence lines. Fiery streamers of *Katyusha* rockets raced towards the enemy, our air force pounded enemy positions, and then our neighbours on the left and right – the troops of General Moskalenko's 38th Army and General Kravchenko's 5th Guards Tank Corps went on the advance. We spent the whole day agonizingly waiting for the order to advance, but it never arrived! Only around 03.00 on 4 November was our battery commander summoned to regiment headquarters. Returning, Pogorel'chenko gathered together his subordinate officers and announced our mission: 'The regiment will go on the attack in the first echelon of the 3rd [Guards] Tank Army towards the Pushcha-Voditsa dachas – Pil'nik – Belichi – Svyatoshino. Forces of the 23rd Rifle Corps will lead the advance.'

Our slumber was instantly swept away, as if by a hand! The crews folded the large tarpaulins that had been covering their vehicles and placed them behind the superstructure, removed the soft covers from the gun barrels, securely fastened their entrenching tools, and thoroughly inspected the optics, wiping them clean time and again, and checked the radio, their submachine-guns, pistols, and the spare instruments and parts for the vehicles and the guns ...

A cannonade to our south had been continuing since the morning of the day before, and time passed agonizingly slowly while we waited for the signal to move out. Only at 09.00 did the regiment begin to set out in a march column towards the south. Having passed the settlement of Yablonka and Height 132.0, we neared the forest edge and moved into our jumping-off positions. Then we went on the advance. There had been no preparatory bombardment within our sector – apparently to achieve the highest level of surprise. Tanks of Lieutenant Colonel Laptev's 47th Guards Tank Regiment were moving through the woods ahead of our tank destroyers in a pre-combat array, and we were followed by the riflemen of Colonel Siyanin's 70th Mechanized Brigade. Colonel Ludvik Svoboda's 1st Independent Czechoslovak Brigade was advancing to our left.

The Germans had mined all the forest tracks, fire-breaks and clearings suitable for tank movement, and in addition had obstructed them with numerous anti-tank barriers: horizontally-laid, thick logs fastened to tree trunks at turret height by cables and clamps. Because of these barriers we had to advance through the forest, breaking and uprooting trees if necessary. The hatch covers on our tank destroyer were closed, but we could clearly hear the rumble of the engines and the sound of trees cracking and falling, sometimes striking the vehicles. Our young driver Viktor Schetnikov did his best not to lag behind his more experienced regimental comrades, driving his vehicle with confidence. Where possible he tried to manoeuvre around the trees, which sometimes scraped along the armour; before striking a tree, he would simultaneously depress the main clutch pedal, so as not to disable the transmission.

Having come up to a complex of dachas called Pushcha-Voditsa, we broke into the enemy positions. Our tank destroyer approached a building made partially of bricks and stopped in some acacia bushes, so I could get our bearings. Having raised the hatch cover part way, I saw three houses engulfed by black-crimson flame – and beyond them the Germans, concealed by the smoke, were retreating to the southern outskirts of the complex. Makarov's self-propelled gun stood just to the right of us, also hidden in the acacias, while the battery commander's was on our left, in a small park. A bit in front of us was a T-34, which was relentlessly firing both its machine guns along an alley at the withdrawing enemy. Enemy tanks and assault guns were using the streets and alleys as fire lanes. A large-calibre machine gun in a water tower off to our side was spraying the battery with lead, pinning down our submachine-gunners. I considered eliminating the position with a fragmentation shell, but wanted to save the ammunition. I ordered Plaksin, 'Vasya, from the machine gun, with long bursts at the tower cupola! Fire!' and thought of Emelyan Ivanovich with gratitude: we had shared one of our trophy machine guns with Khludov's crew. A round cloud of red brick dust erupted from the tower and the enemy machine gun fell silent!

Plaksin began to boast, 'It fears the craft of a master, Comrade Lieutenant!'

I thanked Vasiliy: 'I appreciate the accurate fire!' He preferred gratitude from the commander and his comrades rather than from higher superiors.

Our infantry began to advance bit by bit, mopping up every building from attic to cellar. The perfidious enemy had mined all the alleys and streets practicable for tanks, reckoning that we wouldn't want to crush the dachas or smash the fruit orchards. Three tanks and two tank destroyers – one of them Vasya Rusakov's – had already struck landmines. Our armoured advance was stymied. Fortunately, mine-clearing tanks arrived. Under the cover of fire from the tanks and self-propelled guns, they began to clear passages through the minefields. Our battery advanced to the centre of the settlement through one of these cleared passages.

The short November day was waning, and the cannonade began to settle down in the evening. Attentively scrutinizing the southern outskirts through my commander's panoramic sight, I noticed a truck moving along the Germans' defence line, screened by some trees and stopping from time to time. Aha, it is delivering ammunition – we don't need that at all!

'Valeriy! Ahead of us, on line with rotunda, there's a vehicle! Fire!' I ordered.

'Understood, the vehicle is to be destroyed. A high-explosive round, load up!' Korolev ordered as he lined up the gun on the target. Within a minute, he shouted: 'Shot!'

The gun thundered! The vehicle seemingly staggered, began to smoke, and shells in its back began to explode, illuminating the trees and buildings around it with bright flashes. Several German gun crews reacted to our shot at the same time. One shell ploughed the ground directly in front of our tank destroyer. A second one struck a nearby tree, bursting in a huge fireball. A third one, frightening us with a loud ringing sound, glanced off the right side, knocking off the box containing the spare parts and tools. Only the low light of dusk saved us from a direct hit, but the whole fighting compartment was illuminated with the flame of the explosion.

'We're on fire!' Vitya Schetnikov yelled in reflex. 'If we don't get out of here we'll burn up indeed! It's time to scram!'

'Viktor, start up! Forward and left, stop in the bushes!' I ordered Schetnikov.

The move was just in time. Armour-piercing shells streaked through our former position. Yes, we might have perished just like that! I hadn't even had time to think it over and rejoice over our narrow escape from the quick work of the German gunlayers, when something heavy smacked me in the head! Everything went dark before my eyes, and then I saw bright stars. As if in my sleep, I heard the sound of an explosion behind the superstructure and began slowly to drop into the fighting compartment. Plaksin, sensing that something was wrong, immediately closed the hatch. I came back to my senses when explosions roared right around the tank destroyer and I could hear the bursts of submachine-gun fire. Overcoming the pain and buzzing in my head, I slightly raised the hatch cover and took a look: our submachine-gunners were firing on the attic and throwing grenades into the dormer window of a two-storey building standing nearby.

When everything calmed down the deputy for technical services Ishkin ran up, jumped up on a track and stretched out his hand to me, then shook hands with Korolev, Plaksin and Schetnikov.

'That grenade was meant for you, my dear comrades!' Ishkin said anxiously.

'What grenade are you talking about, Vasiliy Vasilyevich?'

'The one that was intended for your open hatch! But instead it bounced off your hard noggin and deflected to the right of your vehicle, where it exploded! That is what saved you. Then Lieutenant Trubin's platoon made short work of those grenadiers.'

He sighed with relief. Wasn't it a miracle? To deflect a grenade with my head!

Of course, there were miracles at the front. Sometimes I'm asked if my attitude towards religion and God changed during the war. I may say the following: nothing changed for me – I had faith before the war, during the war, and have faith now. Of course I never openly prayed at war, only inwardly. Overt displays of religion were officially banned.

There were superstitions, and I observed them too. We used to embrace each other three times before combat. Not only the crew but other friends would come up, too. Without words, we would quietly embrace. If someone was thinking about something, was afraid or experiencing a premonition, he kept it to himself. Even so, many wouldn't come back from combat.

People believed. They believed in God, believed in dreams, both evil and benevolent, and believed in superstitions. If you think about it, before the war 80 per cent of the population consisted of peasantry or had a peasant background, and the peasants still had superstitions and religious convictions.

I also had certain dreams. My granny taught me how to interpret them. For example, on more than one occasion I saw raw meat in my dreams, or a fire or fire-brands. In the morning I'd tell the crew, 'I'll be killed or wounded today,' and it would happen – I would be wounded. It was some sort of omen.

On the Approaches to Kiev!

Night fell almost imperceptibly, enveloping the dacha village and the park with darkness. The crescent moon was stingily illuminating the trees and the white walls of the nearby dachas. The enemy fire began to subside. Regimental scouts, led by Lieutenant Grigoriy Matveev, filed quietly past our battery towards the German lines. In a quarter of an hour they were on their way back, advising us that there were no Germans left in the complex. This news made us happy for a while, but also put us on guard. However, we would have no time to speculate – a circular order from the chief of staff Avdievich came over the radio: 'Everyone forward!'

The tank destroyers started to move slowly southward in the darkness, the tanks rolling beside us at low speed. Sappers and mine-clearing tanks, covered by submachine-gunners, operated ahead of the formation. We passed the central alley in the dacha complex, and the sapper platoon commander Vorontsov waved a red signal light at us, which meant 'minefield'. It turned out that before retreating, the Germans had hastily scattered anti-tank mines all over the road and had covered them with dirt and leaves.

We occupied the southern part of Pushcha-Voditsa with almost no fighting. The tanks and self-propelled guns stopped here in the same combat formation that they'd adopted for the advance, while the riflemen and submachine-gunners combed the gardens, parks and buildings for German stragglers or rearguard units. We remained parked for more than two hours, waiting for the order to resume the advance. We could hear the sound of distant artillery and machine-gun fire. There seemed to be no Germans around anywhere, but we were on the alert, for we were anticipating some devious action from the enemy.

Around midnight, high-level commanders began to rush and bustle about the settlement. We thought that the Germans had broken through some-where or were counter-attacking with a large force, but soon we learned that the 3rd Guards Tank Army commander Rybalko had come up and, without communicating with the corps commander, had issued a combat task directly to the 70th Mechanized Brigade's commander Siyanin: to advance down the tram line towards Pil'nik–Belichi Station–Svyatoshino. Within half an hour, our unit also began to move up to the line of deployment.

Apparently, Rybalko had passed along a similar order to all the other formations, for the entire army went on the advance simultaneously. The scene was grand and astounding! The armoured avalanche fell upon the enemy over a very wide sector of the front, with headlights blazing, howling sirens and roaring engines! Everything quickly became confused. There were the tongues of flame from firing guns. Bursts of machine-gun fire streaked through the night mist with hundreds of dazzling tracers. Between the valleys of the Dnieper and Irpen' Rivers, invisible scenes of night combat unfolded. The enemy was hastily retreating, abandoning matériel and equipment. At dawn our units burst into Pil'nik, catching the enemy rear services by surprise, and continued the advance without stopping. With a decisive attack we captured Belichi Station and cut the Kiev–Zhitomir railroad.

The Battle for Svyatoshino

Leaving a screening force to repulse possible enemy attacks from the west, the units of the mechanized brigade pivoted by 90° and began to advance towards Svyatoshino, on the western outskirts of Kiev. The enemy offered stiff resist-ance; the *Luftwaffe* literally hung over the battlefield, relentlessly bombing and strafing our combat formations and slowing down the pace of our advance considerably. However, low-level enemy aircraft did their best to stay away from our battery, for Vasya Plaksin was firing pretty accurately from the captured machine gun, striking sparks from the bombers' fuselages.

The enemy resistance strengthened dramatically with such massive air support. The battle grew increasingly fierce. Yet just at this moment, a supply vehicle towing two field kitchens drove up directly into the midst of our combat formation and took cover from direct fire in a small hollow. Everyone rejoiced: we were famished! Handing the machine gun over to me, Plaksin crawled out of the vehicle through the lower hatch and in a crouch, covered by the tank destroyer, quickly rushed to the field kitchen and back!

The gunlayer reported to me with a grin:

> Comrade Lieutenant, Private Plaksin has fulfilled the mission of food delivery! I've brought back a full bucket of meat with some gruel – not gruel with some meat! It seems to be from the Fritz's own kitchens. The rear services commander Captain Tumakov himself is in charge of the food distribution today and is making the cook Yarantsev fill full buckets for the crews!

We ate in turns, continuing to fight, and in less than half an hour the almost full 12-litre bucket was empty. It was hard to believe, but we had not had a morsel of food for almost three days, apart from a single mess tin of gruel for the whole crew dispatched from the brigade kitchen on the night before the advance.

The advance was slow, but nevertheless the suburbs of Kiev gradually came into view: Svyatoshino, curtained by smoke; the outlines of the Machinery Factory, and the Red Excavator plant. At this moment, however, on top of everything else, the enemy turned the fire of his flak guns onto our tanks and self-propelled vehicles. The offensive ground to a complete stop. The situation was worsened by the fact that the terrain was open, and only the battlefield smoke concealed us from direct hits of enemy shells. Flashes from ricocheting hits were appearing on one machine after another. A tank in the very middle of the battle formation exploded. Our self-propelled gun was rocked several times as well. I began to worry about the fate of the crews and vehicles – it was madness to advance through the well-prepared zone of intense defensive fire across absolutely open ground. Just then, at this critical moment, *Katyusha* rocket-launchers thundered with several salvoes, pulverizing the enemy defence lines. Powerful air strikes by bombers and Il-2 ground-attack planes followed. Taking advantage of the enemy confusion, our tank companies and gun batteries made a rapid lunge and gained a foothold on the settlement's outskirts, which allowed us to find cover from enemy fire behind the houses and buildings.

Recovering from the blow, the Germans partially re-established their system of fire. Tenacious street-fighting broke out. Our battery, together with tanks and infantry, was approaching a large brick building. Immediately a couple of dozen machine guns, anti-tank guns and mortars opened fire from the windows and embrasures. Our riflemen were pinned down; the tanks and self-propelled guns took cover behind remaining buildings, in gardens and in the ruins of houses. The thick walls of the brick building in which the enemy was lodged easily withstood the impact of our armour-piercing shells, and the well-protected

Germans were intensifying their fire, which began coming from a growing number of emplacements.

'Valeriy, fire at the embrasures!' I ordered the gunlayer, and then replicated the command to Makarov's crew. The first shell exploded below an embrasure; the second one flew into a window and one enemy gun was silenced. One more gun was knocked out after several more shots. Makarov's crew and other tank destroyers of the battery also silenced several weapon emplacements. An hour later the Nazis were capable of firing only from several guns and machine guns. Resuming the advance, our three tanks and five self-propelled guns bypassed the building around the side where the guns had already been suppressed. Svyatoshino was now in our hands, but some fighting was still going on.

Chapter 8

The Pursuit to Fastov

On My Own in the Village of Khotovo

That afternoon, after we had seized control of Svyatoshino and the 70th Mechanized Brigade had set up a solid defence line to bottle the Germans inside Kiev, the 9th Mechanized Corps command pulled our regiment out of the line and subordinated it to the command of the 71st Guards Mechanized Brigade, led by Hero of the Soviet Union Colonel Luppov.

Leaving Svyatoshino as the sun was setting we advanced to the south-west. A motorized rifle battalion, reinforced by a tank company and two batteries of our 1454th Self-propelled Artillery Regiment operated as the forward detachment of Luppov's brigade. Our SU-85 self-propelled guns represented the detachment's main strike force. Powerful in its composition, mobile in terms of speed and manoeuvrability, the forward detachment kept dislodging rearguard enemy units from settlements on our line of advance. So rapidly was this being done that the Germans had no time to set fire to the abandoned villages and instead ran for their lives under cover of the night. However, we failed to take the village of Gatnoye from the march due to the presence of a significant force of withdrawing enemy. Luppov responded by rapidly deploying the brigade's main force and striking the village from three directions simultaneously. The enemy resistance immediately collapsed. It was not a retreat but a panicked flight! In their haste to escape, the Germans began to abandon their guns, vehicles, carts, and a lot of ammunition and equipment. Only their panzers maintained good order, repeatedly checking our advance through rearguard skirmishes from chosen positions. Over the night of pursuit, they managed to destroy two tanks and knocked out a third; they also immobilized two of our SU-85s. However, the enemy didn't get off easily from these rapid actions either. They left behind two burned-out tanks, and one that had become stuck in a swampy stream basin. With this the German armoured rearguard ceased holding temporary positions and joined the retreating troops.

The enemy was fleeing along all possible roads and so hastily that traffic jams were not infrequent. Our forward detachment was catching up with these motorized columns and smashing them, littering the road from the village of Chabany to Khotovo with destroyed enemy vehicles and equipment. At dawn on 6 November we captured the large settlement of Khotovo by a simultaneous attack of the forward detachment from the north and the 71st Guards Mechanized Brigade's main force from the west. The enemy had not expected such a sudden appearance of our troops. The engagement was brief, but fierce. The Germans managed to set ablaze two of our tanks, which had been the first to penetrate into the centre of the village. In general, though, the enemy failed to put up serious resistance and had to withdraw.

Here we managed to liberate several thousand Kiev civilians, who the Germans were forcibly driving to the west for slave labour. The event was as happy for them as it was for us. The residents of this large village were no less happy to be free of German occupation. The bright morning sun lit the liberated village, its people and the Kiev civilians, who thronged the streets as soon as the fighting had ceased. People with tears in their eyes rushed to embrace us, but some of the locals, having armed themselves with axes, guns and pitchforks were helping the submachine-gunners round up German stragglers and bring them to the brigade headquarters.

The events of that day changed with kaleidoscopic speed. The units of the brigade took up an all-round defence: we could not allow the enemy to escape from Kiev, nor could we allow his reserves to approach the besieged city. Our battery entrenched on the south-western outskirts of the village, and the crews were already preparing fire data. The other units were also urgently selecting and taking up suitable firing positions. Motorized riflemen and submachine-gunners were digging in on the slopes of heights. Sappers were laying mine-fields west of the village. One battalion of the brigade was combing through the adjacent forest.

The regiment commander summoned battery commander Pogorel'chenko, and the platoon commanders Fomichev and me to the command post. Unimaginable noise engulfed the village! The triumphant locals were plying their liberators with milk, vegetables and fruit. Children weary of longing for their fathers to return refused to let go of the soldiers' arms.

The command post was located in a one-storey wooden school building. As we were approaching it, we were surprised to see a staff bus with German officers aboard it pull up in front of the school. They were taken prisoners straight away! About twenty officers were captured with not a single shot fired. It turned out that they were returning to their own headquarters, which had been located in the very same school building that now housed our command post! A lieutenant colonel was the senior officer in rank – he said that fighting in Kiev was continuing.

We returned to the battery. The atmosphere was calm; German bombers were hitting the nearby forest, but by this time we had no troops there. Making use of the lull, the crew went into the hut nearest to the vehicle to have breakfast. The Germans had gathered in Khotovo about 800 head of cattle, ready to be shipped to Germany. We got our hands on the herd and our commissaries snapped very quickly into action – every crew was issued with a butchered calf. We gave this calf to the hostess, but since we were short on time, we also gave her some tinned meat, so as not to trouble her with the carcass, and asked her to cook a pot of Ukrainian borsch. The hostess – her name was Maria – added a variety of vegetables and greens, and cooked such a tasty borsch that we began to drool from just the sight and aroma of it – none of us had ever had an opportunity to taste such borsch before! For the breakfast, Vasiliy Vasilyevich Ishkin opened a prize from among the German supplies captured the night before – a bottle of French rum. It was a large one, probably no less than two litres. The hostess gave us cups, we poured out the rum, and we drank to the hostess's health and to our combat success. We had just started in on the borsch when a captain, the commander of the motorized rifle battalion, ran up to the hut and shouted 'Germans!' from the doorstep.

We immediately forgot the food! Everyone instantly rushed out of the hut without thanking our hospitable hostess.

Having dashed out ahead of the crewmen, I climbed into the driver's seat and moved the SU-85 into a firing position. A large column of enemy infantry and artillery was coming into view on a hillock covered with a sparse deciduous grove from the direction of Khodorovka, which was a village south of Khotovo. They were already about 2 kilometres from the battery, in column formation, and to all appearances seemed unaware that the Russians would greet them with fire so far in their rear. My crewmen came running up. We were still tipsy: the rum had proved to be quite strong! By this time, however, we had gained so much experience that we operated like clockwork. We decided to let the Germans come closer. Once the column had entered open terrain about a kilometre away, the battery opened fire. Machine guns began to chatter from the trenches. The closely-grouped shells were falling accurately among the targets. The Germans quickly deployed into a combat formation and began furiously to dig in and to deploy guns in firing positions. By no means could we allow them to entrench! The battery commander decided to attack the enemy with three self-propelled guns. The 'follow me' signal arrived from the commander's machine. 'Forward!' I ordered Schetnikov.

In a minute three SU-85s – the battery commander's in the centre, mine and Fomichev's on either side, rushed towards the enemy at full speed, while Makarov's and Rusakov's crews fired at the enemy anti-tank guns, preventing them from taking up firing positions. Through my periscope, I could clearly see that the enemy crews and guns were being blanketed by geysers of earth and black smoke. Machine-gun bullets were striking splatters of sparks from the armour of our trio. However, the supporting crews did their job well and the Nazi gunners failed to achieve a single hit on any of the self-propelled guns. All three SU-85s closed on the enemy positions almost at the same time! Within minutes, the enemy guns were smashed and the gun carriages mangled. Eight burning tractors could be seen through the smoky haze – work done by our battery comrades! While the battery commander's vehicle was overrunning the last gun, the gunlayers Lapshin and Korolev set ablaze an armoured halftrack each – two of the four that were escaping towards Khodorovka.

'If there wasn't so much dust, the bastards wouldn't have gotten away alive!' Korolev lamented.

Indeed, the dust raised by the explosions refused to settle down, offering concealment to the fleeing enemy. Several machine-gun bursts rattled on the tank destroyer's superstructure again. Sparks appeared on the other vehicles too. This was fire from enemy infantry deployed on the hill, which had pinned down the motorized riflemen that were approaching in support. The battery commander's and Fomichev's self-propelled guns took off to bypass the hill, while I approached it directly. The engine roared as the machine slowly made its way up the slope over deep and loose sand. About 100 metres from the crest, where the Germans had dug in, our engine suddenly stalled! Schetnikov was an inexperienced driver, a young lad really, only 19 ... My God! I just recalled that I was only 20 at the time – and I used to feel like such an old guy next to him, based on my combat experience and command position. The engine stalled and he didn't know what the problem was. The Germans were right in front of us! They were watching us from behind the crest. I ordered: 'Come on, fix it!' Then I opened the hatch, showed myself from the turret with the captured MG-42 and yelled in German: '*Ergebt euch!* Surrender! We guarantee your life!'

The incoming fire slackened. I repeated my demand, 'Surrender! We guarantee your life!'

The firing stopped, and the Germans slowly began to rise. There were about 100 of them. Placing hand grenades nearby just in case, I glanced at Schetnikov – cold sweat was trickling from his forehead. I told him: 'Viktor, stay quiet, try to switch it on with the side clutches disengaged.'

The surrendered men drew nearer. I ordered: '*Waffe hinlegen!* [Drop your weapons!]'

The Germans laid their rifles and submachine-guns on the ground.

'*Wer hat die Uhr?* [Who has watches?]' I asked, knowing that the rear-echelon men would snatch them anyway, and it would be better if we took them – we really needed them.

Vasya Plaksin made the rounds among the prisoners with a helmet. Watches filled it to the brim. Then I directed the Germans towards the regiment's location and off they went – on their own, because I had no one to escort them.

Even to this day I don't know why the Germans had surrendered. It might have been the offer to spare their lives ... or perhaps they'd been spooked by the self-propelled guns moving around their flank?

After that, without moving from the spot, we captured two more groups of prisoners. Altogether there were 375 men. Later we counted the captured weapons: 75 per cent of them were submachine-guns, and the remainder were rifles. It was just the opposite for our infantrymen, the large majority of which carried rifles right until the war's end.

Having guessed from afar that our vehicle had broken down, Vasiliy Vasilyevich Ishkin, our brave deputy commander of technical services, had crawled up to the SU-85 while we were still receiving fire from the Germans. Then, after sending the prisoners away, he quickly made the repairs together with Schetnikov, and only then did my guys notice Ishkin's torn overalls and the bloody patch on his right shoulder.

Soon Pogorel'chenko's and Fomichev's self-propelled guns came into view, moving barely above idle speed: a group of twenty to thirty German prisoners was walking ahead of each. The Germans were walking with sullen faces, trying to maintain their alignment. Their firearms, which had only been recently firing at us, were now piled upon the self-propelled guns. These prisoners were also sent on to Khotovo, but now under the escort of submachine-gunners.

In general, Petya Fomichev, the 1st Platoon commander, didn't take prisoners – he would sooner crush them beneath his tracks. His family had remained under German occupation and he had heard nothing from them since the start of the war. Petya believed that the Germans had executed his kinfolk. He was born in 1916 and before the war he had been a collective farm chairman in the village of Belyi Verkh in Orel Oblast.

Germans. In combat, I showed them no mercy. Here it was a simple matter: either you would get him, or he would get you. I would never shoot prisoners, though. Why do it? There were special organs to deal with them. There might be a peasant among them – not a Nazi at all – or a Frenchman who'd been forced to fight for the Führer and couldn't care less about Hitler. For this reason I never shot them; I ruled it out as a matter of principle.

I can add that neither I nor the crew received any special recognition for taking these prisoners. Not a medal or even an expression of gratitude – nothing. The higher commanders were totally indifferent.

When we returned to the regiment happy and excited, dusk was already settling over the village. Along the way together with Ishkin we dropped by our hostess's hut for a minute. Maria was distressed: 'My God, you didn't have time to eat, you ran off hungry! Let me give you your dinner now!'

Instead, having thanked the kind-hearted woman, we said our farewells and departed. There was a real festive atmosphere in the streets of Khotovo.

Near the regiment's ambulance, soldiers were dancing with the girls from Kiev and the local girls to the accordion of its driver, Borya Zaprudnov. In some places people were shouting 'Urah!' In some places they were singing, and Colonel Luppov's guys were tossing the brave Anya high into the air and then carefully catching her. We asked Ishkin the reason for such joy and he gladly announced:

> Firstly, we successfully repulsed three attacks by large enemy forces and didn't allow the enemy to break through to Kiev or to break out! Secondly, Kiev has been liberated! And thirdly, all the troops that participated in the liberation received an expression of personal gratitude from the Supreme Commander! It means that our 1454th Regiment got it too!

As night fell, the combat units began to form into columns, preparing for another march ... Forty-five years later Pavel Pavlovich Pogorel'chenko, Vladimir Nikolaevich Shishkov and the author of these memoirs had an opportunity to visit this village again, which was so memorable to us. Khotovo had changed beyond recognition. There were brick houses instead of huts, and instead of the old wooden school there was a brick one – large and bright with all the necessary classrooms. We couldn't find Maria's hut or the woman herself. In the village only a few elderly men were left who could recall those days. However, a monument to the soldiers who died fighting for it had been erected in the village centre. Pity, we failed to find Maria – it would have been great to see her again.

The Death of the Regiment Commander

One dark November night we were marching towards Fastov. As we approached the town of Vasil'kov, I managed to pick up a Moscow broadcast on the tank's radio and suddenly heard: 'To the glory of the gallant fighters of the 1st Ukrainian Front, in honour of the liberation of the capital of Ukraine, I order the firing of a salute of twenty-four salvoes from 324 cannons!' It was the first salute given with such a large number of cannons.

We approached Fastov before dawn.[1] Street-fighting in the city was still going on. We knew from the regiment commander's order given before our departure from Khotovo that troops of General Panfilov's 6th Guards Tank Corps and Colonel Yakubovsky's 91st Separate Tank Brigade were in action here. Although we arrived late for the main show, the enemy was still putting up tenacious resistance near a fuel depot. The crews of Lieutenant Porshnev's 4th Battery, commanded by Lieutenants Samoilov, Steblyaev, Tomin and Savushkin played a decisive role in the outcome of the action. Porshnev's men got behind the Germans and knocked out four tanks, and this broke their resistance. The enemy abandoned the depot – his last stronghold – in panic, without even setting it on fire.

When it grew light and the city was fully liberated, we rolled up to the fuel depot. We wanted to refuel our self-propelled guns with diesel, but to our great surprise we found only purple-coloured fuel in all the cisterns. It was our first time to come across synthetic fuel.

With no delay the troops went on the advance to the south-west along the Unava River. Our battery together with the 2nd Battalion of the 70th Mechanized Brigade mounted on our vehicles were operating as part of a rearguard detachment, charged with the task of preventing a surprise enemy attack from the rear. Here, regiment commander Samyko was killed. Knowing that our troops had already entered the town of Popel'nya, he rushed towards it in his Willys jeep, moving well ahead of our tank destroyers. While crossing a railroad, his jeep ran into an enemy ambush and came under fire from machine guns and submachine-guns. Filatov – Samyko's driver – managed to back the jeep up by several metres, but after being mortally wounded by a second bullet, he toppled over onto the regiment commander. The commanders' aide-de-camp Junior Lieutenant Vladimir Ivanov was also killed. Badly wounded, Samyko, his deputy political commander Gritsenko and the regiment's senior surgeon Muratova got out of the car and, returning fire from pistols, took cover in a roadside ditch. The odds were too long, though, and all of them were killed.

Our rearguard detachment moved in the wake of the brigade. We saw signs of recent fighting in almost every settlement, and in Romanovka we came across Germans who had just entered the village from the opposite direction. The enemy was taken by surprise and failed to put out any organized resistance. Several dozen enemy troops were annihilated in a quarter of an hour, and five vehicles and three guns were destroyed. The rest managed to disappear into an adjacent forest.

It was already dark, there was a cold drizzle falling, and we decided to make a long stopover in the village of Zhidovtsy. We placed three self-propelled guns in firing positions, while the motorized rifle units took up positions near the school, the church and on the slopes of the Unava River valley. Two SU-85s – mine and Fomichev's – were detached for reconnaissance duties. Battery commander Pogorel'chenko gave us our task. He was being billeted in the hut owned by Ivan Mel'nik, situated across the street from the school. The friendly hostess, named Maria Fedorovna, offered us dinner but the battery commander politely declined: 'Thank you, but dinner is going to be late.'

Then he unfolded his map on the table. Each tank destroyer, accompanied by a squad of submachine-gunners, would conduct a reconnaissance patrol: Fomichev to the west, towards Lozovka and Kilovka, and I – to the north, towards Kornin.

As we approached Kornin, it was already the dead of night. The silence was such that the village seemed to be uninhabited, and given the unclear situation, this always made us particularly uneasy. A sergeant – the submachine-gunners' squad commander – and I crept stealthily (lest we bump into sentries!) up to the outermost hut, followed by two young submachine-gunners. The latter looked like boys in comparison with the sturdy figure of the sergeant. We took a listen. There were no signs of life. We gently tapped on the window. No sound again. However, one of the soldiers heard whispering in the cellar. Standing to one side of the concealed door, I said quietly: 'Everyone out of the cellar.'

An old man was the first to emerge. His elderly wife followed him. Happy to see their own side, they told us that partisans had attacked a German column near a bridge earlier that evening, sparking a fierce engagement that could be heard for about an hour. Then the Germans had been firing artillery, and some had come through the village just recently, which is why the old people were hiding.

'Are there Germans in the village now?'

'Hard to say; maybe a few.'

We had to find out if there were still Germans around. The old man agreed to lead the sergeant and two submachine-gunners to search for them, and all four disappeared into the darkness of the night. I returned to my vehicle. We waited for the return of the group for forty long minutes, prepared to rush to their assistance at a moment's notice. Everything turned out well, however – the Germans had left the village. Thanking the old man for his help, we returned to Zhidovtsy along the same route.

The Night March

We hadn't finished eating – it was either dinner or breakfast, when three trucks pulled up in front of the school. By order of Siyanin, the commander of the 70th Mechanized Brigade, the motorized battalion boarded the trucks and departed towards Fastov.

Pogorel'chenko failed to get in touch with the regiment command post, and the battery set off towards Popel'nya an hour before dawn. We moved along a dirt road through the thick coniferous forest. Weighty boughs of fir and pine trees hanging over the tank destroyers curtained the sky like a solid, dense tent, allowing us only rare glimpses of the scattered clouds and twinkling stars. We moved slowly through the pitch blackness, keeping our rear red lights illuminated so as to avoid collisions. We were on guard – with no infantry, moving through a forest at night raised a real risk of coming across enemy tank-hunting teams. In such a forest, they would present a great threat to us not only at night, but in the daytime as well. We stopped from time to time and took a listen. Sometimes we could hear the sound of machine-gun bursts and shell explosions, muffled by the forest.

My SU-85, which had the MG-42 German machine gun, moved at the head of the column, followed by the battery commander's vehicle. Approximately halfway en route, it seemed to me that someone was moving up in front of us. I decided not to waste time on reporting it to the battery commander: 'Viktor! Full lights on!' I ordered Schetnikov.

It turned out to be a column of two-wheel carts, but it was hard to tell if it was one of ours because of the distance and darkness.

'Viktor! Catch up with the carts! Vasya, have the machine gun ready!' I ordered the crewmen, and the tank destroyer with its full lights on hurried to catch the cart column, blinding the men driving the carts.

'Comrade Lieutenant, those are Germans!' Schetnikov shouted into the intercom.

'I see! Pass them on the right and stop!' I ordered the driver and reported the situation to the battery commander.

The other self-propelled guns came up to the carts also with their lights on and stopped on both sides. It was a rear transport unit. The soldiers were old by our standards of those times, although most likely there was no one older than 40 among them. They were transporting all kinds of everyday supplies and clean underwear, which we confiscated immediately. We needed a change after all, for we hadn't had one for quite some time! The prisoners were trembling, most likely because of fear rather than cold. Their faces seemed to be dark blue in the pre-dawn twilight, their eyes – big and motionless. Pogorel'chenko and I explained to them that they would have to follow the first self-propelled gun and if any of them tried to escape, all of them would be shot on the spot.

The battery commander told me, 'You know what to do in case of combat, so keep the machine guns and hand grenades handy.' Then we continued the march along our route.

It had already become light, but the column was moving slowly because of the six two-horse carts we had captured. The carts were pulled by a dozen well-fed horses and urged on by the battery commander's self-propelled gun. Eleven captured soldiers sat in the coachman's seats, hanging their heads and timidly glancing at the machine gun: its barrel was unwaveringly pointed directly at the German transports. Near a railroad crossing we came across a place of recent fighting, and dozens of German corpses lay scattered around it. Our prisoners stirred, but didn't venture an escape, even though the forest was right up against the road.

From ahead of us to the right, near Popel'nya, we could hear the sounds of fighting with unremitting submachine-gun and machine-gun bursts. Deputy chief of staff Senior Lieutenant Arkhipov met us near the first houses and directed the battery into its positions. While the crews were setting up the vehicles, Arkhipov managed to tell us that the main enemy forces had been destroyed the previous night by the vanguard, led by the brigade commander Luppov, and that up to an infantry battalion had been wiped out and sixty prisoners taken. At that moment the arriving main forces of the brigade were destroying the last pockets of resistance. The village contained large depots with foodstuffs, ammunition and fuel, and many tractors, horses and carts had been seized. The men had found a safe full of German reichsmarks and plenty of abandoned arms and ammunition in the German positions.

We also handed over our prisoners and the captured supply carts and horses to a collection point, and then immediately set to digging emplacements for the SU-85s. The regiment spent the entire day digging in and camouflaging positions. Our crews did it with utmost meticulousness, for our battery position was at an intersection of two main roads, which was the anticipated target for an enemy attack.

Destruction of the Motor Vehicle Column

On 8 and 9 November 1943 the weather was good and sunny, and the *Luftwaffe* wouldn't leave us in peace. Junkers and Messerschmitts bombed our positions in small groups. The rear services lost several trucks, which deprived the regiment of the capability to lift and transport all of its material reserves at once, and in case of a retreat threatened the loss of part of our supplies. The truck carrying the officers' gear was destroyed too, and we were left with no ammunition for our personal sidearms and nothing to replace our everyday field uniform.

At dawn on 10 November, we heard the rumble of tank engines, and the strain in the companies and batteries, which had been on high alert for three days now, began to grow. Soon reports came from the front line that five tanks were approaching Popel'nya from the direction of Kamenka. The crews of the tanks and self-propelled guns positioned on this axis waited anxiously at their guns and gunsights for their appearance. Soon the first steel monster emerged from a low-growth forest and stopped about 800 metres from us. It was a Panther! Four explosions appeared on the frontal armour of the enemy tank within several seconds – the crews of our battery had fired a salvo at this 'predator'. Although the tank didn't catch fire, its deafened crew began to leap out of the turret, gripping their heads – all five tankers. Submachine-gunners immediately opened a heavy fire on them from the trench-line. The other tanks pulled back.

Deputies of technical services Lobanov, Ishkin and Sapko ran towards the immobilized tank. Within about fifteen minutes they had managed to start the engine, and soon the 46-ton tank with its 700 horsepower engine was roaring into our lines. We set it up in a firing position, having turned it towards the enemy. Now all of us had a chance to examine it and feel it with our hands. We found four deep dents on its frontal armour and not a single hole! The tank was handed over to the 'dismounted' crew of Lieutenant Tolya Savushkin, which set to studying the new machine immediately, scrutinizing its engine, armament and gunsights so as to make full use of the combat and firepower of the captured tank.

The enemy's withdrawal was only temporary. Soon massive air and artillery strikes fell on our defence line. The earth began to shake and houses began to burn. The chief of staff Avdievich and the deputy of technical services Vasilyev were wounded; the chief of rear services Tumakov went missing. The crews incurred losses too. Our regiment command suffered serious casualties, and only the deputy regiment commander Major Mel'nikov remained capable of acting. Mel'nikov summoned Ishkin and me. The commander of the mechanized brigade Luppov was also present.

Mel'nikov immediately began the meeting:

> The situation is very grave. There are only twelve self-propelled guns and one tank still operational in the regiment, and there are only twenty combat vehicles left in the brigade. We have to hold out until the arrival of the corps' main forces. I'm giving you a special task. It is necessary to break through the German lines near Lozovka and Kilovka and spread panic in their rear. Possibly, they will divert some tanks from the attack formation or will suspend the advance in response. I'm giving you a squad of submachine-gunners and three drivers in case you capture German vehicles. You must take off immediately. You will report every hour over the two-way radio.

The major finished giving his instructions and shook my and Ishkin's hand. I was somewhat surprised by the handshake. Mel'nikov was a dryish man and commonly wouldn't shake anyone's hand. However, this time apparently he had reckoned that we wouldn't come back alive ...

As far as I could understand from the conversation between the brigade commander and Mel'nikov, this was Luppov's idea: with one crew to break into the German rear, to confuse the enemy and, having waited for the arrival of the main forces, to break out of encirclement. The newly-appointed regiment commander should have headed the operation, but Mel'nikov didn't go with us – he didn't dare do it.

We left the regiment command post alarmed by the idea of such an un-imaginable combat assignment. On our way back, we mulled various scenarios for plans and possible routes into the enemy rear. We reported to Pogorel'chenko about the mission and said goodbye to the other crews.

We moved out towards the north-east along a little-used forest road. The SU–85's engine was working at just above an idle, almost noiselessly, no louder than the sounds of the surrounding forest. The men were extremely alert and watchful – everyone was aware that the Germans were somewhere nearby. We studied the familiar village of Zhidovtsy for a long time from a concealed position in the woods; once convinced that there were no Germans in it, we skirted around it. We crossed the Unava River near a water mill. The weather had deteriorated; rain mixed with wet snow began to fall, and visibility declined. When we approached Lozovka, the rain stopped, thank God, and we could observe the village well. It seemed that there were no Germans present, but there were three trucks in a hollow, and some people gathered around them. We gunned the engine and drove towards them at full speed. The crowd scattered, but having noticed that there were no black crosses on the self-propelled gun, the people stopped. They turned out to be simple peasants who were draining oil and petrol from the vehicles – the locals used a mixture of them in their kerosene lamps.

Having left the SU–85 in the hollow, Ishkin and I climbed a nearby slope and from the top of it saw a huge herd of black horses. Six Germans on horseback were driving the herd westward. We gave a signal to the self-propelled gun that there would be firing and hid in a roadside ditch. When the riders approached within pistol-shot range, Ishkin and I opened fire. The horse-thieves returned fire from submachine-guns, but spotting the self-propelled gun they turned around and galloped away. We drove the SU–85 around to the front of the herd and turned them around, getting them moving in the opposite direction. Then reversing the tank destroyer, we continued moving along our assigned route.

West of Kilovka we suddenly saw a whole vehicular column of fleeing Germans. A group of seven light vehicles was leading the column, followed by a fuel truck, then a long line of trucks! The head of the column was approaching Kilovka and its tail-end was almost near Kotlyarka, 5 kilometres away. I immediately stopped the vehicle and gave a command: 'Valeriy! At the light vehicles! Fragmentation rounds! Fire!'

The cars looked like matchboxes from a range of 2 kilometres, but Valeriy blew one up with his second shot. The other light vehicles disappeared into a forest.

'At the lead vehicle! Fire!'

The new command followed and seconds later the fuel truck – a larger target – exploded. Panic ran down the length of the column through the mind of every driver! The drivers began to leap out of their trucks and run into the woods, leaving the engines running. The trucks at the end of the column began

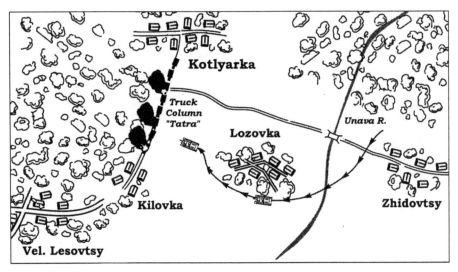

Map 4. The destruction of a German truck column west of Kiev, November 1943.

to reverse, trying to escape that way. Our tank destroyer moved in. Vasya Plaksin fired at the fleeing men from the machine gun, while the submachine-gunners employed their PPSh submachine-guns. Soon it was all over. Leaving the vehicles on the road, the Germans fled.

We approached the column. They were huge Czech-made Tatra trucks, practically bursting with material and foodstuffs. The pedantic Germans – very careful proprietors – had sorted everything into exemplary order: there were military supplies, equipment, pillows and footwear in some machines; foodstuffs like cheese, sausages, bread and butter in other trucks; and in others – chickens, ducks, rabbits, etc.

Several minutes later a group of adolescents carrying rifles, carbines, and an assortment of submachine-guns from different countries came running up from Kilovka. They introduced themselves as partisans. I requested: 'Lads, run back to the village quickly! Tell the people that every driver and tractor operator should get here immediately!' Then I added, 'Hide your firearms, for if you come across Germans now, they'll shoot you dead.'

Nine drivers came up quickly with a large number of other people. I announced: 'Take whatever you need from the vehicles, and then get out of here. The Germans may return shortly!'

Ishkin selected the Tatras with more useful loads and assigned drivers to them, forming a column of twelve trucks to send back to the regiment. Suddenly an artillery shot thundered from the edge of the forest. The shell exploded near the SU-85, and Viktor Schetnikov and Vasya Plaksin were severely wounded by splinters. I managed to detect the gun's location, jumped into the self-propelled gun, and silenced the German gun with two shells. The locals scattered as if blown by the wind: everyone rushed back to the village with loot – some with blankets and boots, others with food items.

We laid Viktor and Vasiliy on fur coats and examined their wounds. It was obvious that they wouldn't survive. Ishkin lined up the column of twelve Tatras and led it back to the regiment under the escort of the submachine-gunners. Gunlayer Valeriy Korolev and I stayed behind the enemy lines near the destroyed column. An unsettling silence reigned. The doors on some of the open truck cabins were tapping from time to time from the wind.

'Comrade Lieutenant, what now?' Valeriy asked. I looked at the 3-kilometre-long columns of huge trucks – each one was comparable to a twin-axle freight car and each one was fully loaded. No way we were gonna leave all these goodies for the Germans!

'Grab your seat,' I ordered my only crew member left, 'and keep a sharp look-out. But first of all, elevate the gun up to its limit so that we won't smash it against the vehicles. We're going to crush them!'

I myself sat at the levers and began to smash the trucks. The Tatra trucks were rolling over and falling heavily into the roadside ditches as I shoved them with my vehicle. The SU-85 was being tossed about as if in a strong storm. One moment we were listing to the left, the next moment to the right. The nose would rise upward, and then we would drop back down onto the road. We kept battering the enemy column until the last truck. When dealing with that one, the tank destroyer dropped so heavily onto the ground that the engine stalled and wouldn't start again. Taking a good look around, we noticed German tanks in the distance were coming down the hill from the direction of Popel'nya. Enemy artillery in Kotlyarka began to zero in on us.

'What are we going to do, Comrade Lieutenant?' Valeriy asked anxiously, watching the tanks through the binoculars. 'Here, take the driver's seat,' I said and quickly removed the engine partition. 'Press the starter button.'

Valeriy turned the engine over, while I had a look: the line connecting the manual priming pump and the filter had broken – diesel oil was spraying from it like a fountain. I felt relieved – we could fix it! Within a minute or two, I had connected the broken ends and wrapped the connection with black insulation tape. We pumped the air out of the fuel system and the engine started! Valeriy's face brightened and he began to respond more calmly to the explosions. I also sighed with relief and looked around. Thousands of hens, ducks, geese and rabbits, freed from the smashed Tatra trucks, were running everywhere.

'Where shall we go, Comrade Lieutenant?' Valeriy asked excitedly. 'The Germans are all around us!'

'Wherever we go, we'll be fighting them! Now start the engine and go forward, into the Germans' rear!'

Once the SU–85 had rolled into a hollow and out of sight of the Germans, we turned by 90° and headed towards Lozovka. We stopped in some bushes about a kilometre away from the village. It was already growing dark but we discerned more than twenty tanks in the orchards at the western end of the village.

'How's the engine running?' I asked.

'Almost normally. We're losing power in fourth gear across this field.'

'Stay here, I'll climb that hill and have a look.'

From atop the low hill, I identified the closest enemy tank – it would be our first target. It was a heavy tank, but we would have a flank shot. The tank destroyer climbed the slope, which was overgrown with bushes, and stopped at the top. With two armour-piercing rounds into its flank, Valeriy set the tank ablaze. The remaining tanks immediately returned fire!

'Comrade Lieutenant, what shall we do if they come at us?' Korolev asked with trepidation.

'It's not likely they will! We've fired on them, and the situation for them is unclear – they're anxious, lest there's a tactical trap or they'll drive right into an ambush. Start the engine. We're heading back to Zhidovtsy!' Yet I thought to myself: 'God knows who is there now – our troops or the Germans?'

It was already completely dark when, having evaded artillery shelling, we stopped at the bridge leading into Zhidovtsy near the water mill. We listened. It was quiet in the village; not even a dog's barking was heard. We decided to cross and enter the village, though I was apprehensive about driving the SU–85 over the narrow, wooden bridge at night. Holding my breath, I slowly drove the heavy combat vehicle across the bridge, occasionally detecting the sound of cracking wood from the planked bridge. Valeriy was anxious too. He stood in the hatch with the machine gun, ready to open fire.

At last the bridge was behind us. I sighed with relief and stopped the vehicle by the first hut. We climbed out of the machine and I gently knocked on the window. The door creaked; the proprietor came out and looked us over with apprehension.

'Are there Germans in the village?' I asked him, with no introductions.

'There weren't any today, but I don't know about now,' the old man answered.

We thanked him and said goodbye.

'All right, Valeriy, hop into the driver's seat and carry out my orders to the letter. Our life depends on this if we happen to come across any Germans.'

The tank destroyer rolled slowly and quietly through the village. The huts were already wrapped in the night darkness, but their white walls were still clearly visible. We stopped by the familiar school. Hearing the low rumbling of the engine, Ivan Mel'nik and his wife Maria Fedotovna came out and ran up to us. It appeared that there were no Germans in the village. They invited us into the hut right away. While we were talking, a group of armed villagers approached the tank destroyer. Their leader introduced himself as Vasiliy Belokur, and then he introduced the members of his group: Ivan Yary, Vasiliy Shimchenko, brothers Vladimir, Mikhail and Nikolay Aksenenko, and a few more men. They were sturdy men, all armed with our PPSh submachine-guns. They had already heard about our raid into the German rear. We gave them two boxes of German pistol rounds – 360 in each, and asked them to get us diesel: we had only enough fuel for about another 30 kilometres. Valeriy and I immediately set to work repairing the engine, while Belokur's men took up an all-round defence encompassing the church, the school, and along the bank of the Unava River. Around midnight Belokur's head peered into the hatch: 'Comrade Lieutenant. There are some men across the Unava, laying low and keeping silent, near the road leading from Kornin. It looks like they've noticed us.'

'Stay well-concealed and keep your eye on them. If you hear German speech, shoot with no warning,' I advised the group commander.

The unknown men across the river slipped away about thirty minutes later, having undertaken no action. We never found out who had been there, but decided that they had been enemy scouts reconnoitring the village.

Before dawn several armoured vehicles with infantry approached from the same direction and stopped on the opposite bank. We fired three flares towards them. They began to bustle about, moving back and forth, and we could hear orders spoken in German. It served as the signal for Belokur's submachine-gunners – they opened fire. Valeriy and I fired two high-explosive rounds too. Although we failed to hit any of the armoured vehicles in the darkness, the Germans hastily pulled back, leaving behind their dead. We were also afraid that we would have to pay for this minor success, if the Nazis returned and broke into the slumbering village with a similar group of halftracks and infantry. We would be unable to use our main gun inside the village, and could only rely upon the captured German machine gun, which we had kept with us since Kursk. Fortunately, however, not knowing much about the situation, the Germans decided not to test us again and everything turned out well.

At dawn we could hear the creaking of cart wheels, and soon Valeriy and I saw Yary and Shimchenko – they were bringing us a barrel in a horse-drawn cart. We instantly felt a sense of relief: we would be able to refuel our vehicle. Using a hose inserted into an opening in the barrel, we siphoned the barrel's entire 200 litres of diesel into our fuel tanks without spilling a single drop. Seemingly now everything was alright; the engine was running better and the tanks were half-full of fuel, but I was still concerned. I hadn't been able to get in touch with our regiment's command post in over twenty-four hours. Apparently, yesterday we'd been out of radio range, but tonight we were much closer. We could only assume that the regiment was either in a heavy night action or had already left Popel'nya. We decided to have a snack to make up for yesterday's missing breakfast, lunch and dinner, and then to force our way through the German positions to our regiment in Popel'nya.

Belokur's guys were still on watch at their outposts; Valeriy and I entered Mel'nik's hut. Maria Fedotovna placed a full dish of soft-boiled potatoes, dilled cucumbers and fresh, ripe tomatoes on the table, and we opened two tins of American Spam. Together with our hosts, we dug into the food with great appetite. We ate rapidly, from time to time glancing at the window and watching the main intersection in the village. Suddenly our keen ear caught the rumble of a tank engine. Everyone rushed out into the street. We listened closely. It sounded like a diesel engine – so it was one of our machines! It was coming from the direction of Popel'nya – and becoming more distinct! Valeriy and I ran to meet the approaching vehicle, leaving our gracious hosts at the gate.

Several minutes later, the battery commander's self-propelled gun rounded a corner from behind the church, turned down the street in our direction, and stopped near our SU-85. Pogorel'chenko quickly jumped down, shook our hands and briefly informed us about the situation:

> We've broken through the encirclement. Currently we're conducting a fighting withdrawal to the south-east, towards Paripsy and Savertsy. Fomichev's been wounded, though, badly wounded, and we have to save him. We are trying to force our way into Fastov with our crew only, to get him to the local hospital. It's his only chance to survive. We have already bumped into German tanks three times.

Pogorel'chenko finished his report and glanced up. I hopped up onto Pogorel'chenko's vehicle. My battle comrade Petya Fomichev, the 1st Platoon commander, lay stretched out and unconscious behind the superstructure on a tarpaulin. His head was fully wrapped in bandages, except for slots for his eyes, nose and mouth. Holding back tears, with difficulty I found a faint pulse and thought with hope that Petr might survive due to his vigorous constitution. Unfortunately our hopes weren't realized. We found out later that he died in the hospital on 31 January 1944, having never regained consciousness.

We were running low on ammunition. Pogorel'chenko gave us seven shells from his allowance and began to hurry to be on his way, taking Volodya Aksenenko from Belokur's group as a guide. Before leaving, he advised me, 'You hold out here for the time being. You might have to give cover to our troops when they are pulling out of the pocket, then act according to the situation.'

We hugged each other tightly three times, as was the custom in our unit before going into battle, and Pogorel'chenko climbed into his machine. The SU-85 rushed off in the direction of Fastov.

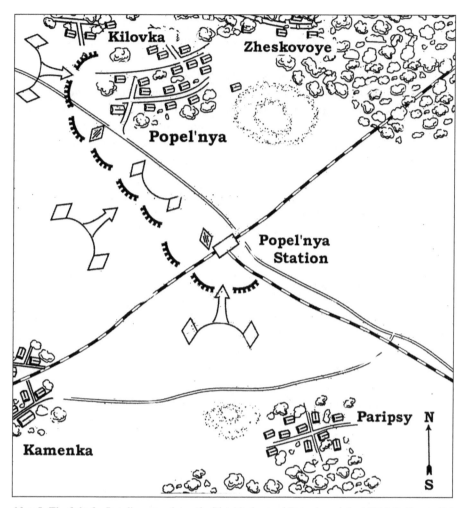

Map 5. The fight for Popel'nya involving the 71st Mechanized Brigade and the 1454th Self-propelled Artillery Regiment.

About 14.00, suddenly two horse-drawn carts with our soldiers emerged from the forest at a gallop, coming from the direction of Popel'nya. From them, we learned that a fierce clash with German tanks had recently occurred near an aerodrome there,[2] and that our units had suffered heavy losses. This group – all that remained of a rifle platoon – had managed to set two tanks ablaze using Molotov cocktails and to break out of the pocket. Somewhere along the forest road they had ambushed a German supply column and had captured these horse-drawn carts.

Our little army in Zhidovtsy had been reinforced; now there were fourteen of us – a much more impressive force! On top of that, Vasya Shimchenko from Belokur's group asked to join my crew as the driver. That meant there were now fifteen of us! After some quick instructions, Vasiliy, a tractor driver by trade, immediately started to handle the SU-85 rather well.

Once it became clear that no one else was going to arrive from Popel'nya, we headed east towards the village of Erchiki, leaving the horses and carts that the soldiers had captured with Belokur's group. As we were pulling out of Zhidovtsy, which had become like a second home to us, we noticed high above a Focke-Wulf reconnaissance plane, which had always been a harbinger of an air-raid. So it was this time as well. I had just managed to replace Shimchenko at the levers, when four dive-bombers caught up with us. During their first pass, the SU-85 was rolling at high speed with sharp zigzags to the left and right – and all four bombs exploded behind us. As they dived on us a second time, I abruptly stopped the vehicle and reversed – the bombs exploded on the spot where the machine had just been! While the planes left to circle around again, we managed to scoot into a village and park beneath a sycamore tree. The *Luftwaffe* men lost track of us! Of course, they guessed that we had hidden under a tree, but they didn't know under which one, and there were many of them in the village. They had to leave with nothing for their pains. We'd won the duel between the single self-propelled gun and four Stukas. Once the aircraft were gone, my tank riders rose up from the armour and noticeably started to celebrate and chatter, even joking as they helped each other shake off the dirt from the explosions.

We encountered only an artillery crew with a 76mm gun in Erchiki – there were five artillerymen headed by a sergeant. The village itself was nearly empty of people; everyone had hidden in anticipation of the approaching fighting. We learned from the few remaining locals that if we proceeded in the same direction we were taking, we would come across Germans, and that they had already seized Zhidovtsy behind us. We decided to hold here for the night, then to head towards Fastov in the morning. While the riflemen and the artillerymen were digging in, I went with Shimchenko to take a look at a narrow neck of land between two ponds, which we would have to use when leaving Erchiki, since there was no other way out for us. Shimchenko walked next to me and was gloomily silent – he was obviously keenly worried for his family back in Zhidovtsy: he had five children. We examined the boggy isthmus; it left much to be desired, but we couldn't be choosy. We returned to our position.

About 04.00 we heard the sound of engines from the direction of the village of Chernavka, and soon a German column emerged from the nearby forest and headed towards Erchiki. A tank and two halftracks slowly advanced at the head of the column, followed by several trucks loaded with infantry. We waited until they were well clear of the forest and allowed them to climb out of a shallow valley.

'At the tank – fire!' I ordered the gun crew in the trench and Valeriy, who was sitting at the gunsight of our SU-85. Two shots thundered almost simultaneously. Both shells exploded just next to the tank, which stopped. The surprise fire brought the rest of the column to a standstill too. The snake-like column convulsed and began to split apart. However, the Germans instantly recovered from the surprise. The tank fired back first! After that both armoured personnel carriers began to fire from large-calibre machine guns with their sharp, metallic staccato. Then submachine-guns and machine guns of the infantry joined the fight. However, after our second salvo the tank burst into flames! The dark silhouettes of two crewmen scrambling out of the turret flitted through the greyish-blue smoke. Our machine guns spoke up, vying with each other. The ageing, moustachioed sergeant was mowing down enemy infantry from the captured MG-42. The tank was burning, and the enemy began to withdraw towards the forest. As they pulled back, the armoured personnel carriers continued to hammer our position and thin ranks with the fire from their powerful machine guns. A shell from Valeriy exploded next to one of the carriers, just as it was entering the woods. The other vehicle didn't manage to escape, though, without getting a taste of our shell. We saw flames, but both halftracks managed to disappear into the woods.

As soon as the Germans vanished into the woods, the shooting stopped. In the silence that followed, I could hear the groans of wounded men. Having ordered my crewmen and the machine-gunner to stay where they were, I walked over to the gun's position and infantry trench to check on them. As I approached the gun, I saw a shell crater about 10 metres from it – a fragment from this shell had knocked the panoramic sight off the gun. Three of the crewmen had been wounded by shrapnel, and the commander was shell-shocked. Three of the riflemen had been lightly wounded, too, and soldiers were hastily bandaging the wounds. We placed the most badly wounded men on a tarpaulin behind the self-propelled gun's superstructure – it was warmer there because of the engine.

In the midst of this flurry of activity, the 12-year-old Anya, Mel'nik's daughter, unexpectedly appeared. Her father had sent her to warn that large German forces were on their way towards the village. I thanked the girl and quickly sent her back home out of harm's way. Having removed the cannon's breechblock, since the gun was useless without its panoramic sight, we pushed the gun and its remaining shells into a hole, covered them with dirt, and disguised the location with thatch and tree branches.

With twilight starting to fall, our SU-85 moved out and reached the boggy neck of land between the two ponds. It was risky to enter this extremely swampy mess, which had been churned by wheels and tracks. We had to fashion something like a corduroy road quickly, so we brought up thick logs and placed them one and a half metres apart. Once that work was completed, I ordered Shimchenko to slowly drive the vehicle across. Valeriy stood in the hatch giving the driver directions over the throat microphone, while I and all the others except the wounded stood on the opposite side, ready to bring more logs and, if necessary, cover the crossing with fire. Kicking up the logs with its tracks, the vehicle crawled across the sticky black mud, further churning the boggy ground between the two reservoirs and gradually settling ever more deeply into the quagmire. Nearing the exit, the self-propelled gun had sunk into the muck nearly up to its superstructure. Just then, we heard the sound of motorcycle engines! 'Get ready for combat!' I ordered immediately.

Three minutes later two motorcycle riders popped out from behind the corner house. Coming under the riflemen's fire, the Germans immediately began to turn around. One of them was killed before he could get away. The other one, certainly wounded, by some miracle managed to disappear around the corner and darted away. Now we had to expect the arrival of enemy tanks, while our self-propelled gun had lost all traction and its tracks were throwing up fountains of muck. We decided to place the biggest log we could find beneath the front end of its tracks. We had to drag it through the icy, muddy slush. There were about 3 metres left before we reached the vehicle, when the Germans re-entered the village – this time with three sidecar motorcycles carrying passenger machine-gunners.

'Valeriy! Open up with the machine gun!'

Valeriy opened traversing fire on all three motorcycles, hosing them with a long, sweeping burst. The Germans quickly dismounted and took cover behind a hillock. Then all three of their machine guns began to chatter. A fire-fight erupted. Our soldiers from the opposite bank immediately joined in. We were sitting in the middle of it, stuck in the bog. Bullets hammered the SU-85, forcing us to take cover behind the hull. Our bodies were growing stiff from the freezing water, our hands and legs were refusing to obey us, but most of all I worried for the wounded men lying on the engine deck. The situation was becoming grave – I was aware that the Germans would be capable of outflanking us once it grew dark, and then they wouldn't let us break out of this quagmire at any price! I issued a fresh order: 'Valeriy! Come on – from the main gun! Fire!'

A wounded artilleryman heavily tumbled into the fighting compartment and loaded the gun with one hand. A shot roared, followed by two more! Then at last we heard the buzz of a departing motorcycle – one motorcycle!

With a lot of difficulty, we manhandled the log into position in front of the machine and staked it down with spare track pins. The engine revved. The tracks caught hold of the log and pulled it under them. The nose of the vehicle lifted, and then the SU-85 suddenly leaped onto firm ground. Our group stayed near a few outlying huts, preparing for a night march, though we didn't know yet for sure where our own troops were. We still had no radio contact with the regiment.

Breaking Through to Our Lines

It grew dark and the self-propelled gun slowly headed north-east towards Fastov along back roads well known to Vasiliy Shimchenko. The wounded men lay behind the superstructure, while the rest were clinging to the brackets attached to the armour for tank riders. Valeriy and I were standing upright in the hatch on the commander's and gunloader's seats. He was with the MG-42, while I had the ten remaining grenades handy. We raced through two German-occupied settlements at full speed, firing fiercely from all submachine-guns and the machine gun. Both times the Germans were surprised and slow to react, opening fire only when we were already distant.

Once it grew light, we quietly parked in a patch of woods. We shared whatever food we had with each other. When it became dark again, we resumed our movement. We avoided villages and main roads so as to avoid encounters with enemy tanks. We had virtually nothing left to use against them: we were down to three shells. Nevertheless, no matter how careful we were, as we approached the road between Kozhanka and Dmitrievka, we almost bumped into a large enemy tank column moving across our path. The night saved us – thank God, they didn't notice us. Hiding in some tall vegetation about 200 metres away, we watched as the long caravan of German vehicles rolled past with switched-on lights – tanks, assault guns, trucks, cars, artillery tractors and armoured personnel carriers. Rearguard units would likely be following the column at a distance of 2–3 kilometres – as a rule they consisted of tanks and motorized infantry, so we would have to slip across the road before their arrival. We had only a little bit of time!

'Everyone, prepare for action! Driver, push on!' I issued the command and the self-propelled gun began to converge on the tail-end of the enemy column.

Leaping out onto the high road, the tank destroyer cut into the column, isolating its tail-end vehicles carrying infantry. The Germans had not anticipated any threat. A storm of machine-gun and submachine-gun fire opened up, and with hand grenades and ramming by the self-propelled gun, we quickly over-whelmed the enemy. During these tragic minutes for the enemy, not a single shot was fired on our group! Some of the vehicles moving ahead of the tail stopped, but didn't turn around or fire on us. Most likely, they couldn't under-stand what was happening behind them. Then, however, enemy flares streaked into the sky – it was a signal for action. Too late! Literally within two minutes we had already disappeared into the forest and out of reach of the foe.

A couple of hundred metres into the woods, our SU-85 emerged onto a forest track and we stopped. It was dark and quiet in the woods ... but we couldn't yet recover our breath, our hearts were still pounding in our throats, and the sounds of screaming wounded, smashing metal, submachine-gun bursts and grenade explosions still rang in our ears. Everyone spoke in a whisper, keeping his weapon at the ready – the enemy was nearby and we could come across him at any moment.

I dropped down into the fighting compartment and located our position on the map. We were in a large forest west of Fastov. The forest road we were on led to a settlement called Veprik. I decided to move down this road until the situation became clearer.

All this time, my heart had been aching over the possible fate of Vasiliy Shimchenko's family, ever since we had learned in Erchiki that the Germans had occupied Zhidovtsy. The Germans might have shot all of them had they learned that he had joined the Red Army. Thanking him for his help, I told Vasiliy to head home.

Only in 1970, when visiting Popel'nya and Zhovtnevo (formerly Zhidovtsy) did I learn from Ivan Afanasievich Mel'nik and the deputy editor of the *Peremoga* newspaper Viktor Vasilyevich Romanenko that Vasiliy had safely made it home back then. Unfortunately I wasn't able to meet with Vasiliy himself.

Returning to our story, back on that distant November night of 1943, the SU-85 was rolling through a dark, unfamiliar forest, with no lights, and coming across no one. We moved northward, not knowing where our troops were, or which side was holding this forest through which we were moving. This uncertainty in the night-time forest oppressed us all. Everyone stared tensely into the darkness, snatching at their weapons whenever an owl or an eagle owl shrieked – it was amazing how much like human beings they sounded.

Only at dawn did we reach the forest edge near the village of Veprik. Our troops were holding it! We found out at the 9th Mechanized Corps' advanced command post that our 1454th Regiment was stationed near the settlement of Trilesy, about 15 kilometres from Fastov. In Fastov we handed our wounded over to a hospital, and about midday we arrived at our regiment's positions with our tank riders. Both friends and commanders rejoiced over our unexpected return. It turned out that after those three days, our crew had been added to the list of casualties. Thus our self-propelled gun's raid into the enemy rear came to an end.

In 1976 I chanced to visit Lozovka and Kilovka on Victory Day. After the Great Patriotic War, these villages had been merged into one – Mirolyubovka. Older locals still remembered clearly the dramatic events of 1943 and told us that stories had grown up around our SU-85's raid into the enemy rear. According to these stories, Valeriy and I had rampaged through the Germans' rear for nearly a month, sowing terror among the occupiers: we hid in woods in daylight hours, and emerged at night to destroy the enemy. There was no end to the number of Fritzes and the amount of their matériel that we had destroyed!

Together with the locals we also remembered those armed civilians that had recruited drivers for that column of Tatra trucks. I already knew the fate of one of them, Modest Mitseruk: he had graduated from the Kharkov Tank School and later arrived in our regiment in Nikolaevsk-on-Amur as a lieutenant. Checking his papers, I asked: 'Do you remember the events of November 1943 near your village?'

'Of course I remember.'

'Why did you join the Tank School?'

He answered with pride: 'Because back then, I and some of the guys had climbed the water tower and watched as one self-propelled gun smashed an entire German column. I gained faith in the power of armour. Look, now I am a tanker!'

Chapter 9

Von Manstein Attempts Another 'Backhand Blow'

Brusilov: 'Thank You, Brothers, for Such a Battle!'

We remained for several days in a coniferous forest near the settlement of Kozhanka and its namesake railroad station. We repaired and did maintenance on the machines and prepared ourselves for further combat. On the same day that we had returned from our raid, my crew received replacements for Vitya Schetnikov and Vasya Plaksin, who had both been mortally wounded. Sergeant Ivan ('Vanya') Gerasimov was appointed as the driver-mechanic and Private Nikolay Sviridov as the gunloader. Losing no time we began to do repairs together. The guys showed their worth and by evening we had made the tank destroyer fully ready for action. During the ensuing lull I managed to get familiarized with the new crewmen to some extent. Ivan was from Yaroslavl' Oblast, Nikolay – from Kursk Oblast. Both were 19 years of age with incomplete secondary education, and both were *Komsomol* [Communist Union of Youth] members. I questioned them in detail on their knowledge of the vehicle and its parts; their ability to replace other members of the crew; and on the use of the gunnery, observation and communication instruments and devices. I went over basic situations with them and pointed out their slightest misunderstanding or error in response, until I was certain that they understood everything that is essential in combat.

On the night between 19 and 20 November 1943, the regiment together with Colonel Siyanin's 70th Mechanized Brigade was relocated to the area of Brusilov – a district centre in Zhitomir Oblast – charged with the task of stopping a large enemy tank grouping.[1] Its armoured spearhead had already reached Krakovshchina and was lunging towards Kiev.

We approached Brusilov in the night. Deputy chief of staff Captain [formerly Senior Lieutenant] Arkhipov showed us the positions for the battery and we began to move into them in the darkness without waiting for dawn. My platoon, consisting of two SU-85 self-propelled guns, was deployed on the edge of a forest, 2 kilometres south of Brusilov, facing German-occupied Morozovka. Together with Pogorel'chenko we selected a position for each SU-85. The night was very dark; patches of night sky with spangles of stars and the bright moon rarely peeked through the leaden clouds, occasionally illuminating the hill overlooking Morozovka and Krakovshchina for a moment.[2]

To the right of us, a company of 120mm mortars was deployed; ahead of us and also to our right, a platoon of 45mm anti-tank guns was digging into position. The battery commander's and Rusakov's self-propelled guns were digging in south-west of us. The main forces of the regiment were entrenching on the western edge of the forest near Brusilov. The thin platoons of the 70th Mechanized Brigade were widely scattered into defensive positions along the edge of the forest. I thought: 'A counter-attack is expected, but the regiment is scattered, platoon by platoon . . .' Obviously, we didn't have enough strength to cover the large sector we had to hold, even if the infantrymen of the 70th Mechanized Brigade in the front lines were taken into account.

In the pre-morning dawn, an easterly breeze was carrying from everywhere the sounds of chatting soldiers and shovels at work. Both of my crews had worked through the night with almost no rest, sometimes diving into the unfinished emplacement to escape enemy fire – an enemy mortar kept firing from the direction of a farmstead, and tracers from bursts of a large-calibre machine gun in Morozovka were skirting the height. Fortunately the soil was sandy clay and light, and by dawn we had managed to dig out and disguise emplacements at both the main and reserve positions – admittedly with no slit trenches for the crews. The faces of all were flushed from the effort, dense steam was rising from the overalls, but no one would admit fatigue. After moving the self-propelled guns into their emplacements, we were ready for a rest when breakfast was delivered. We ate in silence, everyone lost in his own thoughts.

I hadn't managed to get back to my self-propelled gun when a German artillery barrage began, and the *Luftwaffe* appeared overhead. Several bombs exploded in our sector, pulverizing the trees behind the positions. When I reached my SU-85 in a running crouch and took my seat in the fighting compartment, the shells were already bursting frequently all over the defence sector – among the infantry, artillery and self-propelled guns' positions. A dust storm engulfed the whole area of our deployment; neither the front-line trenches, nor the nameless height separating us from Morozovka, not even the platoon of anti-tank guns could be seen. The gunsights and observation devices were covered by a thick coating of dust and it grew dark inside the self-propelled gun. We feared that we would be unable to use aimed fire, and as soon as the barrage began to lift we rushed to wipe the optical devices clean. Makarov's crew did the same. The infantry soldiers dug each other out, bandaged their wounded comrades, and worked to restore destroyed sections of trenches. There was no doubt: the enemy would attack after such an intense and prolonged shelling.

At about 10.00 on 20 November we heard the rumble of engines from the directions of Morozovka and Krakovshchina. Soon tanks began to emerge on the hill in front of us, Tigers in the lead, firing their main guns and machine guns on the move. They were already approaching the advanced outpost line that had been set up by our foot soldiers a kilometre in front of the forward trench, when three waves of German infantry appeared from behind the hill one after another. The situation began to deteriorate with each minute. The 'Forty-fivers' [45mm anti-tank guns] opened fire at the Tigers prematurely, and the enemy didn't fail to take advantage of the mistake! Our men had not managed to fire even a dozen shots when the tanks switched their fire onto them and blew both guns into pieces within a few minutes – we watched as the wheels and gun-carriages of what used to be the guns flew into the air. Only two men out of the two gun crews survived – we dragged them into the trenches of the mortar company and provided them with first aid. I was bitterly thinking: 'There it is – the role of the commander! He opened fire too soon … He inflicted no damage on the enemy and almost all of his guys are now dead.'

The coughing of mortars began to sound frequently from behind us to the right – the neighbouring mortar company had begun to fire on the enemy infantry advancing behind the tanks. The company commander at the observation post skilfully adjusted the mortar fire, forcing the German infantry to take cover in shell craters and depressions. The tanks halted at almost the same time, and the infantry began to crouch behind their steel hulls. There was no point in firing at the Tigers from such long range and against their frontal armour. However, we couldn't allow the Germans to reach the forest either. I decided to close with the enemy tanks and to strike their left flank, positioning our tank destroyers to obtain shots against their side armour. I sent Makarov the command 'Follow me!' with signal flags and immediately ordered my driver, 'Ivan! Forward!'

Gerasimov reversed out of the emplacement with no delay and raced forward. A strip of trees with dense underbrush stretched towards Morozovka from the very forest where we'd been positioned. We passed the wreckage of the smashed 'Forty-fivers' and rushed to meet the enemy at high speed, concealed by the strip of trees and bushes. The vegetation flashed by on the left, masking our green self-propelled guns from the eyes of the enemy crews.

'Vanya, stop!' I ordered over the intercom when my tank destroyer drew level with the lead enemy tank. 'Left 90°! At the lead tank with armour piercing! Aim beneath the turret! Continuous sighting! Fire!'

A flurry of activity commenced within the vehicle – the movement of levers, pedals, flywheels and handles, the chambering of the round and at last the distinctive clank of the closing breechblock. The crew was in action and they were operating harmoniously! The orders had been carried out instantaneously, the implementation of each was reported concisely and I even had to tell the men to calm down.

'Armour-piercing ready!' shouted the gunloader.

'Shot!' Korolev replied as he immediately pressed the trigger.

In a second, a plume of greyish-blue and black smoke belched from out of the Tiger, followed by two tongues of bluish flame!

'At the nearest tank! Same aim! Fire!'

Another German tank burst into flames. Makarov's crew destroyed the left-most Tiger of the attacking wedge. The remaining tanks screened themselves with smoke, and now we could discern only dark silhouettes through the smoke at which we had to fire. However, we managed to knock out three more tanks. Makarov's crew knocked out three more. The remaining tanks began to withdraw at last. They were backing up in reverse, and Valeriy managed to send one more shell in pursuit of them. Having emerged from the smokescreen, the Tigers opened fire on us from long range with their powerful 88mm guns. Just at this moment, our machine was jolted by a heavy thump inside the fighting compartment. Immediately I tossed out a smoke grenade in front of the vehicle, to make the Germans think that we were on fire. Makarov's self-propelled gun received two glancing hits too, and both shells exploded next to the super-structure. The remaining German tanks disappeared behind the height.

When the shelling ended I leaped out of the SU-85 and gasped at what I found. A hole gaped in the frontal armour! Moreover, the two fuel tanks, the antenna socket, and the log we were carrying for self-extraction from bogs had been knocked off, and the right flap was bent. I quickly climbed back into the vehicle, and through the smoke within the fighting compartment, I saw an unexploded shell! To our good fortune, it was an armour-piercing round. If it had struck the ammo rack after penetrating the armour, however, the SU-85 would have turned into a pile of scrap iron, and nothing would have remained of the crew. I threw it out of the fighting compartment with relief. Having signalled to Makarov 'Follow me' I ordered Ivan to return to our position.

At the forest edge we were met by Ishkin, the deputy chief of staff Stepanov, and Senior Lieutenant Panov, a reporter from the *Vpered, na zapad!* [Forward, to the West!] newspaper. All of them firmly shook our hands, and Vasiliy Vasilyevich showered both crews with kisses. The mortar company commander also came by with his adjutant, and then an appetizing lunch was delivered.

'Thank you, brothers, for such a battle!' the company commander exclaimed, raising an aluminium flask in his hand. Having offered the toast, he continued:

> Frankly speaking, I thought, the Tigers were going to crush us! I couldn't believe that two self-propelled guns would take on a dozen heavy tanks with a counter-attack. And when you drew even with

them, turned, and struck them with fire I couldn't believe my eyes! Then I saw one tank catch fire, and then another, then the third … Eight Tigers burned out! So we grabbed lunch for you. It isn't a sin to drink to such an action!

By the way, we didn't even receive medals for those eight Tigers. To be honest, though, my parents received 4,000 roubles – 500 roubles for each Tiger![3]

In Ambush near Yastreben'ka

The 70th Mechanized Brigade and our 1454th Self-propelled Artillery Regiment fought fiercely to repulse several more attacks in the area of Brusilov on 21 November. Then suddenly, as usual, on the night between 21 and 22 November, our regiment was shifted to Yastreben'ka, which was located about 10 kilometres east of Brusilov. The enemy had switched the axis of his main attack to this point, having assembled a lot of tanks and infantry near Divin and Vil'shka.[4]

We entered the village of Yastreben'ka from the north, our column stretching over 2 kilometres. The white huts made the pre-dawn mist more transparent, but the smoke rising from the chimneys still seemed to be almost black. The head of the column stopped near the southern outskirts of the village. We switched off our engines. Suddenly, instead of the exhaust fumes of burning diesel, we sensed the inexpressibly dear smell of freshly-baked bread, which prompted acute feelings of warmth and joy, but also a yearning for home, hearth and family.

'Officers to the regiment commander!' deputy chief of staff Arkhipov yelled.

Once in his presence, Major Mel'nikov gave the units their combat assignments:

> The enemy has switched to a twin-pronged advance from Divin towards Khomutets and Vil'shka with a large force of tanks and infantry and massive air and artillery support. Our troops have had to begin to withdraw on both sectors. The regiment has been ordered to take up a defence line on the southern and south-western outskirts of Yastreben'ka in order to prevent an enemy breakthrough to the north.

Then turning to me, Mel'nikov added, 'And you, Lieutenant Krysov, are to move your platoon up to that southern grove on Hill 187.7 and to organize an ambush there.'

Up on the small hill, a rifle battalion of the 70th Mechanized Brigade was already positioned on defence. The battalion was commanded by our old

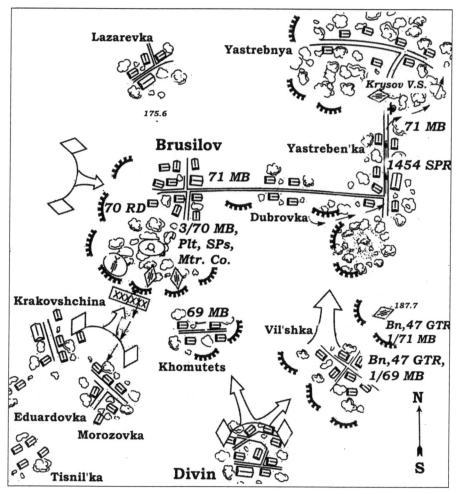

Map 6. The positions of the 9th Mechanized Corps of the 3rd Guards Tank Army during the fighting of 19–23 November 1943.

acquaintance – the same Senior Lieutenant Yuriy Smirnov who had once thanked us for our action against enemy tanks. Makarov and I greeted him with handshakes, and I reported on our assignment. The commander made a good impression – he was tall, with a courageous, suntanned face marked by a large scar. Two combat Orders on his chest told of his considerable combat experience. There were few men left in his battalion – no more than thirty fighters, but on the other hand there were about a dozen machine guns and everyone, including the commander, had a submachine-gun. I also noticed a fair amount of anti-personnel and anti-tank grenades in niches within the trenches.

While searching for a position for our vehicles together with Makarov, we came across some old tank emplacements, now overgrown with grass and small bushes. What a find! Without any delay we moved our self-propelled guns into them. The crewmen rejoiced, spared from hard labour digging the emplacements, but we did as well – the enemy could have turned up at any moment, and we had no time to dig new emplacements.

We coordinated our actions with the riflemen and machine-gunners, and then together with Makarov and the gunlayers we conducted a thorough preparation for firing from our ambush position.

'Comrade Lieutenant, didn't you sense the aroma of fried potatoes and freshly-baked bread back in the village?' Korolev asked.

'Open the tins of stew!' I calmed down the dreamer. 'Let's eat our own local cuisine straight from the can, with crackers, and wash it all down with a little water.'

We had our breakfast by the gun breech, periodically glancing at the enemy tanks standing in combat formation on the northern edge of the village of Vil'shka. The heavy tanks looked like small, earthen-coloured matchboxes, and only through the binoculars did I manage to discern that they were pointed towards Yastreben'ka – in other words, directly towards us.

The First Enemy Attack

As always, enemy aircraft struck first with an attack on Yastreben'ka, and then pounced on our grove with about fifteen bombs. The earth rocked! Huge pine trees were uprooted. Thank God, the brigade's flak gunners managed to down one bomber, so the enemy pilots started to bomb from a higher altitude, which reduced the accuracy of the bombing.

Once the bombing finished, we hadn't had time yet to restore our positions when enemy artillery and rocket-launchers got down to business – they opened heavy fire on the regiment and brigade positions, and incidentally on our hill, evidently reckoning that we had troops positioned here as well. I was very much concerned with the situation back in the regiment, for they hadn't managed to dig in yet and now they were under a constant barrage, and such a powerful one that I could not even see the village because of the continuous explosions. The enemy was shelling our hill much less intensely, but three soldiers in the rifle battalion were badly wounded.

At about 10.00, the enemy advanced, before we had time to recover from the barrage.[5] Two more infantrymen had been wounded and one killed by that time in the rifle battalion. Everybody felt really sorry for the KIA, a young, tall fellow who was most likely around 20 years of age. His friends quickly dug a grave for him with tears in their eyes, and then each threw a handful of earth into the grave to a salvo from submachine-guns.

Atop our hill, we had a clear view of the ground stretching between Yastreben'ka and the enemy's jumping-off positions around Vil'shka and Divin. The tanks were moving in front, followed by assault guns, armoured personnel carriers and infantry, which looked like little black dots. The approaching avalanche of Nazi vehicles and men was ominous; the crew became silent and concerned, and beads of sweat broke out on the freckled face of Vanya Gerasimov. Although I was confident that Makarov's crew would not open fire prematurely, nevertheless I decided to caution the commander against it once again. Glancing from the open hatch, with surprise I saw Vanya Tyulenev – a former partisan and now Makarov's gunloader, climbing down from a tree. I called him over to me: 'Why did you climb that tree?'

'With the commander's permission! I counted the German tanks!'

'Well, what's the number?'

'Sixty tanks! Twenty assault guns, about thirty armoured personnel carriers. Perhaps up to two regiments of infantry as well!'

'Good man, Ivan Grigorievich! And tell Makarov not to open fire before we do.'

'Got it, Comrade Lieutenant!'

With that, the gunloader adroitly disappeared back into his self-propelled gun under a barrage from the enemy tank guns. I didn't have any inkling at that moment that these would be my last words with this brave, strong young lad, and that soon he would be dead.

The five right-flank panzers were moving in our direction, periodically firing their main guns and machine guns. They were followed by about a company of foot soldiers. We stubbornly remained silent, refusing to disclose our positions for the time being. The riflemen of the battalion were silent too. We listened to the salvoes of the enemy rocket-launchers, delivering death to our comrades with a howling, metallic moan. Just then our anti-tank guns, field guns and flak guns, apparently gathered from all the corps' brigades, thundered with answering fire at the enemy tanks, and the battle was under way! The self-propelled guns of our regiment began to roar too – they comprised the main force of the defenders. Only eight of the thirteen self-propelled guns that had engaged the enemy at Brusilov remained, but it was still a formidable force!

The enemy tanks were slowly approaching our grove, exposing their right flanks to us. With difficulty, I restrained Valeriy's impulse to press the trigger. My order was keeping Makarov's crew from firing first prematurely. The tanks had now closed to within a range of about 400 metres, and their flanks were now at right angles to our gun barrels.

'Give it to 'em!' I ordered Korolev.

'Shot!' Valeriy immediately replied.

Within an instant, Makarov's crew had struck too. Holding our breath, we froze as we watched our shells. The gun's recoil hadn't even had time to clatter yet when the tank nearest to us burst into flames, followed immediately by another one. While the other panzers were turning towards us, one more of them brewed up – apparently after simultaneous hits from both tank destroyers. The two remaining German tanks began to pull back, screened behind the smoke of the burning machines. Inflamed by the action, the gunlayers chased them with several hits that failed to penetrate, as indicated by bright flashes on the tank hulls. Meanwhile, the fighting men of the rifle battalion had pinned down the enemy infantry, preventing them from rising and forcing them to follow the retreating tanks in a belly-crawl.

The action near Yastreben'ka began to subside as well. Vanya Tyulenev emerged from Makarov's SU-85 and scurried back up the tree.

'The bastards are pulling back! Four tanks are burning in front of the village and three more in the minefields!' Tyulenev called down to us.

'Vanya, get down from that tree! They'll get you for sure, you just wait!' Makarov yelled to him from the hatch.

Everyone was in a festive mood! I should say so – to have repulsed such an avalanche of tanks and infantry. Such things don't happen too often! The self-propelled gun crews and riflemen praised today's men of the hour – the gunlayers Valeriy and Grisha – for their accurate shooting, shaking their hands and giving them friendly embraces. Before this, though, the rifle battalion's fighters hadn't even known them! However, Makarov and I, while sharing the common joy, worried about our regiment, which hadn't managed to dig in before the attack. We could easily imagine how heavy its losses from the enemy rocket-launchers, aircraft and artillery might have been.

The Second Attack

Talking over the situation with the rifle battalion commander, we concluded that the enemy command would either undertake another attack today, having first destroyed our minefields by air attack or artillery fire, or would postpone the attack until the next day, so as to carry out mine-clearing during the night. We believed that the first scenario was more likely and that was why we decided to make sure the men had better shelter from air attack or artillery bombardment.

With no delay we dug slit trenches at an angle to the foxholes used by the riflemen on watch, while for the rest, we started to dig slit trenches beneath our self-propelled guns, which could effectively protect the men from mortar rounds, artillery shells and bombs. Everyone worked quickly and exerted themselves fully, although no one was hurrying them on. Yet the effort was to no

Vasiliy Krysov as a cadet at the Chelyabinsk Tank School in 1941.

Gunner Sergeant Major Mikhail Filippov (on the right) and loader Sergeant Aleksandr Shadrin.

Major Sergey Fetisov, chief of staff of the 1454th Self-propelled Artillery Regiment.

A 45-tonne KV-1 heavy tank advances, followed by infantry.

From left to right: unknown, Porshnev, unknown, Polivoda.

Loading shells for the 76mm gun of the KV-1.

Commanders of the 1454th Self-propelled Artillery Regiment, 1944. From left to right: Major Nikolay Perfoilev (chief of staff), Lieutenant Colonel Petr Melnikov (regimental commander), Major Mechislav Lavrinovich (deputy regimental commander).

Officers of the 1454th Self-propelled Artillery Regiment. Sitting, from the left: Captain Nikolay Polivoda (commander of operations), Platoon Lieutenant Konstantin Liamin, Captain Arkadiy Parsegov (chief of regimental rear services). Standing, from the left: Lieutenant Stepan Sobol (commander of recovery platoon), Senior Lieutenant Petr Glukhovtsev, SMERSH representative, Captain Kharlampiy Surzhakov (deputy of chief of artillery), Major Boris Avramenko (chief of staff), Senior Lieutenant Gennadiy Garshunov, Lieutenant Andrey Domashenko (deputy chief of staff, reconnaissance), Captain Ivan Zoz, Major Max Tasov (senior regimental doctor).

A 30-tonne SU-122 self-propelled howitzer moving forward at speed.

Sergeant Viktor Oleinik, driver and mechanic.

The crew of a KV-1, wearing protective headgear, prepare for action.

Sergeant Major Sergey Amalechkin and Junior Sergeant Mikhail Tvorogov.

Lieutenant Vasiliy Krysov (on the right) with K. Vaulin in 1944 after hospital treatment.

Residents of Yastrebnya village, from the left: G. Ryapetskaya, E. Pozdnyak, M. Ryapetskiy, M. Ryapetskaya.

Senior Lieutenant
Vasiliy Krysov, 1944.

A group of SU-85 self-propelled guns behind the front.

Red Army infantry aboard an SU-122.

Captain Pavel Golubev,
chief of staff.

A typical scene on the Eastern Front: SU-85s
on the move in a snow-bound forest.

Officers and crew pose for the camera on an SU-85.

The article 'Valeriy Korolev fights the Stalinist way. In 3 days he destroyed 8 Tigers', as published in the 9th Mechanized Corps' newspaper *Forward to the West!*, Issue number 186, from 20 December 1943.

Officers of the 1435th Self-propelled Artillery Regiment.

avail! We hadn't managed to finish the slit trenches when the enemy began the artillery preparation for the next attack. The ground containing the minefields was heaving with the explosion of shells and mines! For the next thirty minutes, the Germans tilled the Ukrainian soil with their shells. Then they shifted their fire to the brigade's and regiment's positions, including our grove. We barely had time to scramble into our vehicle and to get the riflemen under cover when the earth began to quake from continuous explosions. Trees began to crack, breaking and falling with a crash onto the withered autumn grass. The commander of the rifle battalion was in our tank destroyer and feeling rather uncomfortable: a nearby explosion would rock the vehicle or illuminate the fighting compartment, giving the illusion that we were on fire. Now and then the battalion commander was checking on his troops through the bottom escape hatch and asking if there were any wounded.

Then I saw the enemy tanks through the commander's panoramic sight. They were moving in combat formations, following in the tracks of armoured personnel carriers apparently sent ahead to detect minefields. Without an order, the gunlayers of both of my machines rushed to wipe clean their gunsights. Soon a red flag appeared on the superstructure of Makarov's SU-85; it meant he was ready for combat. The artillery shelling on our position lessened somewhat. This time, detaching itself from the main force, a group of eight panzers and up to an infantry company advanced on our small force, which consisted of two tank destroyers and a couple of dozen soldiers. The odds were almost five to one in favour of the enemy! The enemy detachment was moving cautiously, and about a kilometre and a half from the grove, split into two equal groups, one of which swung to the south to outflank us. If the enemy grabbed a foothold on this hill, things would be bad for us. The riflemen ran to take up their positions. We had to come up with something! I ordered Makarov to remain on the defence in his present position, and asked the rifle battalion commander for ten men with three machine guns. My SU-85 and the detachment of riflemen hurried to the southern edge of the grove and prepared a hot reception for the flanking tank quartet.

While the enemy assault group marked time behind some hillocks, apparently waiting for the flanking group to move into position before the final assault, we urgently selected main combat positions for the tank destroyer and the machine-gun detachment, as well as two reserve positions for each. We finished just in time! Soon we heard the rumble of engines. The tanks appeared from behind hillocks. They were now moving confidently, without any precautions.

'Comrade Lieutenant, *by no means* will I let them get away with it!' Valeriy said with a somewhat enigmatic smile, using his favourite expression.

'At the right tank, fire!'

The main gun roared. We watched through the spherical cloud of dust kicked up by the discharge as a plume of smoke followed by tongues of flame erupted from the tank closest to us. The three other tanks reversed and disappeared behind a low ridge without firing a single shot in return. Meanwhile, we altered our position and began to wait for our uninvited guests to show themselves again. The crewmen sat in silence, ready to fire. We could hear the sounds of intense combat from the direction of Yastreben'ka, and against its backdrop the more distinct sounds of Makarov's main gun discharging, and the rattle of machine guns from the northern edge of the grove. This calmed us down: this meant that they were fighting steadfastly and still holding their positions.

All three remaining tanks came into view simultaneously, but from a different direction. While their gun barrels swivelled back and forth, searching for us at our old position, Valeriy struck at the central tank. The tank caught fire, but at the same moment our tank destroyer was violently rocked, spattering us with bright flame from the right side. The thought flashed through my mind that there was no smoke inside the vehicle – it meant we were not on fire! Raising the morale of the men, in a firm voice I ordered: 'At the left tank – fire!'

The shell glanced off the target's frontal armour and exploded behind the turret. This alerted the enemy crew that our self-propelled gun was still combat-worthy, so the tank began to reverse behind a concealing screen of smoke. I immediately climbed out of my machine and jumped down onto the ground in order to examine it. I was horrified! The vehicle was badly damaged. The SU-85 was sitting helplessly without its right track, idler wheel and suspension arm, and without the front roller wheel. Such destruction must have been caused by two hits, possibly three. Sensing something bad, the rest of my crew hopped out of the vehicle. I saw fright and bewilderment in their eyes at that moment, and also despair in the eyes of driver-mechanic Vanya Gerasimov.

He squeezed a curse out through his teeth and said in a mixture of pity and anger, 'Bastards, to cripple the machine so badly!'

I tried to calm him down: 'No worries, we'll fix it up. We'll do some more fighting in it yet!'

At this moment we saw Makarov heading towards us, with the driver-mechanic Misha Grechuk and gunlayer Grisha Kovalenko following behind him with their heads lowered. My heart skipped a beat, as I could tell something bad had happened.

Valentin Pavlovich Makarov reported:

> Comrade Lieutenant, the crew has carried out its combat assignment. The attack has been beaten back, with two enemy heavy tanks

destroyed. Our self-propelled gun has been burned out. The gun-loader Ivan Tyulenev has been killed. We buried him near the burned-out vehicle.

Finishing his report, Makarov wiped tears from his eyes without any embarrassment.

The crew took their comrade's death hard, and the loss of the SU-85 dispirited everyone too. I decided not to question the guys about what had happened and sent them back to the regiment right away with a request to the commander to send a recovery vehicle for our self-propelled gun.

'Comrade Lieutenant, even though we're on one track, we're not going to let the enemy through,' Korolev said in an agitated voice as he cleaned the gunsight.

'That's the only way, Valeriy!' I replied, supporting my gunlayer.

The Germans Take Yastreben'ka

About an hour passed after the unsuccessful second attack. The Germans were ominously quiet, concealed behind the crest of a hill and refusing to show themselves in any way. In the meantime the recovery vehicle came up and towed our SU-85 to the rear, leaving it near a windmill between Yastreben'ka and Yastrebnya.

As soon as the recovery vehicle departed, the enemy began another massed artillery preparation for an attack. We clearly saw the avalanche of advancing tanks from our vantage point – they were moving in three echelons. 'This time our guys won't hold out,' I thought and rushed to help portage track links that we were removing from a knocked-out T-34 approximately 200 metres from our position. It was difficult to lug the steel track links at a run – each pair of them weighed more than 24 kilograms [53 pounds]. We also scrounged a roller wheel, idler wheel and suspension arm from the same source.[6] There were three men on the repair team: Sergeant Aleksey Suslov, and Privates Nikolay Dronov and Fedor Shimraenko. All three had a lot of experience in making repairs under field conditions, but the main thing was that Dronov was capable of removing and mounting a 160-kilogram [352-pound] roller wheel by himself, which was pretty hard just to grasp, let alone move.

When the artillery shelling on Yastreben'ka fell silent, we had already managed to drag over and reassemble all seventy-two track links. Now we only needed to link the upper and lower parts of the caterpillar track. However, by now the fighting had ended and it was clear what the result was.[7] Our troops were pulling out of Yastreben'ka and retreating to the north, beyond Yastrebnya. Soon a cavalry unit rode past us. It was followed by motorized rifle units, who were exchanging fire as they fell back. Our self-propelled artillery regiment pulled out after them, covering the retreat. That meant the pursuing Germans were just about to arrive, though we were not yet in running order! Only the gathering twilight was giving us a chance to remain unnoticed and to complete our repairs. Obviously, our guys had forgotten about us in the bustle of the retreat, and now we could count only upon ourselves. The gloomy faces of the repair team and my crewmen reflected the gravity of the situation. We quickly removed the armour plug, inserted the torque wrench and prepared a 'spider' – a device that helped tighten together the end track links of a caterpillar track. We worked in silence, as quickly and as hard as we could – if only we could finish tightening the tracks before the Germans came! All too soon, we could clearly hear shouts and submachine-gun bursts – German infantry was approaching the self-propelled gun! We had to stop our work and take instant defensive measures.

I quickly gave an order: 'Drop the gun to its limit! Open all hatches!' We had to give the impression of an immobilized machine that had been abandoned by its crew. Then I added: 'I forbid opening fire from any kind of weapon or tossing grenades without my order!'

The repairmen with submachine-guns and grenades hid in a hole beneath the self-propelled gun and the crewmen took their seats inside the machine. We held our breaths. First, German tanks passed us about 100 metres away. Infantry followed them, now only about 50 metres away, firing on the move from submachine-guns. Having come alongside the tank destroyer, the submachine-gunners fired several bursts at its superstructure. I understood from their loud conversation that they believed our self-propelled gun to be knocked out and empty. However, I felt relief only when they began to move away. Preparing to climb out of the vehicle, I took a glance out of the hatch and immediately dropped back down: a submachine-gunner was returning to our self-propelled gun! The thump of the German's jackboots when he leaped up onto the vehicle's right flap seemed particularly sharp to us. The night was moonlit and the shadow of the Fritz's head fell upon the turret floor, near the gunlayer's seat. Valeriy pressed himself against the wall of the fighting compartment and Nikolay showed me his widespread hands, linked at the thumbs, as if ready to strangle someone. I understood the signal and nodded, but thought to myself: 'What if the Fritz sticks the barrel of his submachine-gun into the hatch?' However, the German dropped to his knees and stuck his head into the hatch. Nikolay immediately seized his throat in a death grip, preventing him from even letting out a squeak. Now we had about ten minutes to finish tightening and adjusting the track, before the Germans would rush back to look for the missing man. Together with Valeriy, I pried Nikolay's fingers away from the dead German's throat, and we dragged his corpse out of the machine and tossed it overboard. Then we all turned to adjusting the track, and soon at last the self-propelled gun was serviceable.

However, we didn't succeed in getting away unnoticed. As soon as the engine started and the vehicle began to move from its spot, the Germans raised the alarm and immediately opened fire on us. However, we veered sharply to the right in order to follow our regiment's track prints and raced through the Germans' combat formation at full speed, firing from our machine gun and submachine-guns, and tossing our F-1 grenades. Perhaps because the Germans couldn't turn their turrets quickly enough, we managed somehow to slip through without losses and safely made our way back to our unit.

Whenever I am asked about which day of the war was the most terrifying for me, I think of Yastreben'ka. It was frightening when our troops abandoned the village and pulled back to Yastrebnya, leaving our self-propelled gun behind. Now one can grin about the episode, but at the time it was almost cruel. The cavalry had ridden past, the infantry had marched away, our regiment had departed, and there we were alone while German tanks rolled past just 100 metres away from us. I have to admit that the sensation was not very pleasant, but how must it have been for the poor repair team hiding beneath our vehicle? They must have been more frightened than we were. How must it have been actually to see the German infantry through the vehicle's roller wheels just 50 metres away?

The Night Counter-attack

Four tanks of the brigade, five tank destroyers of the regiment and the regiment commander's tank had reassembled on the edge of a forest about a kilometre from Yastrebnya. We set up our self-propelled gun there too, backing it into the bushes, and we were gradually calming ourselves down after our narrow escape from our predicament. The faint rumble of tank engines could be heard from the direction of Yastrebnya, which was about a kilometre and a half north of Yastreben'ka. The night sky suddenly darkened with heavy clouds brought in by a cold wind; a very fine, light drizzle began to fall. Our small units were strictly observing blackout and noise restrictions, trying to preserve the element of surprise as our main trump card in the upcoming action. The regiment and the brigade had suffered heavy losses around Yastreben'ka, especially from the rocket-launchers. The Germans though, who had to advance across open ground strewn with mines, had incurred much more significant losses, leaving about thirty tanks behind on the battlefield. Now, not knowing the real situation, they had stopped for the time being, but were periodically firing tracer rounds towards our forest, and from time to time launching flares over the eastern outskirts of Yastrebnya.

At about 22.00 Colonel Vladimir Vasilyevich Luppov summoned all the officers of the brigade and regiment behind haystacks and issued a short order: 'Comrades officers, we will go on the attack at 24.00! We must recapture Yastrebnya, which we previously abandoned without a fight! We will act with the combined force of the brigade and the regiment.' Then he explained which tanks would move in such and such direction within the two-kilometre-wide sector of the front and concluded by saying, 'I repeat – the attack will begin at midnight.'

Over the next five minutes the brigade's chief of staff Captain Krylov gave directions on cooperation and radio disinformation. As he was finishing, the regiment's scout chief Captain Soldatov walked up to the brigade commander, accompanied by a tall, skinny man who looked around 45 years of age. It turned out that he was a local named Miron Repetsky. He had managed to slip out of Yastrebnya unnoticed under cover of the night, and had come across our scouts out in the fields. Miron Gavrilovich revealed that there were about twenty tanks with infantry in Yastrebnya, positioned on the village outskirts in fruit orchards and vegetable gardens. The brigade commander thanked Repetsky for the valuable intelligence.

We loaded three days' worth of ammunition onto each self-propelled gun: one daily allotment inside the machines and two in crates behind the super-structure. We moved into jumping-off positions in pitch darkness under a canopy of solid, heavy clouds from which a cold, slanting rain was now falling, mixed with snow. The commanders moved ahead of their machines with white signal flags, to direct the vehicles into position, while the drivers followed with difficulty, straining to see the flags through the opened hatches.

Once in position, all of the available armour was deployed across a two-kilometre-wide sector of front, concealed behind haystacks, in ravines, or behind folds in the terrain. A hastily-formed provisional infantry platoon, consisting mostly of staff and men who had been gathered in a sweep of the rear services, was assembled behind each vehicle: everyone was present in the combat formation except for the banner guards. Makarov's dismounted crew and the depleted platoon of submachine-gunners led by Ivan Trubin were behind my SU-85; behind the battery commander's self-propelled gun was the administrative platoon; behind Senior Lieutenant Statnov's machine to our left were the scouts and Mitya and Rema, armed with submachine-guns. Our four tank destroyers were in the centre of the combat formation. To our right were the tanks of the brigade, to our left – the tank of the regiment commander and other self-propelled guns. All the armoured cars were in the second echelon.

Precisely at midnight three green flares soared into the sky, and all the advancing units opened fire simultaneously from guns, mortars, flak guns, machine guns, submachine-guns, carbines and rifles! Then firing on the move, this entire formation rolled towards Yastrebnya. We didn't spare the ammunition, for we had plenty. Sitting behind the superstructure of our vehicle, Ishkin was handing shells from the crates placed on the upper armour deck to the gunloader, and exclaiming into my ear: 'A grand advance! It's grand! Grand!'

Indeed, the spectacle of the advance was impressive. It seemed like an entire tank corps was attacking! The enemy was so stunned by the unexpectedness and ferocity of the attack that he even stopped illuminating the front line, as was customary for him, and was replying with only scattered, random fire.

Slowly advancing, we frequently changed positions, trying to fire each shot from a new direction. Glowing streams of tracers from machine-gun bursts were dissecting the night darkness all across the front of the attack, supplementing the menacing sound of the cannonade from the armoured vehicles with a dazzling light show. Having switched the radio to receive – all the radios were operating on the same frequency by order of the brigade commander – I heard the voice of Luppov himself who was sending orders in the clear to non-existent units: 'Fulfil the orders: the corps must press from the north! Brigade commander, don't delay! Formation, encircle the village from the south! Don't let the enemy retreat to Yastreben'ka!'

In the meantime we kept firing: one or two shots from one location, and then we would move to another location and fire from there, striving to create the impression of a huge number of armoured vehicles. Without altering the rate of advance, we kept moving forward slowly. Then the right-flank tanks and the left-flank self-propelled guns began to outflank the village, to give the enemy the impression that he was being encircled. The enemy fire began to decrease. As we neared the village, we heard only individual gunshots and rare machine-gun bursts. Obviously the enemy had been intercepting our radio communications and had bitten on the disinformation! The Germans were abandoning the village. The interception of our communications by the enemy had played in our favour.

At 02.00 we entered the village. We immediately began creating main and reserve positions, although the men were dead on their feet after many sleepless nights. We worked under constant harassing artillery and mortar shelling, but by dawn the emplacements were ready. Just before dawn, the regimental field ambulance came around, and we sent the wounded commander of the 3rd Battery Senior Lieutenant Pavel Pavlovich Pogorel'chenko to a hospital. After the ambulance departed, Mitya Medin came running up and reported that I was being summoned by the regiment commander. Dmitriy [the name from which the nickname Mitya is derived] and I walked quickly through the pre-dawn mist, frequently stumbling on German corpses as we went.

The unit commanders and heads of the regimental services had already gathered in the well-equipped bunker of the command post. Major Mel'nikov conveyed the corps commander's order to us: 'Not a step back!' No questions followed and everyone dispersed back to their places. On the way back, I found myself under a heavy barrage and had to get back to the battery by short rushes.

I had just managed to inform the crews about the meeting when five German assault guns with infantry advanced towards Yastrebnya from the village of Bandurovka, which was located about 2 kilometres to the west. I allowed them to approach to within about a kilometre before ordering the gunlayers Korolev and Lapshin (who was on Rusakov's crew) to open fire. Large splashes of sparks showed up on the two left-flank assault guns and the two on the right within a few seconds! We were happy with the accurate fire of our gunlayers, and we could hear the infantry from their trenches shouting 'Uraah! Uraah!' as some even tossed their caps into the air. Unfortunately we rejoiced prematurely: the assault guns were able to withdraw under their own power, though they did so in reverse: their crews didn't dare to turn around, fearing penetrating hits on their flanks. However, they didn't attempt another attack – apparently our frontal hits had stunned them, despite their thick armour protection. The infantry retreated after the self-propelled guns.

I fired a white flare immediately after the enemy's withdrawal, signalling a relocation to reserve positions. Gerasimov switched on the engine, the vehicle started off, and then about 30 metres in front of us an enemy shell ploughed the ground and ricocheted away. 'To the right!' I ordered immediately.

The vehicle veered sharply to the right just as a second shell whizzed past at the level of the superstructure, missing us but striking a century-old sycamore tree behind our emplacement. The explosion was so powerful that it blew off almost half of the huge tree.

'That one was ours,' the gunloader Kolya Sviridov joked humourlessly.

We had just managed to set the tank destroyer up in a reserve position when the deputy chief of staff Arkhipov came running up, and breathlessly conveyed Mel'nikov's order to move my battery to the north-western outskirts of the village to repulse a German tank attack heading towards the regiment command post. Several minutes later both of my tank destroyers arrived at the assigned location. We found a Tiger was already in flames out in front of us, but Statnov's self-propelled gun was burning, too. Nevertheless, four enemy tanks continued to advance on the regiment command post, opposed only by Lieutenant Shishkov's command tank. Our two guns fired almost simultaneously at the leading Tiger. The tank caught fire, emitting black smoke and flames. The remaining tanks began to pull back, returning fire as they withdrew. The infantry followed them, crawling on their bellies to avoid the fire from command platoon and scouts – the headquarters' defenders.

The probing attacks on the weak sectors of our defence and the shelling of our command posts and rear areas alarmed our command. Soldatov's scouts scoured the entire village and found two enemy scouts with a radio that had been left behind in the church belfry by the Germans as they retreated. They refused to surrender for quite some time, reckoning that their troops would return and set them free. However, when a T-34 pulled up and a final ultimatum was given, they came down with their hands up. They were SS men. They testified during interrogation that the enemy command had interpreted our night attack as the attack of an entire tank corps.

Almost until the middle of December, we kept repulsing numerous enemy attacks, frequently conducted from three directions simultaneously, with our small force and only insignificant infantry reinforcements. We had to shift our tanks and self-propelled guns from one position to another very actively.

On the evening before our departure from Yastrebnya, the deputy chief of staff for training Glukhovtsev dropped by to ascertain our losses. I handed him the information and asked: 'Petr Andreevich, what kind of losses have we incurred recently?' He replied, 'If we count back to Popel'nya, the brigade and regiment have lost more than 100 men. As for equipment, of the thirteen self-propelled guns that entered Brusilov on 19 November, only three remain.'

I felt uneasy . . .

Chapter 10

Rest and Refitting

We arrived at Levonovka by midday. We were dirty, tired, and thoroughly soaked. Mud was squelching even inside our boots. We were quartered in huts and (what a miracle!) by the end of the day we had managed to dry out our uniforms and footgear and had also washed and warmed up! All of this happened due to the kindness and hospitality of the people of this Ukrainian village. In several hours they arranged a *banya* with a steam bath inside some shack, and supplied it with white-hot stones for us. The facility was such a good one that the whole regiment managed to have a wash in it! It was sad to bid farewell to these kind, cordial locals ... I still remember with gratitude the warmth and care that the villagers bestowed on us.

We received new SU–85 tank destroyers in Levonovka from march batteries that had arrived at the front. Our battery now again had five vehicles, just as it was supposed to have. We felt sorry to part with our old machine – it had been our faithful friend in hard and bloody fighting. The driver-mechanic Vanya Gerasimov suffered more than the others – he walked around our old SU–85 three times and stroked its armour. Valeriy Korolev also couldn't take his eyes off the gun for quite a while – he was silently saying his farewells. The new vehicle lacked the eight red stars for each destroyed Tiger that the old one had, and there were no battle scars on it either – the welded patches, furrows and dents that reminded us of the circumstances of each battle in which they'd been received. Gradually, however, we began to get accustomed to the new machine and gradually our sense of loss faded.

Having refitted and received replacements in a position about 20 kilometres behind the front line, we surmised that an advance would happen any day now and we used every hour to prepare for the oncoming action. We trained, prepared the vehicles for wintertime use and painted them white so as to make them blend in with the snow.

We spent these final days before going back into action in the relative comfort of this forest near the front. We dug deep trenches with spacious trench shelters, covered each dugout with sturdy logs for a roof, and parked our self-propelled guns over these roofs. Inside the dugouts we set up iron stoves with chimneys, and illuminated our living space with 'chandeliers'. How great those chandeliers were! A flattened shell casing, a bit of cloth for a wick, and a plug with an eyehole: just pour some gas-oil or petrol into the shell casing and plug it – and you have light! Necessity is the mother of invention! We also carved out earthen benches into the walls. Generally speaking, we lived in clover – warm, light and cosy! Things like this, when crews lived so comfortably in close proximity to the enemy, occurred very rarely, especially when it was frigid outside, and no one could lay their hand on the armour of his tank destroyer, lest it stick to the metal!

Winter, of course, is the most difficult time for a tanker or a self-propelled gun crewman because of the cold. Our uniforms were cotton, and we wore a field cap in the summer and a helmet in combat. For winter we were issued with quilted pants and jackets – during combat we covered them with our overalls. Sometimes we were issued with *valenki* [felt boots] and fur coats, but never in sufficient numbers for everyone. As a rule, we received such winter gear only on the defence, when we were standing in the same position for a long time. Our clothing would last until we wound up in a hosptial – at the hospital they would replace everything.

At dawn on 22 December, we assembled in a forest north of the village of Khomovka, where we completed our final preparations for the offensive: emplacements for the tank destroyers and slit trenches for the crews. In the evening, a regimental Party meeting took place, at which many were accepted into the Communist Party. Lieutenant Colonel Meshcheryakov, the deputy chief of the corps' Political Department, attended. Initially they took in those who had distinguished themselves in combat. Our crew was selected first. The regiment's *Komsomol* leader Mikhail Gumenny took the floor first. He didn't say much, but pulled out a 20 December issue of the 9th Mechanized Corps' newspaper *Vpered, na zapad!* from his pocket, and read out an article from it that stated on 20 November my crew had destroyed eight Tigers and an artillery battery. The article was entitled 'Valeriy Korolev Fights the Stalinist Way!' In brief, my entire crew was accepted into the Party without first having to pass through the candidate stage. We were congratulated with the words, 'Now each of you is a Communist! That means you must fight even better!'

Makarov's entire crew was also accepted into the Party – during the latest action they had destroyed five Tigers. Gunlayers Nikolay Lapshin, Petr Murzintsev and others followed. To be honest, they didn't have time to hand us our membership cards. We went on the attack, I was wounded and hospitalized, and that was it. I never received my card, so I remained a non-Party man.

Chapter 11

The December Zhitomir-Berdichev Offensive

At dawn on 24 December 1943 we were still occupying jumping-off positions east of the village of Raevka, in Zhitomir Oblast's Radomyshl' District. A powerful artillery preparation commenced that lasted a full hour and marked the beginning of the Zhitomir-Berdichev offensive operation of the 1st Ukrainian Front.

Tanks, self-propelled guns and infantry raced at the same time across the snowy field that stretched over the knolls and hills. With a decisive attack, they managed to break through the adversary's defence from the march – a defensive line that the enemy had been fortifying for more than a month! We were moving at high speed, our tracks throwing up whirling clouds of powdered snow, so our soldiers running behind our vehicles had to fight their way through a real blizzard. Approaching the villages of Raevka and Zabeloch'e, we watched as frightened and half-dressed Germans tumbled out of the huts and rushed towards a forest, scrambling to get fully dressed. Only a few of them were returning our fire from submachine-guns and machine guns, trying to cover the panicked flight of the others.

'Vanya! From the machine gun, at the running Fritzes! Fire!' I ordered Cherevsky who had already mastered firing the captured MG-42 reasonably well.

Bypassing Raevka and Zabeloch'e, the battery reached a hill overlooking the Kiev-Zhitomir highway to the south. The enemy was conducting a heavy blocking barrage on the hill from the direction of the village of Kocherovo; the height, engulfed with the smoke from continuously exploding shells, looked like an erupting volcano. Having reported my thinking to Captain Golubev, who was in our self-propelled gun, I led the battery around the eastern side of the hill, where three tanks of the 59th Guards Tank Regiment were already making their way ahead of us. We went around the hill, and ahead of us stretched the black ribbon of the Kiev highway and the large settlement of Kocherovo, in which the enemy had concentrated his artillery. Having spotted us, the Germans intensified the artillery fire. Golubev, who as before was observing our actions without interfering with my orders, now commanded, 'Accelerate the attack!'

I understood him – the enemy was firing at us from dozens of guns, and we had to gain a foothold inside the village as soon as possible, in order to find cover for the vehicles from direct hits. I issued the command to the other crews with signal flags: 'Accelerate the attack!' Weaving across the field at full speed, the self-propelled guns rushed towards the enemy. The enemy gun crews became nervous and started to fire wildly, fearing the threat of imminent death, which is why they only managed to knock out one tank. During the attack our battery smashed several guns and destroyed halftracks.

Our troops managed to break into the eastern side of the village. The enemy withdrew to its western half behind a line of ponds that divided Kocherovo. That afternoon, the commander of the 69th Mechanized Brigade Colonel Derbinyan committed the second echelon and the Germans began to retreat to the south-west. However, street-fighting continued into the evening.

Retreating along the Kiev-Zhitomir highway, the enemy put up stubborn resistance at every suitable position and slowed our advance. In order to organize a more effective and mobile pursuit of the retreating foe, the brigade commander ordered the urgent formation of a forward detachment, consisting of a motorized rifle battalion, a platoon of sappers, two tank companies, and two self-propelled gun batteries, including ours, and sent us out ahead.

Near the Tsarevka River we unexpectedly bumped into a strong enemy grouping consisting of about fifty tanks and assault guns. A fierce night action erupted. The enemy tanks and infantry were located in favourable positions – on a forest edge separated from the highway by a large field approximately 200 metres wide. We were forced to deploy into a combat formation from our column while under heavy enemy fire, and then needed to negotiate a very deep roadside ditch. Taking advantage of our momentary confusion, the Germans quickly managed to set ablaze one T-34 and to knock out two self-propelled guns and another T-34.

Having deployed into firing positions, using whatever cover was available and the Germans' own illumination of the battlefield, we opened a heavy return fire. The action lasted all night. By morning, our main forces had come up and the enemy began to withdraw towards Korostyshev.

Heavy fighting occurred near the settlement on the Gorodetsk collective farm. On 25 and 26 December we had to beat off fierce enemy counter-attacks here. However, on the evening of 26 December the 70th Mechanized Brigade came up, we resumed the advance, and by midnight we managed to obtain a lodgement on the eastern edge of Korostyshev.

At dawn on 27 December, large enemy forces counter-attacked the 69th Mechanized Brigade and our 1454th Self-propelled Artillery Regiment, and we had to pull back to the area of Kozievka. The city of Korostyshev would only be liberated on 28 December by the forces of the entire 9th Mechanized Corps after crossing the Teterev River – I'll never forget its ice-coated banks.

Our battery, operating in the brigade's vanguard was the first to enter the village of Pilipy. It was night-time, and we could clearly see the straight rows of white huts in the moonlight. It was quiet in the village: obviously the locals were already sleeping and only very few chimneys were still producing a thin stream of smoke from dying fires. There was no sign of any German presence. Suddenly we heard a rumble of engines and the Russian 'Uraah!' from the southern side of the village. Ishkin and I exchanged confused glances: they might be ours, but it wouldn't hurt if we placed ourselves on guard. So I ordered: 'Get ready for action! No shooting without an order!'

A Panther with clearly visible black crosses suddenly came into view, moving in the direction of my self-propelled gun. It stopped next to a hut. Three more tanks marked with crosses halted to its right. Still confused by the Russian cheer we had heard, various thoughts were crowding my mind. What if our troops are using captured tanks? If so, why haven't they alerted us? We might strike our own guys! It was a good thing that our whitewashed tank destroyers blended well against the huts, because it gave us a chance to think for a couple of minutes. Holding our breath, we watched the tanks carefully, as the infantry approached them with more shouts of 'Uraah!' Suddenly an officer leaned out of the hatch of the tank closest to us and shouted something in German! At the very same moment my half-frozen forefinger squeezed the trigger of the signal pistol. The red flare shot into the skies and cannons began to roar. Korolev set a Panther ablaze with his very first shot. Only the commander, his overalls on fire, managed to leap out of the blazing vehicle. Wildly agitated, he first ran in our direction, and then turned around and ran the other way. The flames on the running man were fanned by the wind and quickly engulfed him. The German collapsed and began to roll like a burning torch until he expired. The other tanks were quickly destroyed by accurate shots from the other crews. The Bandera men [pro-German Ukrainian nationalists, followers of Stepan Bandera] who had confused us with their cheers, stopped and took to flight instead of attacking.

On 31 December, my birthday and just before the New Year of 1944, my SU-85 was hit and set totally ablaze during a fierce night-time clash near Korostyshev in Zhitomir Oblast. I was wounded, and I don't even know who pulled me from the burning vehicle. I only regained consciousness in the hospital. I wasn't to return to my 1454th Self-propelled Artillery Regiment after convalescing. The regiment had suffered heavy losses during the fighting in Zhitomir Oblast, and at the end of February 1944 it was pulled out of the line and sent to Berdichev for replacements, and then transferred into the reserve of the 1st Ukrainian Front.

The documents of the 1454th Self-propelled Regiment have been destroyed, and it took me a lot of effort to locate my former comrades using the sparse information that I had retained in my memory since the war. During the war, more than once I had the desire to keep notes, but this was forbidden: if someone found the diary, in which everything was written down accurately and honestly, a penal battalion would have been my next stop. After the war, I so often regretted to discover that I had forgotten the names of people, villages and rivers, and found that key dates and even events had slipped from my memory.

I began to meet with my old comrades only in the beginning of the 1970s, and at these reunions we would compare our memories of certain events and recall their participants. On the basis of these discussions, I have been able to recreate the events I have described in these memoirs.

Chapter 12

From the Front to a Hospital and Back Again

So, I turned 21 on 31 December 1943: my self-propelled gun had been set ablaze and was irrevocably destroyed, and I had been wounded. When I regained consciousness, I found I was in a hospital in Kiev near the Bessarabian Market. Only here did I sense that my shoulder and leg wounds were not a trifle, since because of them I had to remain in the ward during air-raids, and we were bombed mercilessly! Day and night! Although bombs never fell in the hospital area, the medical buildings were shaken as if by an earthquake during each raid. Ambulatory patients were better off, for they could escape to the shelters, cellars and slit trenches, but we who were left behind were shaking along with our spring beds. As we soon found out, the reason for the raids was an underwater wooden bridge that the *Luftwaffe* was trying to destroy. The crossing was not visible from the air, so the enemy never managed to destroy this strategic object.

Several days later we were grouped according to our wounds and transported in a hospital train initially to Kursk, where we spent two days, and then evacuated by rail to the South Urals. The train was unloaded at night at the Argoyash Station about 50 kilometres from Chelyabinsk. The hospital was located in a two-storey wooden school. We found ourselves in the hands of good surgeons and nurses, and surrounded by caring local villagers. Teachers and students of the school visited us daily and even put on amateur performances in the school auditorium. My health began to improve quickly and at the end of February 1944 I requested to be sent to a medical review committee, though I could still feel rather tangible pain in my shoulder and leg.

The doctor in charge of my case, Alexandra Vasilyevna, was a very decent and clever woman. In reply to my request, she said, 'What sort of discharge, if you're still limping? You'll remain here as the commander of a convalescent company.'

I disagreed with her proposal: 'Alexandra Vasilyevna, I'd rather go to the front. After all, I'm only slightly limping, aren't I?'

'Discharge him!' the head of the hospital Medical Captain Kopylova supported me. 'We'll write "lightly wounded" on his record and let him go to the front! With this kind of persistence, he'll only harm himself and if we don't send him, he'll never leave us in peace.'

The bone in my left shoulder had been chipped, but they recorded 'light wound' on my record. I didn't care too much. Having bid warm farewells to the surgeons and nurses and to my comrades in the hospital, I arrived in Sverdlovsk on the same day.

There I experienced everything that I had gone through the year before: the Urals Military District's Personnel Department of Armoured Forces, the 5th Reserve Tank Regiment, and then the receipt of our SU-85 self-propelled guns. Then once again two steam engines in tandem carried us and our vehicles along a 'green street' to Pushkino Station near Moscow, where we disembarked at the end of the second day. After a short march, we assembled in a forest near the Pravda Station. Here, the regrouping of the 225th Separate Tank/Self-propelled Artillery Regiment into the 1295th Self-propelled Artillery Regiment of the *Stavka* Reserve was under way. The tankers and self-propelled gun crews arriving from Sverdlovsk were assigned to this new regiment.

The 225th Separate Tank Regiment had a heroic history. It had been raised near Moscow in the summer of 1942. Once the main direction of the German offensive in the south had been determined, the new tank regiment had been transferred through Central Asia and over the Caspian Sea to the North Caucasus, to the Mozdok area. The regiment received its combat baptism in heavy defensive fighting there. At the end of October 1943 the regiment was withdrawn from the Kursk area to an area near Moscow for rest and refitting, where it was replenished with two batteries of SU-85 self-propelled guns. It acquired the title of a 'Tank/Self-propelled Artillery Regiment', while retaining its numeric designation, and it took part in the liberation of Kiev. Thus, the regiment had taken part in three major battles by the time of the regrouping: the battle of the Caucasus, of Kursk and for the Dnieper.

Major Libman was appointed to command the newly-formed 1295th Self-propelled Artillery Regiment. Lieutenant Rudakov was appointed as the deputy of political affairs, Major Bazilevich – as the deputy of technical services, and Major Chernyak – its chief of rear services. The staff officers and the heads of services came mostly from the old 225th Separate Tank Regiment. I was appointed as the 3rd Battery's 1st Platoon commander, although I had been a battery commander before I was wounded. The explanation for this was simple, and it wasn't the first time this had happened to me. After my first wounding, I had arrived at a new regiment and I didn't know what the staff clerks had written into my file. It turned out that they had stated I was a platoon commander, so I became a platoon commander again. Now I had found myself freshly discharged from a hospital for the second time and the same story repeated itself. It was even funny. When I had been with the 1454th Self-propelled Artillery Regiment, I had never found the right time to drop by the headquarters to have it noted on my identity card that I was a battery commander. Back then I hadn't been bothered too much by it, and even now it wasn't a big concern for me. My main focus was on fighting the Germans!

By the way, the same thing happened with my rank – I fought for more than two years as a lieutenant. To be honest, I didn't pursue ranks – I just wasn't much interested in it. This kind of situation was not uncommon for field officers.

A 35-year-old Siberian, Senior Lieutenant Mikhail Andreevich Voroshilov was our battery commander. He'd been called back out of the reserves, but already had combat experience, including time in the 225th Separate Tank Regiment. He was a little taller than average, broad-shouldered, and had an expressive face with blue eyes. Three deep wrinkles across his forehead made the battery commander look older. By nature he was a resolute, quiet man, and he always treated his subordinates in a direct manner and with respect.

The barracks near the Pravda Station, where we were billeted, had been built with summer in mind and were poorly insulated with additional boarding, so we slept on the plank beds side by side, and were able to get warm beneath the threadbare soldiers' blankets only by morning. We rose at 06.00, managed to shave, wash and have breakfast within an hour and then would spend the whole day with combat training and developing the tactical cohesion of the units. A lot of attention was paid to cross-training the crew members to fill other positions. The command distributed the personnel among the self-propelled guns so that there were combat veterans in each crew and at least one man with previous experience in a self-propelled gun. I was luckier than the rest in this regard as all my crewmen turned out to be experienced front-liners. The driver – Yakov Petrovich Mikhailov – was born in 1910, and before the war he had worked as a steam-engine machinist in Petropavlovsk. By the beginning of 1944 he had already experienced action in the Kalinin, Bryansk and the 1st Ukrainian Fronts, had been wounded and awarded with two Orders, and also had had 2,000 hours of practical driving experience in tanks and assault guns – this experience was priceless!

Sergeant Major Sergey Bykov from Sverdlovsk Oblast's Shalya Station became our gunlayer. He was a brown-haired guy with hazel eyes, taller than average, and sturdily built. He had seen previous action in airborne and tank units and was very familiar with self-propelled guns. He could drive them in difficult terrain conditions and also had a lot of gunnery experience. The gun-loader Sergeant Major Sergey Mozalevsky from Voronezh Oblast's village of Stupino was of the same kind – a physically strong man who had significant combat experience starting from the Winter War with Finland. He could easily replace the gunlayer, the driver, or even the self-propelled gun commander.

Lieutenant Pavel Revutsky was the commander of the second vehicle of my platoon. He was a splendid man and commander! A little bit taller than average, with regular features, burning hazel eyes and a rich head of fine curls, he was extremely charismatic. However, his most important personal characteristics were his sense of humanity and bravery, which were highly valued in the platoon and in the battery. He had received excellent military training, and knew both the combat vehicle and its weapons perfectly. At the age of 20, he already had significant combat experience.

His crews were also good men with combat skills. All of them were from Gorkiy Oblast. Admittedly, they quickly had to replace the gunloader Khukharev: he was so frail and weak that he was unable to hoist the heavy shells, which weighed over 16 kilograms [36 pounds] each. Senior Sergeant Aleksey Bessonov from Bogorodskiy District replaced him as the gunloader. Aleksey could take over any position in the crew: he had plenty of previous combat experience in the 225th Separate Tank Regiment, and had been awarded with a promotion and the Order of the Red Star for combat distinction. Sergeant Ivan Pyataev was Revutsky's driver, and Senior Sergeant Fedor Belyashkin from the village of Koverino was his gunlayer.

A guy from Rostov, Lieutenant Sergey Bakurov, was in charge of the 2nd Platoon of our battery. The second self-propelled gun of his platoon was commanded by Lieutenant Yuriy Vetoshkin from Kirov. Sergeant Major Ivan Sidorin was appointed as the battery commander's self-propelled gun commander.

We became acquainted with each other very quickly. We also became familiar with almost all the officers from the units, headquarters and regimental services over the five days during which the regiment commander was drilling us in combat formations. We also got to know a bit about the regiment commander himself, when he reported to a representative of the People's Commissariat of Defence on the occasion of receiving the regiment's combat banner. We kept busy with combat training for two more weeks after receiving the combat banner. Day after day the self-propelled guns would move out for driving across difficult obstacles, gunnery and tactical drills.

The period of training passed quickly. At the end of 1944 the regiment embarked on two trains at Pushkino Station and headed westward. It was cosy in a soldier's way in the heated railcars and a bit hot from the iron stoves. We sang a lot and swapped combat stories. The regiment propaganda officer Major Kuzyutkin and the Party organizer frequented our battery during stopovers, and informed us about the latest events at the front and in the country, and discussed the international situation.

Both trains made a long stop at Klintsy Station. The dexterous chief of rear services Chernyak used this time effectively – he organized a wash for the entire regiment in a fine *banya* with a sweating room. We managed to launder our uniforms, foot wraps and handkerchiefs, and to iron our pants and combat blouses. By the end of the day we all were looking our best – fresh, neatly shaven and with cropped hair! Our polished boots, shining buttons and snow-white undercollars gleamed! It was a pleasure to see such neat, dashing guys. Our girls in the regiment looked even better, having managed to fit their figures into brand-new uniforms. Probably most of us felt like we were in seventh heaven for the first time during the war. Dancing began spontaneously – here, on the ground near the *banya*. A sudden air-raid dispersed the dancers. Fortunately it was brief and no one was injured. The well-camouflaged trains in the forest were undamaged as well.

On Defence near Kovel

We arrived at the assigned place on the night of 30 March 1944, disembarked at some small rail station, and having made a short night-time march, assembled in a forest several kilometres north-east of Kovel – a district centre and rail hub in the north-western Ukraine, which was occupied by the Germans. Under cover of the forest we immediately built solid shelters for the armoured vehicles and wheeled machines, and slit trenches and bunkers for the personnel. Everything was so well camouflaged that the enemy aviation failed to detect the presence of our regiment for quite some time.

For the first two weeks of our stay, we were busy with combat training and political education, then – up until 4 July inclusive – we held defensive positions near Kovel. We worked to identify targets in the enemy defence lines and to neutralize any detected forces moving into the German front line or into reserve positions. If a new German battery appeared, we'd react immediately and there would be no battery any more! Once we even fired salvoes at a German command and observation post located in the cupola of a Catholic church: we tried to fire only at the windows and apertures so as not to destroy this architectural monument. We learned from partisans that the Germans soon abandoned the post, which meant that we'd been successful. An experienced gunner – Lieutenant Colonel Petr Savelievich Prigozhin, the deputy regiment commander of artillery – directed this shelling. His method was to zero in on the target very quickly with one self-propelled gun, and only then to include the entire regiment in the destructive fire. Once having suppressed or destroyed a target, the regiment would withdraw to its stationing area, where the crews would do maintenance on their vehicles, excited and pleased with the results.

Being on the defence, we used the few free hours between forays up into firing positions for our leisure activities. Our youth won out here: we played *gorodki* [a popular Russian form of skittles], volleyball, and chess; organized wrestling competitions; and sang in the evenings. Sometimes we watched films.

The Germans began to conduct daily bombing and ground-attack strikes on the regiment's positions starting from the latter half of June, after apparently receiving some fresh intelligence. Sometimes they would come over several times a day, dropping 1,000-kilogram bombs as well. Our well-protected and camouflaged vehicles incurred no damage from these air strikes, and no troops were injured either. We had ample warning of approaching *Luftwaffe* raids by aerial observers and communications services, so everyone was able to get to secure cover in time. The regiment remained in this area until 5 July 1944, when the Kovel offensive operation began.

Chapter 13

The July 1944 Offensive on the Kovel Axis

The Fateful Hill 197.2: Day One

The evening of 5 July arrived. Regiment commander Libman summoned the officers to his command post. To our great surprise, Libman entrusted the chief of staff to issue his first battle order. Major Shuliko rose, straightened up, and standing a head taller than the commander, looked around the officers in attendance with a stern gaze, which even stopped the rustling of maps. From memory, glancing at a map, the chief of staff issued the attack order in a precise, commanding voice:

> Tomorrow at dawn, in cooperation with the 68th Kalinin Separate Tank Brigade and units of the 165th Rifle Division, we will go on the offensive towards Dubova – Moshona – Krugel' – Paryduby. Our mission is to seize the line Krugel' – grove two kilometres east of Krugel', with a subsequent advance towards Paryduby–Zabuzhzhya.

In night-time darkness, amid thick clouds of dust, with switched-off headlights the regiment moved up to the start line at a low speed. The drivers were getting their bearings only from the rear tail-lamps of the self-propelled gun rolling in front of them. During a halt, when the engines were switched off, we could hear the buzz of enemy night bombers flying to the east. They didn't notice us, and at dawn, as our artillery was already conducting the preparatory barrage, we moved into the line of deployment without incident.

The artillery preparation lasted for thirty minutes. Then our air force pounced on the enemy positions with bombing and ground-attack strikes. At last the offensive began. Armour and infantry moved into the attack at the same time. Fierce fighting for the first line – apparently, the enemy's main line of defence – broke out. Tanks, self-propelled guns and infantry moved forward slowly behind a creeping barrage. By midday we had penetrated the enemy defence and were approaching the settlements of Dubova and Moshona. These turned out to be heavily defended and here the enemy put up very stubborn resistance. Two of our tanks were set ablaze and quite a few soldiers fell. However, by the end of the day we had captured these settlements, which had actually been incorporated into the defence system of Kovel. The entire crew behaved splendidly in combat, coordinated their actions superbly, and my gun-loader Mozalevsky at my prompting even procured a trophy MG-42 machine gun after we had driven the Germans from their first line.

Pursuing the retreating enemy through the night with occasional clashes against rearguard detachments, we reached the line Krugel' – forest two kilometres east of Krugel' by dawn of 7 July. Our further advance was stopped here by very heavy fire from German artillery, tanks and assault guns dug-in on Hill 197.2, which had been converted into an enemy strongpoint.[1] We quickly concealed the tanks and self-propelled guns behind folds in the terrain, and disguised them thoroughly. Lacking clear targets, the Germans randomly shelled our forest. It was so stuffy and hot that even at night, the forest couldn't spare us from the sultry July air; our crews' overalls were soaked with sweat, and our faces were as grimy as stokers.

As soon as the first rays of the morning sun peeked above the dark-green hem of the forest, the regiment command summoned officers to a meeting in the bushes near the jumping-off line. From here Major Shuliko pointed out enemy weapon emplacements in the enemy's positions, assigned combat tasks and gave directions on cooperation between the armour and infantry in the coming assault. Then the chief of reconnaissance Captain Marchenko showed us where the enemy's assault guns were positioned and explained, 'The enemy's strength is concentrated on Hill 197.2. There is a large cemetery atop the hill there, with headstones, granite sepulchres and marble tombs. All this provides the foe with good cover not only for the infantry, but also his armour.'

Several dozen metres away from us, officers of the 68th Separate Tank Brigade returned from a reconnaissance led by the brigade commander, Lieutenant Colonel Timchenko. I thought, 'There is a formidable force concentrated in this forest: a tank brigade, two regiments of self-propelled guns, three infantry regiments and several artillery battalions!' This was understandable. There were solid enemy defensive positions arrayed against our advancing forces, and its line ran along three dominating heights: 185.7, 181.1 and 197.2.

Tall, overripe rye in the 2-kilometre-wide grain field that separated us from the enemy swayed under the wind. Even the conversation among the crew members who had already seated themselves into the tank destroyers seemed to be loud in the silence before the approaching storm. The enemy lines were quiet too, except for the occasional rattle of a machine gun.

Then our artillery began to roar! Shells raced overhead with a howl, exploding with geysers of earth and shell splinters on the slopes and crest of Hill 197.2. The artillery preparation had not yet ended when the battery commander Voroshilov ran up, yelling 'I will go on the attack in your vehicle!' before clambering into the fighting compartment.

Three green flares fired by the commander of the 165th Rifle Division Colonel Kaladze soared into the skies. Immediately, dozens of tank engines roared as the tanks and self-propelled guns headed menacingly towards the enemy lines. Our self-propelled guns and the infantry followed behind the tanks. The 1821st Regiment of heavy SU–152 self-propelled guns headed by Major Gromov moved in the second echelon as the corps' reserve of General Anashkin's 129th Rifle Corps. Judging from the expressions on the faces of my crew and the communications from the other tank destroyers, everyone was in an elated mood and had no doubts about the success of our assault. Obviously, I was the only one who thought that the preparatory barrage had been too short and not sufficiently concentrated for such a solid enemy defence, and for some reason there had been no air strike at all.

As soon as the tanks and self-propelled guns emerged from the forest, the enemy defence came to life and bristled with fire. Shells began to explode just nearby. Machine-gun bursts were riddling the area. The parched rye caught fire – at first locally, but the fire spread quickly, and the wind drove a line of crackling red flames and long plumes of smoke towards us. It became unbearably stuffy inside the fighting compartment because of the heat and smoke, even though all the ventilation fans and the powerful fan of the engine's flywheel were working. It was hard to breathe, but even more difficult to spot enemy tanks and guns. The flames and smoke concealed the discharges of firing enemy gun barrels, and we had to fire at vague outlines of targets. Our tank destroyer was heading directly towards the hill, about 30 metres behind the tanks and in a gap between them, to allow firing opportunities. Revutsky's machine rolled to the right of us, while the other self-propelled guns advanced on the left.

I took a glance out of the hatch to get a better view of the battlefield and to get my bearings. The T-34s were slowly advancing across the whole front towards the crackling, burning rye, firing on the move from guns and the hull and turret machine guns. The self-propelled guns were advancing in their wake, positioned in the gaps between the tanks – they would stop for several seconds from time to time to fire a shot. Enemy shells were exploding all along the front of the advance and throughout the entire depth of our formation. Shells were either striking sparks from the steel hulls of the armoured vehicles, or they were ploughing up the earth near the tracks. Enemy machine guns were spraying the battlefield with a multi-layered deluge of lead, so intense that our foot soldiers couldn't even move forward in a belly-crawl, and were forced to advance exclusively within the tracks of the tanks and self-propelled guns, sheltered by their hulls.

We left behind the wide strip of burning rye and in front of me to my left I saw two of our tanks burning. I thought bitterly about the burned crewmen, and about what was awaiting the rest of us on this blazing, wind-blown field, which had already gobbled up two tanks during the first hour of action. Quite a few infantrymen had already been killed or wounded too. Gazing intensely at the Germans' ominous defence line I managed to spot a gun that was firing at our tank destroyer, and I immediately ordered my gunlayer over the intercom: 'Sergey! At the gun near the three birch trees! Sight mark 15! Fire!'

'Lane!' the driver reported to indicate that he had found level terrain as the vehicle stopped smoothly.

With a lot of effort I discerned through the obscuring smoke that our shell had burst a bit short of the gun, and adjusted the aim: 'Sight mark 16! Fire!'

'Comrade Lieutenant, the gun's gone!' Sergey Bykov reported.

'Look for it to the left and right of their previous position!'

However, there was already a spurt of flame from the left birch tree. We sensed a hit on the hull and heard an explosion. The left side of the machine was illuminated by fire!

'Short! Fire!' Sergey ordered and fired again.

An instant after the shot we heard Bykov report in our headphones: 'The target's been hit!'

Battery commander Voroshilov periodically stood up in the hatch to survey the battlefield, and then switching the throat microphone to transmit, he would send orders to the commanders. However, he was pressing his luck, and when he rose once again to take a look, a shell glanced off our armour and exploded just off the right side. Voroshilov was wounded in the chest by a splinter. The wound was severe, but he didn't lose consciousness. Bykov and the gunloader Mozalevsky rushed to bandage the wound, having placed the battery commander on a quilted jacket behind the superstructure. I ordered the driver to reverse, got in touch with the 2nd Platoon commander Bakurov over the radio and quickly informed him: 'Sergey, the battery commander's been wounded. I'm driving him to the aid station. Take charge of the battery until I return.'

Bakurov acknowledged the order: 'Roger. Carrying it out.'

The battery commander was still conscious, and was acutely suffering from the timing of his wounding. He spoke up in a very weak voice and I had to press my ear to his pale lips to catch his words: 'Pity . . . failed to take part . . . in crossing the national border . . . The height . . . I order you to lead the battery . . .' With that, the battery commander's strength gave out and he lapsed into silence.

An unfamiliar captain halted our self-propelled gun at the forest edge and yelled rudely, placing his hand upon his gun holster, 'You're fleeing the battlefield, aren't you?!'

Surmising that the captain was a SMERSH[2] officer from the 68th Separate Tank Brigade, I took umbrage at his accusation and brought him to reason:

'I am transporting the severely wounded battery commander to the regimental aid station, Comrade Captain, and I advise you to choose your words more carefully and not reach for your weapon – we've got enough of them inside the machine.'

'All right, take off! But I'll be watching for your return!' the counter-intelligence officer insisted.

We handed our commander Mikhail Andreevich Voroshilov over to Senior Surgeon Grigorov and medic Nadya Naumova, and then gave him some encouraging, parting words. However, even I understood then that I was bidding a final farewell to the battery commander. The chief of staff Shuliko rode up to the aid station in a Willys jeep and, having learned what had happened, ordered me to take charge of the battery.

Upon returning to the battle line, we saw that our troops had hardly made any advance at all in our absence. Three more tanks of the 68th Tank Brigade were on fire. However, I was feeling terrible because of the loss of the battery commander. Somehow it had to have been my fault: he had chosen to ride in my vehicle, because I was the battery's most experienced officer, who had Stalingrad, Kursk, the Dnieper and the Ukraine behind me. Now I was mercilessly cursing myself for failing to warn the battery commander about the details of combat in a self-propelled gun, which differed from those of the tanks he'd been in before. Tankers commonly went into the attack with closed hatches, while we more often advanced with open ones, except for when we found ourselves within enemy formations or lines. I should have thought to tell the battery commander that the open hatch wasn't an invitation to stand upright for more than a few seconds – a sniper or a stray bullet could catch you, and if you heard an approaching shell, you had to duck back inside the vehicle.

The battle was reaching its climax by this time. Our advance had almost stopped; we had nearly run out of ammunition. At the urgent requests of the battery commanders, regiment commander Libman ordered the chief of the transport platoon to deliver shells directly to the combat formation. Putting it gently, under such circumstances, the order was unwise . . .

While carrying out this order, Technician-Lieutenant Lopukhin managed to replenish the ammunition in two self-propelled guns. As his Studebaker truck approached a third vehicle, a German shell struck it, blowing the truck, the ammunition, and the entire supply team into bits. After this, we began to replenish our stock of ammunition back in the forest by withdrawing one self-propelled gun at a time from the action.

One more tank exploded. The self-propelled gun of Lieutenant Aleksey Prokofiev, attacking to the left of ours, erupted in flames next and no one emerged from it – apparently everyone had perished. Having scrambled over to his burning self-propelled gun to check for survivors, I had to return to my vehicle at a run under a hail of bullets. On my way back I noticed two more tanks and another self-propelled gun brew up. I immediately ordered the entire battery: 'Mask your vehicles with smoke pots and grenades!' At the same time I asked the 2nd Platoon commander Bakurov, 'Whose tank destroyer has just been destroyed?'

'Junior Lieutenant Chubarov's, along with the entire crew.'

With every passing minute our plight was becoming more and more critical. I thought: 'We will all be destroyed and won't carry out the task!' At this moment a circular command resounded in the air: 'This is "Sokol" [Falcon]. Everyone forward!' It was the call sign of the tank brigade commander Lieutenant Colonel Timchenko.

The brigade commander's tank raced past us at high speed! In response, all the tanks and self-propelled guns rushed forward after it. Then three tanks struck land-mines simultaneously at the foot of the hill. They had unexpectedly encountered a German minefield there. Taking stock of the situation correctly, the brigade commander ordered everyone to fall back to the jumping-off line. We pulled back, covering each other and the remaining infantry with our gunfire.

While we were returning our vehicles to their former positions and putting them back into combat-readiness, field kitchens brought up our lunch and dinner at the same time. It was growing dark, and after finishing their duties, the tankers gathered in groups to discuss the details of the action that day. An hour after dinner the chief of staff convened the officers and conducted a debriefing, while pointing out the mistakes made even though the order to attack across tactically unfavourable terrain without sufficient artillery preparation had been erroneous. We had advanced against a strongly fortified enemy position across an open field that lacked any trees, or any wrinkles or folds in the ground. The chief of staff's deputies, Captains Korol'kov and Marchenko, went around the officers during the debriefing and quietly, so as not to disturb the meeting, questioned them about their losses and recorded the information. The chief of staff reiterated our orders:

> Comrade Officers, our combat assignment remains the same for tomorrow – to capture the dominating Hill 197.2. This is the key to the whole enemy defence line. There'll be no other order. The attack begins at 07.00. As before, we will be supporting the 68th Tank Brigade and the 165th Rifle Division.

It was completely dark when a Willys rolled up to the ravine, where the field kitchen was located, while the last units were having their dinner after completing their work on their self-propelled guns. The regiment commander Libman, his political deputy Rudakov and a phone operator – the very cute girl

Valya Udodova, who was the campaign wife of the regiment's chief of signals Captain Omel'chenko, got out of the jeep and approached. Incidentally, Libman had recently sent the captain away, allegedly for an appendicitis operation ...

Major Libman on the spot, in the ravine, summoned the officers and curtly ordered: 'Tomorrow Hill 197.2 must be taken at any cost!' Then he indistinctly hinted that we had behaved cowardly that day, before continuing in an imperative tone out of the darkness, 'This is an order of mine and of the army commander!'

Only later did I understand the real meaning of his words. Someone on the command staff had already reported to higher command that the hill had been taken.

In order to calm down a bit, I walked around the battery's area and checked on the sentries manning their posts. On the way back to my vehicle, I came across scouts and sappers led by the chief of reconnaissance Marchenko. Dressed in camouflage cloaks, they were walking towards the German lines, carrying mine detectors and probing rods.

I stretched out next to my crew on the warm deck of the engine compartment, but I couldn't fall asleep, even though I hadn't slept for two days in a row. I was thinking about our orders for the next day. How could we take this hill under such unfavourable conditions? If we attack over the same ground as today, they will destroy all our tanks and self-propelled guns and the hill will not be captured. We would have to outflank this bloody hill one way or another, and gain the enemy rear. Then he will abandon the hill himself. That is when an idea came to me: to attack to the left of the height! According to our intelligence information, the Germans had neither tanks nor assault guns there. There was only artillery, and their gun crews lacked armour protection and couldn't match the rate of fire of the German tanks. This was the enemy's vulnerable spot! But what will the guys say? None of the crew was sleeping, most likely thinking about the imminent action. Everyone knew that it would likely be the last one for any of us, if the attack went ahead as planned.

'This is what I've worked out,' I began, ready for a lengthy debate. 'Let's be the first to get to the German artillery positions between the hill and Krugel' – and smash their guns!'

To my surprise, everyone agreed with me, having estimated that it would be better to take our chances racing towards the artillery for some five to ten minutes, than to be under the devastating fire of numerous anti-tank guns, tanks and assault guns for the whole day.

'Yakov Petrovich, you've got a lot of experience, don't you?' I addressed to the driver Mikhailov. 'You know how to advance on the guns by zigzagging to avoid direct hits. I guess you can manage it this time, too.'

'Well, been there, done that. Certainly, it's a better option,' the old battle-hardened tanker replied with no doubt in his voice.

With that, everyone fell silent. I advised, 'Better get some shut-eye for at least an hour.'

'Hill 197.2 Must be Taken!': Day Two

It was becoming light, the guys were still asleep and I decided to have a shave: I had to look presentable before such an action. An hour before the designated attack the chief of staff summoned the officers for another reconnaissance. As we surveyed the battlefield, combat tasks were specified for each unit, platoon and crew. When the turn of our 3rd Battery came, I suggested my plan of breaking into the enemy rear between Hill 197.2 and Krugel'. Major Shuliko agreed and shifted our battery to the regiment's left flank, while attaching a platoon of submachine-gunners to our battery under the command of Junior Lieutenant Zhurov.

With that, the attack began! Our artillery was just finishing its preparatory barrage. The tanks, engines roaring, were moving out of the forest and deploying into combat formation on the move. Our self-propelled gun still stood quietly – we had to bide our time until the battle was fully joined, to give us a better chance of sneaking through. The platoon commanders Revutsky and Bakurov had been instructed back on the start line to provide cover fire for our self-propelled gun's movement, and then after we entered the enemy's artillery positions, to attack in the same direction.

As on the day before, the enemy opened a most powerful fire on the advancing tanks and self-propelled guns. Our crews were returning fire from main guns and machine guns, slowly advancing and concealing their vehicles with smoke grenades. However, during the first minutes of the action the Germans managed to set ablaze a tank and a self-propelled gun, the one commanded by Ilya Gorelik, who had taken over from the wounded Sasha Grabovsky. The self-propelled gun stopped and became engulfed in flames, and only the commander managed to clamber out of the upper hatch, his overalls on fire. He immediately started to rush away, but because of his movement and the winds, he turned into a running human torch. He was not wearing a helmet and his hair was on fire, too. Screening itself with a smoke grenade, another self-propelled gun pulled up alongside Gorelik's burning vehicle and stopped. Two men jumped out of the operating tank destroyer and ran to intercept the unfortunate Gorelik, hoping to tackle him to the ground and put out the flames. The guys were about 10 metres from Gorelik when he collapsed. Running up to him, they tore away Ilya's burning overalls while rolling him back and forth on the ground, and they managed to extinguish the flames. I watched as they leaned over their prostrate comrade and then removed their helmets. Ilya was dead. Ilya's image flashed before my eyes, just as I'd seen him for the last time before the attack: his handsome young face was pinched and seemed older, and he seemed to be fighting back tears. Apparently, he had a presentiment of his own death. I felt agonizingly sorry for this guy who had died at the age of 18! And in his first attack ...

I repeated the task for the battery crews: 'We're going to attack with one self-propelled gun, and you'll be supporting us from this location. Is everything clear?'

'Understood.'

I addressed my crew: 'Fellows! There can't be seven deaths, but one can't be avoided! Yasha [Russian diminutive for Yakov], by zigzags, let's go!' I ordered to the driver as I gazed into the dark-green forest edge on the western slopes of the hill.

The self-propelled gun started promptly, easily bounded across the infantry trenches, and we raced across the field! Yasha had had so many hours of driving that he steered the vehicle like it was a toy. The enemy line bristled with many gun barrels, but they were still silent. At first our tank destroyer rolled almost in a straight line, manoeuvring only a little bit to avoid a hit from the first shot. Once within about 800 metres of the guns, Yasha began to swerve back and forth skilfully without slowing down. The enemy gunners were still silent. We closed to within about 500 metres, hearing only the shots behind us from the rest of the battery, which was supporting us with fire. Suddenly explosions threw fountains of earth skyward on every side of the self-propelled gun. We kept racing forward at maximum speed. At that moment for some reason, I wasn't thinking about a direct hit; I was only afraid of one thing: stopping! The first glancing hit struck the left side, making the vehicle shudder. The flame of the explosion illuminated the entire self-propelled gun, which apparently created the impression among the German gunners that we were on fire. I thought cheerfully, 'If we're still racing, it means we're not on fire!' and decided not to distract the crews with further orders. There was just a bit left before we reached the forest – around 300 metres. Then we sensed five hits one after another – they were not just shaking us, but even turning the self-propelled gun a bit because of its lower traction at this speed! Now, however, we could see that half, maybe even more, of the gun crews had scattered, while the others were agitatedly bustling about the gun breeches and gunsights. Their fire had become random.

'Sergey! From the machine gun, at the gunners! Fire!' I ordered the gun-loader Mozalevsky, who had fortunately picked up the German machine gun the day before.

While Sergey confidently fired at the escaping crewmen, though without much skill, the Germans managed to deliver two more glancing hits. Then we were on them! Yasha decided not to crush the guns – he simply selected five guns and knocked them over, striking them with jerky turns of the vehicle – it was his revenge against the Germans for attempting to destroy us! Yakov Petrovich stopped the self-propelled gun only once beyond the position of the orphaned and now harmless guns – he had to let the already overheated engine cool down. However, Sergey kept firing long bursts at the fleeing gunners from the machine gun.

Climbing out of the self-propelled gun in order to look it over, first of all we gathered around Yakov Petrovich. Each of us came up to him to embrace and shake hands with the battle comrade – the man who had dragged us safely away from death's doorstep! I sent a signal – three yellow flares – and the tanks and self-propelled guns took off towards us. Then I contacted the regiment command post and reported: 'The first task – to reach the enemy artillery positions – has been carried out. What should we do next?'

'Continue the attack!' was the regiment commander's reply.

Having checked that our vehicle was still combat-worthy, we set out towards Malaya Smedyn'. The fighting was now behind us – the tankers and our battery men had arrived quite quickly!

Once again, we came under enemy fire. Two large-calibre machine guns opened fire on our SU-85 from a farmstead. While we were busy dealing with them, three self-propelled guns from the 2nd Battery led by Misha Zotov and several tanks with infantry mounted on them passed us. The rest of our battery for some reason had not arrived yet. I had no inkling that our comrades in the battery behind us were at that moment beating off an enemy counter-attack, which was why I continued to advance, hoping that the battery would catch up.

Bypassing Malaya Smedyn', our self-propelled gun rolled up onto a plateau somewhat higher than the surrounding countryside. Ahead of us we saw a village, Paryduby, buried in greenery, and about 200 metres in front of it, Zotov's three self-propelled guns were sitting in a green meadow, arrayed into a line. We approached them. The vehicles remained immobile, showing no signs of life. Intuitively I sensed something sinister – some kind of trouble the crews of the vehicles had found themselves in, and on the move resolved to destroy the enemy guns in the village. We had to save the guys!

'Yasha, steer to the left of the self-propelled guns!' I commanded. 'Break into the village!

As soon as we reached a line with Zotov's battery, our self-propelled gun was rocked by a strong hit, and we heard a muffled explosion somewhere below the hull. The fighting compartment was immediately filled with pungent smoke, and on top of that the engine had stalled.

'Is everyone alive?'

'Alive!' they all answered in one voice.

'Yasha! Start it up! Get to cover! Towards the forest!'

The engine roared and the vehicle turned around in a small semi-circle. Bogging slightly in the grassy quagmire, we moved towards the nearest bushes while making slight turns – somehow we could hide in them. We were urged on by hits on the self-propelled gun's hull. Almost without thinking I counted nineteen glancing hits on the rear and sides. Then we were in the forest! It seemed everything was now fine because we were safe, but there was a gnawing in my heart – what had happened to the crews and the submachine-gunners? What had happened to them? Why were they silent? The first thing that came to my mind while the driver was turning the self-propelled gun around so its gun faced the enemy was the following: Where had the swamp come from that had bogged down the SU-85s? My mind recalled the map quadrant that contained the village: there was not a single blue stroke in it that indicated a swamp! Where had that swamp come from? Coincidentally glancing towards the right corner of the fighting compartment, I was stunned: an unexploded shell was protruding through the dissipating smoke behind the smashed radio set! I shivered as if from a chill, and broke into a cold sweat . . .

'Men, everyone out of the vehicle, now!' I ordered in a no-nonsense tone. 'Everyone take cover!'

The men scattered as if by the wind. Holding my breath, I carefully took hold of the shell and turned towards the hatch, afraid that it might catch something or that I might stumble. The shell was still warm, but it seemed to be making my hands and heart numb. It was as dangerous as it was heavy, and I had to get out of the vehicle without letting it slip out of my hands! When I stood on my seat and began to exit through the hatch, I could now see the shell clearly. Scrutinizing it, I saw no nose fuse. I looked at the bottom of the shell, but there was nothing there either apart from the notch for the tracer! I yelled cheerfully to the crew, 'Guys, come out! It's a dud!' and threw the shell on the ground.

We shifted the self-propelled gun to another position which offered a better vantage point to see the village and opened fire at likely positions for the enemy anti-tank guns. The Germans immediately returned fire, forcing us to alter our position after every two or three shots. For about an hour, we traded fire with the enemy's guns, hoping that somehow this would support the crews of the bogged self-propelled guns, but we knew nothing about them and couldn't contact them on the radio, because ours had been smashed. Unexpectedly a squadron of our Il-2 ground-assault planes flew over the forest. Making several passes, they struck the Germans in Paryduby with bombs and machine-gun fire. That is when we saw a figure crawling towards us from the direction of the bogged self-propelled guns. It was Petya Kuznetsov, a submachine-gunner with the infantry detachment attached to Zotov's battery. He had been wounded by bullets in both legs.

'I'm the only one still alive,' the emaciated soldier almost whispered to us. The 17-year-old Petya Kuznetsov from Kalinin Oblast was a handsome and brave soldier, but now with tears in his eyes he was telling us how the Germans had finished off our guys with point-blank shots, but he'd pretended to be dead and crawled out to our position under cover of the air strike. We bandaged his wounds and put him on the floor inside the fighting compartment. Then we turned towards the empty self-propelled guns of our dead comrades, removed our helmets, and fired three volleys in that direction from our pistols as a form of salute to their sacrifice.

It was a sad thing to think that within some half an hour TEN SUBMACHINE-GUNNERS AND TWELVE SELF-PROPELLED GUN CREWMEN LOST THEIR LIVES – Misha Zotov, Ivan Zagvozdin, Nikolay Troshev, Kafiy Yunisov ... No more than two hours ago they had rushed to save the burning Ilya Gorelik. Apparently, everyone has his own fate, and no one has managed to escape from it yet.

Through Enemy Lines

There were only seven shells in our ammunition racks left. We had to cease fire. We thoroughly inspected our self-propelled gun. Two holes gaped in the frontal armour, and a machine-gun bullet had struck the front fuel tank. Luckily for us that the other shell had turned out to be a dud, but it had managed to do a lot of damage: it penetrated the spare tracks attached to the frontal armour, stripped the facing from the interior wall on the right side, and blew away the radio transformers and radio set, before dropping spent into the corner of the fighting compartment. 'Looks like we were all born under a lucky star,' Mozalevsky joked humourlessly as he bandaged his right hip.

Shells began to burst around us again – the artillery resumed fire as soon as our planes departed. Now they were firing not only from Paryduby, but also from Bolshaya Smedyn'. We could hear the sounds of submachine-gun and machine-gun fire to the west, and occasional cannon shots as well. During a short lull Petya told us in more detail how the men of the battery and the submachine-gunners had died. The following picture emerged.

After passing us, the battery had advanced successfully and it was decided to attempt to capture Paryduby from the march. However, they came across the swampy area just in front of the village and the charging self-propelled guns had become stuck, sinking to the bottom of their hulls. The Germans immediately opened fire from anti-tank guns and machine guns. The doomed crews didn't abandon their machines and returned fire. Turning their guns towards targets with great exertion, they managed to neutralize several anti-tank guns. Gradually, one after another, the self-propelled guns were knocked out. Some of the crewmen were killed; others, being wounded, dropped down beside the self-propelled guns with submachine-guns and hand grenades, joining the submachine-gunners. They repulsed an enemy attack. Aware of their small numbers, the Germans closed in from two sides, intending to capture the rest of them alive. Everyone fought courageously and Zotov hurled the last grenade at the enemy in reply to their call to surrender. The Germans shot them from almost point-blank range, and then returned to the village. They gave Petya one more bullet, but he didn't flinch and give himself away. When our tank destroyer had approached the spot, there had been no single man alive apart from him. During the air-raid he had moved away from the vehicles and crawled along the furrow of a track towards our self-propelled gun, lapsing in and out of consciousness along the way.

'It was as if someone was pushing me: you crawl and crawl, although I couldn't do it any more ...' Thus Petya, who had survived by a miracle, concluded his story about this tragedy.

It suddenly came to my mind that in less than an hour, we could wind up encircled, and as if to confirm that thought, shells flying from somewhere in our rear began to explode nearby. We had no one to help us defend, nothing with which to attack – we had to pull back to our own lines.

I pulled out the map and took another glance at the Paryduby area: there was nothing on it to indicate a swampy area around the village. To tell the truth, the map had been produced on the basis of a survey done in 1897 and the area had been reconnoitred in 1911, but all the same a swamp couldn't have appeared on the dry ground over such a period of time! What had the General Staff's chief of its topography department been thinking about?! Over the two years [1939–1941] since the unification of the Western Ukraine they hadn't bothered to check their maps of the area. The Germans, though, had managed to compile very accurate maps of our territory, which we readily used whenever we captured some. Yet now due to someone's oversight or irresponsibility, two dozen soldiers had been killed – gallant fighters, mostly young men from the age of 17 to 24. Only Kafiy was 29 and Ivan Zagvozdin was 34 – not an old age either! They might have lived much longer ...

The self-propelled gun headed through the woods to the south-east, in order to vacate the area under shelling from the direction of Bolshaya Smedyn' and to link up with friendlies. At the edge of the forest, we came across a German trench. We could see soldiers in helmets looking out of it in our direction, some with panzerfausts at the ready. At this time, in the middle of the day, it would be extremely unlikely for the self-propelled gun to break through the enemy lines when the enemy had panzerfausts! However, I didn't want simply to retreat! I began to issue orders to the crew: 'Sergey-1! At the fascists, from the machine gun! Fire!' (This order was intended for Mozalevsky, who was born in 1918.)

'Sergey-2 (I addressed Sergey Bykov in this way, for he had been born in 1923)! Get five hand grenades ready!' and one after another I threw them towards the German trench.

'Yasha! Turn around, pull back into the bushes!'

While we were slipping away from the German trenches I worked out an idea: to return to our lines over a hill that had some sort of tower on top of it. I hadn't yet managed to issue the order, when suddenly we could hear the sounds of close combat to our west! We hurried to the scene of the fighting and closed in unnoticed by the foe. The crew of a T-34 also failed to notice us right away: together with a small group of submachine-gunners, they were resisting an enemy attack. Two enemy armoured personnel carriers and one light tank were already on fire in the rye field – the result of the ambush that the tankers had set up. However, other German tanks with infantry were advancing on them.

'Sergey! At the lead tank! Sight mark 10, from our location! Fire!'

The tank stopped after the first hit and then burst into flames after the second one. The enemy, seeing that some reinforcement had arrived, fell back and disappeared over the crest of the hill with the tower atop it. Our self-propelled gun approached the T-34. A lieutenant – its commander – climbed out of the turret. We greeted each other, assessed the situation and decided to break out together. There was no time for hesitation, because the ring of encirclement was getting tighter. We decided to break out to the south over the eastern slope of the hill with the tower. This tower was not shown on the map, but it became engraved in my memory so well that I still remember it. It was wooden, and for some reason kind of rounded on top. There were likely Germans on the hill, but we weren't receiving any artillery fire from its direction. We mounted the submachine-gunners on the tank and on our tank destroyer, eight men on each machine, and our group quickly headed towards our lines with around 50 to 100 metres of spacing between the two vehicles.

Climbing the slope of the hill, the drivers squeezed everything possible out of the engines, but they also had to manoeuvre, because while the hill screened us from the west, it didn't offer us any protection from the direction of Bolshaya Smedyn' and Parduby. The bursting shells coming from those places were literally surrounding the vehicles! Ricocheting hits on the sides made the entire self-propelled gun shudder. However, as we approached the German trenches, the fire lessened significantly because of the fear of hitting their own side. I was standing in the open hatch as the SU-85 closed on the German trenches from behind. Turning around, the Germans opened a heavy fire on us from machine guns, submachine-guns and anti-tank rifles. Hand grenades flew into the air. Inside I was somewhat relieved, though – there were no *faustniki* [infantry tank hunters armed with panzerfausts] in the enemy trenches! At this time, the Germans still had few of these dangerous weapons; they had just begun to produce them in mass numbers. The fire from the trenches was not dangerous to the crews inside the armoured vehicles, and our submachine-gunners quickly dismounted and took cover behind the tank and self-propelled gun. However, two of the submachine-gunners were wounded.

Then we were at the German trenches, the submachine-gunners rushing ahead of us, firing on the move and hurling hand grenades into dugouts. Our self-propelled gun began to iron the trench, while the T-34 rolled along the defence line, raking the frightened Fritzes with its two machine guns. Our Sergey Mozalevsky was also firing long bursts from the machine gun at the Germans fleeing into the forest. Taking advantage of the enemy's momentary panic, the submachine-gunners headed for the top of the hill, and our armoured vehicles followed them.

As soon as we left behind the enemy positions, the artillery again opened a drumbeat of fire from Paryduby and Bolshaya Smedyn'. As we climbed towards the crest of the hill, the engines were screaming, seemingly ready to tear free from their frames. The machines were rolling at the limits of their abilities – they couldn't speed up any more nor could they manoeuvre! However, with tremendous effort the driver-mechanics managed to squeeze out little zigzags from the vehicles, which protected them from a direct hit. There were now only several dozen metres left before the crest, when the T-34 suddenly stopped and immediately burst into flames. A man leaped out of the turret hatch. Only one! The Germans immediately opened fire from machine guns and submachine-guns. Traversing bursts were mowing the rye around the belly-crawling tanker.

'Yasha, stop the machine behind the crest!' Having reached the salvation of the reverse slope, the SU-85 stopped immediately.

'Sergey, grab the machine gun, we're going to save the tanker!' I ordered Mozalevsky and we headed towards the burning tank. A few submachine-gunners who had emerged from some slit-trenches and shell craters joined us.

Approaching the crawling man, I recognized that he was the tank commander. About a dozen Germans were already running towards the wounded lieutenant – they wanted to capture him alive. Yet the commander kept persistently crawling towards us, firing back at the oncoming Germans with his pistol. However, when Mozalevsky's machine gun opened fire and two hand grenades I had thrown burst next to the pursuers, the Germans dropped to the ground, then turned around and pulled back, firing as they moved. The lieutenant was extremely weak because of his wounds and the loss of blood, so we had to carry him to the self-propelled gun on a tent half. We bandaged his wounds and laid him on the floor of the fighting compartment next to Petya.

Then there we were – at long last we had passed through the German defence lines! We were in no-man's-land. When we left behind the sector of the German artillery shelling, I pulled out a map and began to assess the best way to reach the regiment without exposing ourselves to enemy gunfire, and how to circumvent bogs and cross the highway, which was exposed to enemy fire. Suddenly we heard a moan from some nearby bushes, and then a weak cry, as if coming from underground: 'Brothers, save me!'

Apparently, hearing Russian conversation, a man was calling for assistance with his last bit of strength. Having learned lessons from devious and clever German provocations, I took two submachine-gunners with me, and holding my pistol ready, I plunged into the bushes with them. Within several steps, we came upon a terrible scene: an infantry sergeant was lying on the grass, writhing in the shade of a large willow cluster. His abdomen had been ripped open and his guts had spilled out. The sergeant was a skinny guy about 30 years of age, and he was fully conscious. I gingerly picked him up and carried him over to the vehicle, then laid him on a mat that we had kept under the tank's engine.

'Brothers, give me some water,' the sergeant squeezed out through his pale, cracked lips in a half-whisper.

Grabbing a canteen, Bykov quickly poured a mug of water and gave it to the wounded man. He avidly gulped down the first one, then two mugs more, and large drops of sweat exuded on his pale, bloodless face. A medic – one of the submachine-gunners – washed his hands with alcohol and cut apart the combat blouse and undershirt on the wounded man. Fully exposing the terrible wound, he then cautiously tucked the man's intestines back into his abdomen, then bandaged the wound and covered the wounded man with a trench coat. His pain and suffering were horrific and almost unbearable to witness.

'Brothers, shoot me!' the sergeant cried out with the last of his strength as he began to lose consciousness.

I still had hope that we would be able to get him back to our lines and this man would survive somehow, although I knew that he had almost no chance to survive: he had been lying there too long with an open wound under the scorching sun, in the dust, expecting at any minute that the Germans would come across him. Having arranged the wounded men on the floor of the fighting compartment, we mounted the submachine-gunners on the armour, and the self-propelled gun headed towards our lines across the large expanse of no-man's-land that had been created after our capture of the three dominant hills. We came under artillery fire two more times, but saved all the men – except for the sergeant we had picked up, who died just before we reached our lines.

After a short, lively reception we placed our SU-85 in a firing position in the centre of the battery's line, and the crew worked without rest until dawn building a dugout. Meanwhile, the repair team was welding up the holes and scars on the body of the self-propelled gun.

The next day, having had some sleep, we examined the former German positions on Hill 197.2 and their entire system of defence. It was virtually an unassailable fortress! Each tank and assault gun had a revetment, each anti-tank gun – a semi-revetment, and all had been constructed from granite and boulders. Only direct hits by bombs or especially heavy artillery might have destroyed this bastion. The infantry too had been so well-sheltered that it would have required flame-throwers to clean them out. Nevertheless, we had taken Hill 197.2!

Currently the sappers were clearing minefields from the slopes and foot of the hill. Here we saw for the first time what the German spherical anti-tank mine looked like. Before that, we had only encountered the dreadful results of its work: when an armoured vehicle's track rode over it, the device would throw a burning liquid 40 metres up into the air and the tank or assault gun would be burned out.

We Go Over on the Defence

About midday the regiment commander summoned the officers to his command post situated in the former German command-observation post: the Germans' retreat had been so hasty that they had not managed either to mine or to blow up their trenches. The German post was astounding with the solidity of its construction and its creature comforts: battery-powered electric lights, comfortable furniture and even a travelling wine bar. We considered it too luxurious by our wartime standards. The post had a splendid view through its embrasures of the surrounding countryside even without optical devices, all the way down to the forest that had served as our jumping-off position. In addition, with stereoscopes the Germans could definitely see all of our former positions from Krugel' to Hill 185.5 inclusive.

Major Libman stood up, looked around everyone present, and then began to deliver his talk smoothly, occasionally glancing at his notes:

> We've carried out the army command's task, having captured Hill
> 197.2 and the other dominating heights from which the enemy was
> blocking our advance to the Western Bug. All enemy counter-attacks
> aimed at regaining possession of these strongpoints have been repulsed.
> Nevertheless we've suffered heavy losses. Seven of the regiment's
> self-propelled guns have been irrecoverably destroyed, and almost all
> of them have been damaged and require serious repairs. Our losses in
> personnel comprise about forty men. The 68th Tank Brigade has lost
> almost all its tanks and tomorrow will be withdrawn for refitting. It

means we have no resources to continue the offensive. We have to restore all available self-propelled guns to combat-readiness within one week and at the same time to defend the regiment's sector. That means that all repairs and maintenance work will have to be done at the firing positions, in dugouts.

Then the chief of staff spoke up:

Comrade Officers, each battery will be attached to a rifle battalion of the first echelon and will hold the battalion strongpoint in co-operation with it. Before 12.00 of 10 July every crew will have to create two reserve firing positions each apart from the main one. The pioneer battalion together with the sappers from the rifle units will lay mixed minefields in front of the defence front by this time.

We remained here for a week, working to put our remaining self-propelled guns to full combat-readiness and to prepare for our next attack. We knew that the Western Bug River and Poland were not far away ...

'With all Due Military Honours'
The long-awaited morning of 17 July 1944 arrived. Unlike the previous time, our artillery conducted a powerful artillery preparation and at the end of it *Katyusha* rocket-launchers fired a few salvoes.

The well-repaired and seemingly rejuvenated self-propelled guns easily and quickly rolled into the attack together with the SU-152 assault guns of Major Gromov's Heavy Artillery Regiment and units of the 165th Rifle Division. We were advancing in the same direction as we had on 8 July – towards Paryduby. This time, however, we were attacking the village not head-on, but with a double envelopment. Despite the losses incurred from our artillery and aviation, the enemy put up a stubborn resistance. He returned heavy defensive fire from guns deployed a kilometre behind the village, which checked our advance and forced us to exchange fire. Only after two *Katyusha* salvoes could we resume our forward movement. Our battery broke into the western outskirts of Paryduby together with a rifle battalion of the first echelon. Fierce street-fighting broke out with fluctuating success; in some sectors the combat became hand-to-hand. Only when the battalions of the second echelon joined the action did the Germans begin to pull back to the centre and northern outskirts of the village.

Our self-propelled guns were advancing through the village in a right-echelon combat formation towards the enemy artillery positions on the hillocks situated behind the village – the German guns were firing intensely from there and inflicting heavy losses on the infantry. As we approached the village's central street, our advance was stopped by two German tanks that were firing down the full length of the street. We started to trade fire with them. The enemy tanks were in previously prepared positions and could not be reached by direct attack.

I sent an order over the radio in the clear: 'Revutsky! Outflank the tanks with your platoon and destroy them!'

Our other self-propelled guns, concealed behind houses and in gardens, were advancing slowly, briefly stopping to fire single shots. The enemy tanks were somehow shifting their positions unseen by us. However, their crews became so absorbed in the gun duel against our three self-propelled guns that they didn't notice Revutsky's platoon take position on their flank. Both enemy tanks blazed up almost simultaneously from hits on their sides, and their on-board ammunition began to explode immediately, belching crimson-black plumes of fire and smoke. Moving up to the burning tanks and hiding behind their smoke, we pivoted our guns towards the hillocks and struck at the artillery positions with fragmentation shells. It was so unexpected that the gun crews fled in panic towards a forest, suffering heavy losses as they ran.

The German commanders committed all of their reserves into action on the eastern outskirts of the village, and who knew how the battle would have ended, if Gromov's SU-152 regiment had not arrived from the second echelon. His crews set ablaze three heavy tanks from their 152mm howitzers with their 48-kilogram shells in some half an hour; the others began to withdraw, unable to withstand the unfolding slaughter.

The turning-point of the battle had arrived. The machine guns in the German pillboxes fell silent too. We had essentially encircled them, and having realized the situation, their occupants began to emerge from the pillboxes. Tossing aside their weapons and raising their hands, they were turning themselves over to the mercy of the conquerors.

An almost unnatural silence fell over the village. Soon villagers began crawling out of their shelters. They joyfully threw their arms around our necks, simultaneously vying with each other to tell us with tears in their eyes how nine days ago on 8 July the Germans had finished off some wounded Red Army soldiers. I immediately understood that they were talking about Zotov's group.

The prisoners were now standing in two rows beside the outermost pill-box, their heads lowered, though some of them were looking down at their abandoned weapons with obvious regret. Some lads from huts on the outskirts of the village, who had witnessed the massacre, were peering into the prisoners' faces, and one of them recognized three of them who had executed our wounded and were now hiding behind the backs of the prisoners in the front row. Senior Lieutenant Viktor Permyakov, the commander of the submachine-gun company, ordered the three to be brought out of the line-up. At the same time they grabbed their commanding officer, who had ordered that the wounded Russian soldiers and officers be shot.

Right here, on the spot, on the outskirts of the village in front of the local residents and the trembling prisoners, Permyakov briefly announced the sentence: 'For the massacre of the wounded! Shoot them!' The submachine-gunners raised their weapons, and the accursed murderers got what they deserved.

Time was pressing – we had to keep pursuing the retreating enemy with no delay, but the division command allowed the regiment to bury its dead comrades. We went out to that sinister bog where the self-propelled guns had become stuck, and found our dear regimental mates. They were laying one next to the other, just as death had caught them. The Germans hadn't touched their Orders and medals. Ants were already creeping over the blackened faces of the dead. My heart shook ...

We buried our battle comrades with full military honours. Three rifle salvoes rang out and the bodies, wrapped with sheets, were lowered down into the fraternal grave. The regiment and the villagers stood in silence with uncovered heads, wiping away their tears.

Chapter 14

From the Western Bug to Siedlce, Poland

We Prepare for a River Crossing

An hour after the liberation of Paryduby the regiment resumed its advance together with the 165th Rifle Division, which was operating as the vanguard of General Anashkin's 129th Rifle Corps. By the end of the day we approached Zabuzhzhya – a large settlement situated on the opposite bank of the Western Bug – on Polish territory! Here the division was to force a river crossing and to cross the national border, which was creating quite a stir among the soldiers and officers.

We encountered no German troops on the near bank. Our troops pulled back into a forest about a kilometre from the anticipated crossing site and dispersed to build rafts and boats, which we would be using to cross the deep river under fire. The enemy didn't notice our troops, which had made a timely withdrawal into the depths of the forest, and continued to retreat now to the north, still on the near side of the river, in the direction of Pulemets and Svitiaz Lake.

We began to prepare for the river crossing meticulously, but in secret. Emerging from the forest before the onset of nightfall was banned. A small detachment was sent in pursuit of the enemy rearguard in order to divert his attention from the area of the crossing. The scouts and the pioneers would have one night to reconnoitre and mark fords for the self-propelled guns. The task was difficult and dangerous. The river channel was up to 100 metres wide here, and the current was swift. It was going to be hard enough just to find one ford, let alone several. Moreover, the reconnaissance would have to be done in the direct proximity of the enemy. A ford would have to be established in a location where firstly, the self-propelled guns wouldn't find themselves immediately under fire from enemy pillboxes as they emerged on the other side; secondly, where there would be sufficient room to deploy into combat formation and engage the enemy; and thirdly, where the ground on the other side of the ford would be firm enough to support the heavy weight of the self-propelled guns and to resist becoming a morass from all the water draining off the vehicles and their churning tracks as they emerged.

The chief of reconnaissance Marchenko included three platoons into the combined reconnaissance detachment – a scout platoon, a pioneer platoon, and a platoon of submachine-gunners led by Lieutenant Gulyaev. As the detachment passed our battery's position, I noticed that all the pioneers were carrying rubber hoses with wooden floats and rocks with ropes – apparently the latter were going to serve to weight the men down. I became interested and asked about their gear. One of the pioneers replied:

> This time we're going to reconnoitre under water, but we have to breathe somehow. So the guys invented this gear to replace diving suits. You see, the float has a hole in it. We'll stick one end of the hose through it, and breathe through the other.

The reconnaissance group returned about 02.00, cheerful and excited by having carried out their mission superbly – they had located fords and a concealed hollow on the other side, although the Germans were illuminating the river with flares and even searchlights throughout the night, and occasionally raking the channel and our bank with machine-gun fire just in case.

My guess is that no one in the entire regiment slept the night before the crossing. Deputy division commander Lieutenant Colonel Prigozhin, together with Lieutenant Colonel Filippov, the artillery commander of the 165th Rifle Division, was compiling data for indirect firing by the artillery and self-propelled guns. The self-propelled gun crews together with the technical service personnel were preparing the vehicles for crossing the deep, broad river by fording: they were sealing the vision slits, closing vents to prevent water penetration from above, and putting together breakwater planks. The deputy of technical services Bazilevich went around all the vehicles, meticulously checking the seals, giving advice, showing how to do things properly, and scolded some for poor work.

'Who seals the side vents this way?!' he exclaimed, reprimanding Lieutenant Volkov's crew loudly to ensure that the other crews heard him. 'You're going to suck water into the engine and drown it! Then the Fritzes will smash you in the middle of the river!' He wasn't finished yet and pounced on another crew – its young gunloader had caulked up the exhaust manifolds.

Crossing the Western Bug

The morning of 18 July was sunny. About an hour before the assault crossing, the regiment commander summoned the officers to the edge of the forest for a reconnaissance. The chief of reconnaissance Marchenko showed us the paths our vehicles would take down to the river and the crossing sites. The chief of staff Shuliko issued instructions on cooperation during the crossing, while creating the bridgehead, and the subsequent battle to take Zabuzhzhya. The start times and sectors of advance were clearly specified. He concluded with the signals for calling down artillery fire and for shifting it into the depths of the enemy's defences.

We anxiously returned to our vehicles. During the commanders' reconnaissance, the crews had already moved the machines up into firing positions, closer to the crossing area, and made them ready to open fire. Every crew had extra shells for the artillery preparation in addition to the normal combat allowance.

Soon the preparatory shelling began. A second later, the 165th Rifle Division's entire artillery and Gromov's 152mm self-propelled guns joined in the barrage. The opposite bank of the Western Bug became cloaked in dense black smoke from continuous explosions. Barbed-wire entanglements, chunks of logs from German bunkers and pieces of steel from destroyed equipment whirled into the air. We had just expended the shells for the preparation when the attack signal – a series of red flares – soared into the sky. The stunned enemy was literally stupefied and didn't fire for several minutes. During these minutes we rushed to the river at top speed. The self-propelled guns with the most experienced drivers led the way. Our vehicle was the first to reach the right-hand ford, while the SU-85 of the battery commander of the 1st Battery, Sergey Dvornikov – the left one. Hoping that the water wouldn't reach the top of the superstructure, I stood in the hatch opening in order to get a better view and to be able to respond quickly to the rapidly changing situation. Yakov Petrovich drove the vehicle down to the river channel like the wind, and without slowing, plunged into the river. As the self-propelled gun was flying into the water, the first German shell whizzed right past the hatch cover. I instinctively ducked into the fighting compartment. The SU-85 moved across the ford like a torpedo boat, pushing a high wave of water in front of it that even reached the gun itself, while exposing the river bottom behind it. Submachine-gunners several metres behind the vehicle were running across the exposed, sandy riverbed, trying not to lag behind the vehicle so as to keep their feet dry. The rear vents were closed, but the engine's powerful ventilation fan was working like a water jet, creating a large circular spray of water. The exhaust pipes were emitting a dark bluish-grey smoke, which mingled with the spray from the engine to form a vapour-like cloud, which made it difficult to see the soldiers running behind us. When the vehicle reached the middle of the ford, water appeared on the floor of the fighting compartment and steering compartment. It concerned me, but also cheered me up: we would be able to reach the Polish bank with such a minor leak. Exiting the river, we clambered over a hump and stopped in the hollow in order to make the machine combat-ready.

It took us ten minutes to drain off the water and open the vents and vision slits, and then we were ready for battle. We had to give our scouts credit. Their skilful action had guaranteed the operation's success. The submachine-gunners quickly took up positions on the western slopes of the hollow to cover the assembly of the 165th Rifle Division's regiments here. When I reached the positions of the submachine-gun platoon headed by Zhurov, the commander of the 1st Battery Dvornikov and the commander of the 4th Battery Istomin were already there. From this vantage point we got a good look at the pillboxes that guarded the exits from the river. Their guns and numerous machine guns were belching continuous deadly fire and we would have to advance directly towards them. It wasn't possible to bypass them or to suppress them, but to attack them was tantamount to suicide! We contacted Lieutenant Colonel Prigozhin over the radio, and Dvornikov on behalf of all of us asked that the pillboxes be blanketed with smoke shells, in order to blind the occupants.

Several minutes later, the ground in front of the pillboxes was enveloped in dense smoke, and the self-propelled guns attacked, followed by infantry and submachine-gunners. The enemy pillboxes continued to fire heavily from guns and machine guns, but now they were firing blindly. We broke through the line of pillboxes without losing a single machine! Just minutes later, we ran into the first line of enemy trenches guarding Zabuzhzhya. Just before the attack, we had watched as German vehicles pulled up to this line and disgorged soldiers – apparently they'd been urgently relocated to here from another sector of the front. Now, falling upon the enemy, our self-propelled guns were overrunning these trenches. The riflemen and submachine-gunners came to grips with the foe in hand-to-hand fighting. The majority of the enemy soldiers resisted stubbornly and fought fanatically to the last man. Only a couple of dozen of them laid down their arms and surrendered.

While we had made short work of the enemy in the first trench line, as soon as we emerged from the smokescreen and headed towards a second trench line on the outskirts of Zabuzhzhya itself, enemy assault guns and artillery opened fire on our vehicles. We had to manoeuvre, to take cover in gardens and behind houses, and to shift position after every shot. However, we continued to expand the bridgehead, though very slowly. With incredible difficulties and heavy losses, we fought for every house, and one after another they were falling into our hands. Our battery burst into a garden and crushed two guns and several large-calibre machine guns that had been holding up our infantry. However, very soon the enemy artillery opened such heavy fire on this garden that we had to abandon it and urgently find different cover. That's when I noticed twenty enemy tanks deploying into a combat formation. They immediately advanced towards us, accompanied with at least a regiment of infantry! The enemy counter-attack had begun.[1]

I urgently ordered my platoon commanders over the radio, 'Revutsky, Bakurov! Move over to that cluster of houses and consolidate your position there!'

As usual the enemy tankers were counting upon the impregnability of the armour on their heavy tanks and were advancing directly towards us, slowly and insolently. Recalling a similar situation back at Kursk, I ordered my men, 'Battery! At the lead tank! Fire!'

The simultaneous hit of five armour-piercing shells and resulting explosion blew the turret off the Tiger, and a jet of flame blazed from the hull, sending a plume of blue-grey smoke into the air. I sent a new order without delay, 'At the second one on the right! Fire!' The second target erupted in flames.

The other enemy tanks began to scatter around the field, trying under the cover of smoke to find more concealed positions. Now we could see nervousness and uncertainty in their actions. To the left of us, another enemy tank brewed up – the work of Istomin's battery. The tank destroyers' guns were booming on both sides of us. Together with the infantry, we continued to advance slowly, driving into the depth of the enemy's defences. Unable to withstand the pressure, the enemy fell back – and the bridgehead kept expanding.

Behind us, my keen ear sensed that the 152mm howitzers of Gromov's regiment, which was advancing in the second echelon, had stopped firing – it meant that they had managed to knock out the enemy pillboxes. Their guns and machine guns had fallen silent too. Glancing back, I saw with joy that the heavy self-propelled guns were approaching and in my mind praised the tactical acumen of the rifle division commander Kaladze: he had selected just the right moment to commit the heavy regiment into the fighting at a crucial point in the battle.

Very soon Gromov's guys set ablaze two tanks from their heavy guns, but by now we were taking losses too: the Germans had destroyed two self-propelled guns from our regiment and a heavy one from Gromov's regiment. However, recognizing that the odds were in our favour, the German command declined to continue the counter-attack and the enemy tanks began to withdraw.

Exploiting this tactical success, our troops occupied the whole settlement of Zabuzhzhya and seized the entire German defence line. Our battery found itself on the western outskirts of Zabuzhzhya, and just in case we immediately moved into favourable combat positions. By evening our bridgehead had expanded significantly. All night long, the main forces of the 129th Rifle Corps moved into the bridgehead, and with their night attacks, they further expanded our lines on captured Polish ground.

The Polish people gradually began to emerge from their shelters, and chatted in a friendly manner with our soldiers and officers. Some sought medical assistance for injured family members, while others requested medicine for illnesses, just in case. All of them, though, were interested in the future fate of Poland. Such questions were normally handled by our political officers, and they always said the same thing: 'You will decide what will happen with Poland after the war, and our duty is to liberate your country from the Nazis.'

Many of them asked if there would be collective farms in Poland. As we understood it, they were very much concerned about them. However, our propagandists always replied the same way to this question: 'It will be up to you to decide.' In general, these initial encounters were very warm and cordial; the locals treated us with fruit, and the conversations lasted till morning.

Over the following days, we continued the advance in the north-west direction. Now, though, we were on Polish territory!

The Battle for the Village of Stulno
Somewhere on the approach to Lukow the 20th Tank Brigade left the 165th Rifle Division to rejoin its 11th Tank Corps. Once again we would have to operate in the place of tanks.

On the night between 27 and 28 July we halted in a forest. The men had not slept for several days in a row. The fierce fighting for every village and settlement had exhausted everyone so badly that we were falling asleep on the move, but nevertheless the first thing we did as always was to service and resupply the vehicles with fuel, oil and ammunition. While we were occupied with these chores, the chief of rear services Chernyak organized a tasty dinner. Everyone ate with great appetite, but now with our bellies stuffed we felt even sleepier. Having checked the immediate guard posts and set up the officers' watch, I took a seat on the engine hatch and immediately dozed off. However, once again I didn't have a chance to get some sleep.

Around 01.00 the chief of staff summoned me to the regiment's staff vehicle. I found his deputies and assistants tightly huddled together around maps spread out on desk shelves that had been attached to the walls of the truck's cargo hold. I reported on my arrival, and then Major Shuliko spread out a map on a little table, and under the dim light of a lamp fashioned from an artillery shell, with a colour pencil he showed me the line that my battery was supposed to reach, and said:

> We have to capture the settlement of Stulno. You'll be operating with a rifle battalion. According to aerial reconnaissance, there is up to a battalion of infantry reinforced with artillery in the village, which is why you'll be attacking at dawn. Only a surprise and resolute attack will bring you success. The captain – the riflemen's commander – will get his orders from his division commander. Report to me over the radio every hour on the hour.

In conclusion, Major Shuliko shook my hand and wished me luck. When I returned to the battery, the rifle battalion commander was already waiting for me – his battalion was already mounted on the self-propelled guns. We exchanged greetings under the light of a torch, synchronized our watches and compared our maps, which had the situation and mission plotted on them. Time was pressing, and I quickly went over the mission with my platoon commanders in five minutes. They in turn conveyed it to the crews.

At about 02.00 our column headed out along a dark forest road. The captain and I were sitting next to each other behind the commander's hatch cover of my machine. The self-propelled gun was slowly moving at the head of the column, trailed by Revutsky's machine with infantry mounted on the armour. The infantry was equipped with light machine guns, submachine-guns, grenades and two flame-throwers, giving the assault team considerable firepower. An advanced reconnaissance detachment was moving in advance of the column, hopefully to prevent a German ambush of our main force. We maintained communications with Revutsky's self-propelled gun via pocket torches.

The forest made the shadows even darker, the road was practically invisible, and only rarely did patches of dark-blue sky with bright stars and the thin crescent of the moon appear between the heavy bands of scudding clouds. The tank destroyers' engines were running smoothly at low speed, and their sound was so soft that sometimes we could hear the shriek or noisy flight of a hunting owl. The battalion commander and I strained our eyes, vainly peering into the night – it was pitch-black. That we hadn't heard a single shot calmed us down. The Germans were not expecting our approach from this direction. However, at every turn in the road, the commander of the advanced reconnaissance patrol would let us know by the green light of his torch that the way was clear.

Just before dawn we noticed a somewhat lighter patch up the road – it was a sign that the edge of the forest was just ahead, and we couldn't go any further. The column quietly closed up on Revutsky's self-propelled gun, on either side of which, spread along the forest edge, were the rifle battalion's scouts. I noticed that they were all prepared to open fire at any moment, although neither the scouts nor our forward reconnaissance detachment had encountered any enemy. Mentally, I was applauding the combat skills of the rifle commanders.

Stulno was situated ahead of us on the right. Silently, the column moved along a forest road and deployed into combat formation opposite the village.

'Thank God, we've managed to deploy before sunup,' the rifle battalion commander said right into my ear, before jumping down from my vehicle.

Red flares soared into the sky over a broad sector of the front. The Russian 'Uraah!' rang out. The main guns of the self-propelled guns began to roar in sequence, pounding the enemy defences with high-explosive shells. It was still so dark that the fiery bursts of our shells were barely visible through the pre-dawn haze, but we could surmise the panic in the enemy camp caused by such an unexpected and terrible reveille. Between the thundering reports of our 85mm guns, I could hear anguished shouts, orders and the screams of wounded. The self-propelled guns moved out on the advance, and firing from short halts, approached the enemy defence line on a broad front. With about 800 metres left before the first line of trenches, the self-propelled guns began to zigzag to throw off the enemy aim. The foot soldiers were trying not to lag behind the machines, firing intensely from machine guns and submachine-guns on the move, and terrorizing the enemy with their loud-voiced 'Ura-ah! Ura-ah!' Their battle cry resounded all across the assault front.

'Battery! From short halts, concealed with smoke grenades! At the guns! Fire!' I ordered the crews over the radio. The gunlayer replied right away, 'Brief stop!' and at the same moment I tossed out a smoke grenade.

Within a second, our shell reached an enemy gun, which disappeared in the black ball of an explosion. The thunder of our battery's 85mm guns seemed to be coming from everywhere. Several enemy guns had already been destroyed, but still the enemy anti-tank fire was quite heavy. Flashes of shell bursts were appearing on one after another SU-85. Our own self-propelled gun was taking its share, too – enemy shells kept finding us time and again with glancing hits! However, we were coming closer and closer to the enemy lines and their artillery positions.

At last the Germans began to waver. The accuracy of the German gunners began to drop, though the remaining guns were firing just as heavily. There were now about 500 metres to the trenches – it seemed that with just one more spurt, we would be overrunning the enemy guns concealed immediately behind the infantry trenches!

However, just then I glanced at the other attacking self-propelled guns, and I saw Sergey Bakurov's vehicle shudder and then come to a halt. Then two more – Vanya Sidorov's and Vetoshkin's – came to a stop. All three vehicles had been immobilized, but all were continuing to fire from the spot, supporting our attack. I turned my eyes back towards the enemy and rejoiced! Enemy gunners were fleeing in every direction, abandoning their guns.

At just this moment, my drivers Yakov Petrovich and Vanya Pyataev without any orders trebled their speed and hurled their vehicles at the enemy trenches. The macabre dance began! The multi-ton fighting machines began to smash and iron the trenches of the accursed Fritz. Mozalevsky was mowing down fleeing Germans with the machine gun. The gunlayers, having abandoned their gunsights, were hurling hand grenades at the enemy infantry. Our riflemen, with the aid of flank fire from their machine-gun platoons, wouldn't allow the entrenched enemy troops either to stick their head out or to return fire, and cut down any attempting to flee. Thus, an enemy attempt to counter-attack was disrupted almost before it could start.

The self-propelled gun crews didn't let the Motherland's infantry down – they helped it out a lot! We had already burst into the artillery positions. My vehicle was rising and falling for the fifth time – it meant that our Yakov Petrovich was crushing the fifth enemy gun beneath our tracks. Pyataev had smashed no fewer – Ivan always acted boldly, to the point of recklessness in attacks. Of course, we had been lucky that the enemy had not a single tank or assault gun in Stulno. There had been no *faustniki* either. That was why our victory came after only about an hour of fighting.

A portion of the Nazis surrendered after the counter-attack had been thwarted. The rest established themselves in two brick buildings and stubbornly returned fire from machine guns and submachine-guns for quite some time. They also had a remarkably effective grenade-launcher, who kept pinning down our infantry and forcing them to hide behind buildings time and again with his accurate lobs. But when two of our self-propelled guns pulled up in front of these buildings and fired high-explosive rounds into embrasures in the buildings, the Germans ceased fire immediately and dangled white cloths from the windows. Then they began to come out with their hands up. As each emerged from the building, he threw down his weapon, and the pile of rifles, submachine-guns, machine guns, and boxes of ammunition grew in front of our eyes. Then each joined the file of prisoners without any orders.

I counted forty-three prisoners. There were a lot more enemy dead. We had suffered painful losses too, but much less than them, even though we'd been on the attack.

Wasting no time, the battalion and two operating self-propelled guns took up a defence line and organized sectors of fire to repulse any enemy counter-attack. I had about half an hour before the next radio report. I left Revutsky to act on my behalf, asked the rifle battalion commander to give me two submachine-gunners for an escort, and walked past the smashed enemy anti-tank guns towards our immobilized SU-85s. All three vehicles appeared to be badly damaged; there were even holes in Siforin's and Bakurov's machines – they'd been lucky not to catch fire. We'd need a couple of hours to repair one of the self-propelled guns, which had both of its tracks broken and a damaged suspension arm. The other two would need at least five hours of repair work.

Not even an hour had elapsed since my report to the chief of staff when the emergency repair team headed by the mechanic Sergeant Major Shpota showed up. Sergeant Ivan Kostylev followed them in his Studebaker and distributed shells to re-stock our supply. The mechanics set about their business straight away, and the crews of the damaged vehicles joined them.

I didn't have time to run back to my self-propelled gun for the next scheduled radio contact, so I checked in with Shuliko from Vetoshkin's self-propelled gun. Using a procedure table and a coded map, the chief of staff gave me an urgent order to move my battery to a forested area 3 kilometres south of the Lukow–Brest road by 14.30, to join forward elements of Colonel Kaladze's 165th Rifle Division already positioned there. My battery had been detached to support the infantry.

Having plotted our route on the map, I showed the commanders of the damaged vehicles the place where they would have to arrive after completing their repairs, and they marked the route on their maps. I ordered Bakurov – the 2nd Platoon commander – to contact me over the radio at the beginning of every hour. Without waiting any longer, Revutsky and I went back to our vehicles, climbed into them, and started them up. As we passed the rifle battalion, we stopped for a minute. The infantrymen were already fitting out their positions, making full use of the former German dugouts and trenches. Two Maksim heavy machine guns stood on each flank. I informed the rifle battalion commander about the order I'd received, exchanged farewells with him and his soldiers, and headed off to the destination point.

Massacre in a Polish Forest

West of Stulno, we came across a narrow river with a muck-bottom and boggy banks. We stopped to examine the crossing. Near the road leading to the ford, we found the debris of a light SU-76 assault gun that had been blown apart by a powerful high-explosive mine, and the fragmentary remains of its crew. It was clear that it had happened just recently – oil spilled onto the ground was still burning and the rubber on the wheel rims was smoking, but there was nothing left of its crew – not even really enough to bury. The scene, as always, made a painful impression on everyone. I thought how cruel the war was – it had swallowed four young men in a flash, and not one of their family or kinfolk would ever find out that they'd been blown to pieces near some muddy Polish river.

There was no time and no point to do any kind of engineering reconnaissance. So as to avoid striking another lethal mine, I ordered Yakov Petrovich to shift about 50 metres to the right and to cross there. I ordered Revutsky to follow and stay directly in our tracks. We both managed to get across that ill-fated river safely, but without having identified the crew that had died there.

For the next 15 kilometres, we rolled along dirt roads through a forest, passing through only one settlement. We arrived at the advanced command-observation post around 14.00, a whole thirty minutes ahead of schedule. I reported to division commander Kaladze upon my arrival and placed myself at his disposal.

'I was expecting a battery, and there are only two of you. Why aren't all five here?' the colonel asked, shaking our hands.

'A third one will be here in about an hour, the other two in about four hours. They are still under repairs after an engagement.'

Kaladze responded with some brief instructions:

> If that's the case, then let's do it this way. You will move to the Lukow–Brest highway with a platoon of heavy machine guns and take up a defence there. There are no Germans there yet. Your duty is to prevent the enemy from using the highway to move men and matériel. Block the road very firmly and maintain your position until the rifle units come up.

We mounted a machine-gun platoon with two Maksims on the armour and moved slowly through a low coniferous forest. Fir and pine trees 3 to 4 metres high fully enveloped the vehicles, their spreading branches frequently and painfully lashing my face, forcing me to duck my head behind the hatch cover. Strangely, but each time I was ducking to avoid another 'slap in the face', Colonel Kaladze's words involuntarily came to mind: 'There are no Germans there.' At some point, my 'sixth sense', which had been sharpened at the front, started to tingle and I became uneasy. I just sensed that Germans were here, and not far away.

I ordered the self-propelled gun to stop. Climbing out of the machines, the five of us, three officers and two driver-mechanics, armed with submachine-guns and hand grenades, slipped noiselessly through the woods towards the Lukow–Brest highway. As we approached it, we could clearly hear the sound of engines and the rumble of moving heavy equipment. Judging from the sounds we were about 100 metres from the highway. We crept forward and then dropped onto our bellies: a few enemy armoured personnel carriers were racing down the road at top speed; trucks with crews in their back were towing guns; more trucks were carrying infantry, and other light vehicles were rolling by! A unit, seemingly no smaller than a motorized regiment, was rushing to reinforce some unknown group.[2] The length of such a column might extend over 30 kilometres! They were moving confidently, totally unaware of our presence. I decided to attack. In a few words, I gave the crews and machine-gunners their tasks:

> We will drive into the column with our two vehicles. My self-propelled gun will turn left and crush the fascists in that direction. Revutsky will turn right and pursue the tail of the column in the opposite direction. Each vehicle will be supported by fire from one machine gun. Continue until the complete destruction of all vehicles and combat equipment has been achieved.

We had to creep forward almost to the road itself, in order to assess the character of the roadside ditches. They appeared to be 1 metre wide and very deep. I gave the order: 'We're going to leap over the ditch at right angles without stopping.'

We didn't walk back to our vehicles – we ran back so as not to miss such a favourable moment for a surprise attack. The self-propelled guns rolled towards the highway quietly, but quickly. About 30 metres from it, we stopped to let the machine-gunners dismount and then immediately raced towards the road at high speed. Yakov Petrovich managed to accelerate the vehicle so well that it almost flew over the ditch and, landing with a hard jolt, we right off the bat struck an armoured personnel carrier with the left edge of the front armour, sending it into the opposite ditch upside-down. Pivoting, we started moving down the enemy column like a battering ram, smashing and overturning vehicles and equipment with our momentum, armour and mass. Seeing my tank destroyer coming, some of the drivers of the forward vehicles panicked and tried to turn away; others were turning around or unsuccessfully trying to overcome the roadside ditches to hide in the woods. The rest, having abandoned their vehicles, fled into the forest. However, the vehicles in the rear, unaware of what was happening in front of them, continued to roll forward, and vehicles began to collide. Finally, all movement stopped and complete chaos and panic engulfed the road. Even so, Yakov Petrovich kept shoving vehicles over and knocking them into the deep roadside ditches. The machine-gunners fired long bursts from the forest at the remaining fascists, preventing them from slipping away into the woods. Machine-gun bursts also caught those who were climbing out of crumpled vehicles.

For a second I opened the hatch cover to see how Revutsky's vehicle was doing. All I could see was the rear of his tank destroyer, its exhaust pipes belching smoke. Having smashed into a truck towing a gun with one track, his self-propelled gun was continuing to move towards the next victim, briefly dragging the half-smashed truck behind it. There was complete chaos over where Pavel was.

One could only imagine the condition the Germans were in. A mighty armoured self-propelled gun was breaking up the whole column! Both Maksims chattered exuberantly from the forest, chopping the wood planking on the trucks into chips as Germans poured out of the vehicles and scattered in every direction, seeking cover. Some managed to escape intact, but others were trampled or caught by the machine-gun fire.

The nose of my vehicle rose again, before abruptly dropping back onto the road, lifting open the hatch cover before slamming it closed again – one more enemy vehicle was smashed. A Maksim hidden in the forest was firing so intensely that once its bullets even struck our armour, forcing me to duck down. However, just before that I had managed to glance at Revutsky's self-propelled gun once again: it was racing up the road, catching up to another vehicle, while stretching from the clearing where we had entered the road up to the top of a slope, there were dozens of vehicles and guns scattered and burning on the sides of the roads and in the ditches. Some lay on their sides, others – upside-down. Certain that Pavel and his crew would carry out his assignment successfully and not let any vehicle escape unpunished, I contacted him nevertheless: 'How is it going?'

'Great! We've smashed up to half a hundred vehicles; some were towing guns. We are destroying enemy troops with hand grenades and submachine-guns. The engine has begun to overheat, and the Germans are fleeing quite quickly,' Revutsky rapidly relayed.

While I was talking, Yakov Petrovich kept wreaking havoc on the tail-end of the enemy column, trampling, toppling over and knocking aside halftracks, vehicles and trailers left and right into the ditches. Surviving Fritzes were fleeing, leaving behind dead and wounded next to the smashed machines.

I can't resist saying it time and again: Yakov Petrovich Mikhailov was a top-notch driver; probably the most experienced one in the Army. It is painful to think that later, after being transferred to a different crew, he was killed in action. Over all these years I can't get rid of the thought that had we stayed together, he might have survived.

About 10 kilometres from where we had entered the road, we smashed the last vehicle. We had reached the end of the column. Revutsky's machine was out of sight – it had gone far in pursuit of escaping vehicles. Assuming that other columns might turn up, I ordered our vehicle to move into the bushes. We also had to let the overheated engine cool down. As soon as the self-propelled gun stopped, I contacted Bakurov over the radio and warned: 'Cross the river west of Stulno following our tracks, or you may strike a powerful anti-tank mine.'

Immediately after that, I contacted Revutsky again. Pavel reported, 'I've smashed about twenty more vehicles! Pity, I've let two cars get away – they fled at high speed.'

Listening to the platoon commander's report, I never took my eyes away from my binoculars. Suddenly I saw a new column consisting of five armoured halftracks and a couple of dozen motor-cars pull out onto the road. Was it the rearguard of the destroyed regiment?

I addressed my crew: 'We're going to fight them. We'll let them approach to about 150 metres and then strike the personnel carriers. Then, drive back onto the road to give the motor-cars a workout.'

Mozalevsky found room for himself on the right-hand side of the upper hatch, ready to open fire on those who would try to escape. A deathly hush reigned inside the self-propelled gun. Behind us in the distance, our Maksims were breaking the silence with short bursts. They were of no help to us now; they were too far away to provide fire support. During these strained minutes each of us stared at the steel hulls of the rapidly approaching enemy vehicles.

I ordered Bykov: 'At the lead armoured carrier, with an armour-piercing round! Fire!'

The blast wave raised dust and dry needles, obscuring our vision of the road, but the dust had not yet settled when we saw a burning armoured vehicle! The halftrack behind it was unable to brake in time and ran into the first vehicle's burning rear. The fifth halftrack began to back up until it collided with a truck rolling behind it. The third and fourth halftracks were hastily turning around, trying to drive off to one side. Panic and confusion set in among the motor-car column, too – the lead vehicles were running into each other, while the tail vehicles were trying to reverse and escape.

'Comrade Lieutenant! It's time to crush them!' Yakov Petrovich suggested, grasping the levers impatiently again and again, apparently having lost his usual composure.

'Sergey-2! At the left armoured personnel carrier! Fire!' I ordered the gun-layer, at the same time indicating targets to Sergey-1 (Mozalevsky) to fire at from his machine gun.

'Comrade Lieutenant, the carrier is on fire!' Yakov Petrovich called out, vigilantly observing the action through his periscope built into the cover of the driver's hatch. A moment later, a burst from a large-calibre machine gun struck the hatch cover, striking sparks and causing Mozalevsky and me to dive into the fighting compartment. The burst had been fired from the fifth halftrack. Right away, another one that had pulled over to the right opened fire from a gun mounted on it and from its two machine guns.

'Sergey-2, at the one on the right! Fire!'

'Roger, firing at the right one!' the gunlayer repeated the order before pressing the trigger. 'Shot!'

By the time the gun's breech-block had clanked as it ejected the shell casing, the third halftrack was belching smoke. There were two more left. 'Sergey-2, strike the others!'

However, Sergey, though an experienced gunlayer and quick in action, failed to catch them. One was screened behind the burning vehicles, while the other had managed to cross the roadside ditch and had disappeared into the woods.

'Take that, you bloody Fritzes!' Sergey yelled spitefully as he sent another shell at a truck following the halftrack.

Just then, the rear vehicle, having reversed by about 50 metres, began to turn around near a small bridge leading to a dirt road. Mozalevsky fired several bursts at it, but the driver kept going, trying to complete his change in direction and to escape.

At last the Germans came back to their senses; the moment of complete shock had passed and, having understood that there was no chance to escape the fire of the Russian gun, they began to leap out of the backs of the trucks and take up positions in the ditches. We began to receive fire from submachine-guns and machine guns. Two gun crews began to unlimber their guns and turn them towards us. Now it was time: 'Yasha, it's your turn now, go for it!'

The self-propelled gun easily took off from its spot and raced towards the enemy column, like a horse bolting from a starting gate.

'Sergey, put the machine gun down, I'm going to switch to hand grenades!' I ordered Mozalevsky.

He handed me one bag with grenades, took another one for himself, and together we began to employ our 'pocket artillery' with no delay. The grenades flew out one after another, exploding amid the groups of Nazis hiding in the ditches. I hurled grenades into the left ditch, Sergey into the right one. We constantly ducked inside the fighting compartment after each throw in order to avoid return volleys of gunfire coming from both roadside ditches. The grenade explosions drowned the rattle of machine guns and submachine-guns, but we could clearly hear the bullets pinging against the self-propelled gun's armour.

In the meantime Yakov Petrovich was doing his job: he was skilfully ramming the enemy motor-cars into the ditches, pushing them until they toppled over. The vehicle was shaken twice and heavily listed to one side – that was when Yakov trampled the guns with one track. The surviving crews and infantry, losing the will to resist, fled while returning fire on the run.

'Sergey! Use the machine gun!' I ordered the gunlayer. Then I heard Revutsky's voice in my headphones: 'There are no vehicles left. I am approaching Biala Podlaska; the Germans have opened fire from there. I have decided to withdraw.'

'That's the right decision, pull back to the clearing where we started!'

Glancing at the map case, I reckoned that Pavel had driven the Germans pretty far – he was 20 kilometres from where we'd begun our work. When Yakov Petrovich was crushing the last machine which hadn't managed to escape, I stuck my head out of the hatch. Now without any 'obstacles', the self-propelled gun was smoothly racing on the asphalt of the highway! I decided to turn around and head back.

In less than half an hour the tank destroyer was already near the clearing where we had begun our work. Pavel's self-propelled gun was already waiting for us there. I congratulated and thanked both crews and the machine-gunners for the successful combat action.

A rifle battalion reinforced with artillery, mortars and a machine-gun company arrived to replace our battery in holding this tactically important sector of the highway. A captain – the rifle battalion commander – approached Revutsky and me, greeted us, and congratulated us on our big success before relaying that the division commander was waiting for us at his command post. Colonel Kaladze received us cheerfully and also congratulated us – it appeared that he had already been at the highway and had seen the results of our work. While we were reporting and speaking to the division commander, Vetoshkin's self-propelled gun came up. Colonel Kaladze invited the riflemen's commander and the tank destroyer officers to have lunch with him. We didn't reject the invitation from a high-level commander – all the more so since we hadn't had a morsel of food since the day before. Our crewmen were led by a quartermaster sergeant major to a waiting field kitchen.

During the lunch, having poured everyone a half glass of vodka, the division commander raised his glass in a toast: 'Let's drink to your battle success! You've done a great job! Tell Major Libman that he must award all the crewmen with Orders! One no lower than the Red Banner!'

We drank to the rifle battalion commander as well, for just that day he'd been promoted to the rank of major. After lunch the division commander summoned the battalion commander with the brand new badges on his shoulders, and then issued new combat orders to us: 'It is necessary to capture a bridgehead across the Krzna River and hold it until the arrival of the division's main forces.' Then he proceeded to trace the assigned route on the map, listing the succession of settlements through which we would pass. The rifle battalion commander and I plotted the route on our maps and jotted down the listed farmsteads and settlements in strict order on the back side of our maps. By the end of the same day, having waited until Bakurov's and Sidorin's self-propelled guns had rejoined with us, we set out on our new route.

From Line to Line

Our forward detachment was small in numbers but mobile, with rapid movement capabilities and not insignificant firepower. It was already growing dark when we, passing through a large Polish village, suddenly saw a large horse-drawn convoy heading into the centre of the settlement. Naturally, we took it for a German column, since we were in the vanguard and as far as we knew there were none of our troops ahead of us. We decided to open fire on the convoy but the major stopped his soldiers in time. Together on my self-propelled gun, we caught up with the trailing cart and saw two of our own older soldiers sitting on the two-wheeled cart, smoking hand-rolled cigarettes.

'Which unit are you with, where are you going?' the major asked.

'We're from the rear, catching up with 185th Rifle Division,' a moustachioed corporal replied.

Those are rear area troops for you! They'd almost run into the Germans!

'What sort of division are you trying to rejoin, when there is nothing but enemy in front of you?' asked the major.

The corporal swiftly stood up directly in the cart, then cupped his hands around his mouth and yelled to the whole convoy, 'Stop! Stop!'

A senior lieutenant of the quartermaster services came up to the major and presented himself as the commander of this rear area unit. The major replied, 'Where the hell do you think you're going? There are Germans in front of you! Stop immediately and take up a defence on the western outskirts of the village!'

We bid farewells and our detachment continued the march. We entered a large village on a bank of the Krzna River already at night. A German unit, which had been defending a bridge across the river, put up almost no resistance and retreated to the opposite bank.

The rifle battalion and our self-propelled guns took up defensive positions around the near end of the bridge, and the major and I went into the nearest house. The owners were having dinner under the light of a kerosene lamp. Discovering that we were Russians, they received us with a mixture of joy and apprehension. Nevertheless, they invited us to share their meal with them. However, we refused, politely referring to the lack of time.

The rifle battalion commander unfolded his map on the table and asked the host to indicate where there was a ford across the river. The peasant pointed to two locations on the river, but both were about 10 kilometres from the village.

The major and I hadn't yet had time to discuss the situation, when a signals officer from the regiment, Lieutenant Nikolay Volkov, rode up on a horse and gave me a verbal order from Major Libman to report to the regiment command post together with my battery within two hours. The rifle battalion commander became worried: it wasn't safe to remain here without the self-propelled guns, when there were only sixty-two men left in his battalion and not a single anti-tank gun or even a mortar, but Colonel Kaladze's order remained in effect. He was still supposed to cross the water barrier, establish a bridgehead, and hold it until the arrival of the 165th Rifle Division's main forces. The major was in a most difficult situation! How was he supposed to capture and hold a bridgehead with just a handful of men? There was nothing, though, that he or I could do. We both believed that the Germans must have broken through somewhere, and that a mortal danger was now hanging over the regiment command post and division's rear area.

To raise the major's spirits and as a warning to the Germans, each of our self-propelled guns fired three times at the Germans on the opposite bank, and with this farewell salute to the rifle battalion, the major and I wished each other luck. I ordered the column to pull out.

Lieutenant Volkov rode in front of my self-propelled gun to lead the way. I sat on the closed cover of the driver's hatch and was thinking about how much a man can be changed by the position he holds. Take Kolya [Russian diminutive for Nikolay] Volkov, for example. As a self-propelled gun commander, he had always worn dirty overalls and was often unshaven. In a word, his appearance was not very dashing. If I can put it simply, Volkov was a coward. There were only a few people like him among us, the tankers and self-propelled gun crews. Volkov had always used a variety of ruses to avoid combat. One day his engine had stalled, another – his transmission was broken. Then he had apparently offered himself as a signals officer to the regiment commander. Now his former slovenly appearance had changed; just look – he was a dandy in a freshly-pressed uniform, new forage cap, gleaming new belt, and with a fine officer's map case. He was perched on his mount like a true cavalryman – a hero on a steed! Just like a Guardsman! And this entire metamorphosis had occurred over just two days! Bykov, who was sitting on the superstructure, suddenly spoke up over the intercom as if he'd been reading my thoughts: 'Comrade Lieutenant, look, Volkov's a real fop, isn't he?'

Volkov's horse was moving at a trot and occasionally disappeared from view. How quickly the freshly-baked staff officer had forgotten that a self-propelled gun was not the regiment commander's Willys. Yakov Petrovich had to drive the machine in second and even third gear in order to keep up with our guide, or at least keep him within visual range.

At Regiment Headquarters

About midnight we reached the regiment's area. The command post and headquarters were located on a large estate, engulfed by an enormous fruit orchard. The old *palazzo*, covered with decorative vines, seemed to be gloomy and uninhabited. The windows, covered from the inside with blackout paper, were reflecting the cold moonlight, which gave the building an even more dreary appearance. A high brick wall surrounded the manor like a rampart. It had two gates: the front one and a service one.

We drove into the yard. The first thing that struck me was that nothing indicated an emergency situation. Nevertheless, we parked our vehicles in a combat formation and immediately got busy replenishing the fuel, lubricants and ammunition. As we serviced the machines, we could hear sentries at the gate asking for the password and giving replies in a low voice. Nearby were the headquarters' vehicles, and standing a bit apart from the others, next to the commander's tank, loomed a huge Tatra truck equipped as the regiment's mobile command post. Above the entire vehicle park, the orchard was bursting with fruit under the bright moonlight. We could see heavy garlands of cherries, and large fruit glowed on the apple and pear trees. Then suddenly I thought, what if Libman was a coward, and had simply become frightened to spend the night in this fortress of a manor house? The Germans might come unexpectedly and capture or destroy his headquarters – after all, the enemy wasn't far away. What if that was why we had been called back, leaving the defenceless infantry behind?

Having requested permission, I entered the commander's mobile command post, and I was shocked again by its luxurious amenities! A long table stood in the middle, a battery-powered electric bulb suspended above it. Two beds, chairs and a wardrobe stood by the walls. I was immediately gripped with a sense of indignation over this extremely blatant comfort relative to our everyday lives at the front. Libman was sitting behind a small table, eating with a great appetite; an unfinished bottle stood in front of him. Signals operator Valya Udodova was sitting in the opposite corner with earphones on her head, working at a wireless set. I began to report on the successful execution of our combat assignment: 'Being under the temporary direct command of division commander Colonel Kaladze, the battery . . .'

I wanted to report on the action on the highway, and to relay the division commander's order to decorate the two crews. Waving his hand dismissively, Libman interrupted me:

> Report later. Within an hour, you will set out as a forward detachment together with a platoon of the regiment's submachine-gunners and a rifle battalion. By tomorrow morning, we must seize the settlement of Wyglanduwka, a suburb of the city of Siedlce. You're now free to go.

He wouldn't even listen to me! What could I do?!

'Understood!' I uttered. 'I am to take Wyglanduwka at dawn!'

I spun around and exited, intentionally slamming the door behind me to express my protest against such callous treatment! The regiment commander hadn't shown the least bit of interest in whether or not there'd been losses in the battery, or any wounded, or even how the men were doing: whether or not they had been fed, or how much sleep they'd been getting. In fact he had driven me away – he'd issued an order and then gotten rid of me. Why should he care? He was sitting here, having his dinner, with a bottle on the table and his girlfriend nearby – what else did he need?

Let's just take a closer look at these PPZh, for example [PPZh, *pokhodno-polevaya zhenshchina* or 'campaign field wife' is a play, of course, on the initials of the Russian submachine-gun, the PPSh]. Having a campaign wife was a common thing at the front, beginning from the company commander level. There was no such thing at the platoon level, but in a company there might be a female medic or signaller.

Lev Abramovich Libman was a short man, not very glib or handsome, but quite a successful womanizer. He simply had to call one up – and that was all! Just try not to comply! Libman's wife somehow found out about his PPZh Valya, and came to the front: she showed up one day, raised a scandal, and generally speaking gave Libman a dressing down. Grigorov, the senior regimental surgeon later wrote me about this in a letter. Seemingly Libman settled down after the incident. After all, Valya had not been his only mistress – many girls had passed through his command post.

There were few women in our regiment, and their lot was not enviable. Take Lyuba, for example – a 17-year-old girl. Libman used to call her up too. She told me once: 'I don't want to have his child.' She was already worried that she had become pregnant. Soon after that she was wounded and sent to the rear. Such was the life of a female at the front. War is not a woman's business . . .

Of course, not all men were like Libman, but in general the headquarters' staff officers didn't care too much about us, the field officers – they were mostly concerned with career games. Results were the main thing to report up the chain of command; how much blood it had cost, how many losses, didn't matter much, and often they knew nothing about them. For example, for my three combat exploits by that time, I had not even received a single commendation, much less a medal. That huge column of Czech Tatra trucks near Popel'nya? Nothing. Those eight Tigers? Nothing. The destruction of the motorized regiment on the Lukow–Brest highway? Nothing, even though the 165th Rifle Division commander, not my own commander, had said: 'Nothing lower than the Red Banner! You've earned it! Pass this on to Libman!'

With respect to awards, a lot depended on personal relationships with the regiment commander, his political deputy, the battalion commander and the battalion political leader. Showering them with nice captured items meant a lot, too. We field officers had no time to deal with such things; due to this, we – who remained alive – ended the war with just two or three Orders. I received three Orders during the war: two Orders of the Red Star and the Order of the Patriotic War, 2nd Degree. One Red Star was for a series of engagements: in one action I had crushed two guns; in another I had knocked out three tanks. Altogether in the war I knocked out nineteen tanks and set twelve ablaze, including eight Tigers and one Panther. I also received the second Red Star for a 'group of engagements', as well as the Order of the Patriotic War.

I returned to my comrades from Libman's command post. They were waiting for me. The crews had a quick dinner. Then I met with the rifle battalion commander and Vanya Zhurov – the commander of the submachine-gun platoon. We would be cooperating with them. We reviewed all issues of coordination in detail in case we encountered the enemy during our march to the allocated line, and sketchily went over the attack on Wyglanduwka. We would clarify the rest once we got there. Then I ran over to the dispatch post: there were two letters waiting for me – one from home and the other from Vasiliy Vasilyevich Ishkin, with whom I had served together in Mel'nikov's [1454th] regiment before being wounded. I had no time to read the letters – I stuck them in my pocket. On my way back to the vehicles I came across Sergey Dvornikov – the 1st Battery Commander. We exchanged a few words about the recent fighting, I told him briefly about the fighting for Stulno and the massacre on the highway. He was astonished: 'Vasya, your battery is charmed! The 2nd Battery has lost all of its vehicles, I have only three tank destroyers left, Istomin – two, and yours is still intact!'

I replied:

> Go on with you, Sergey! I was lashed pretty well near Paryduby, yesterday I was battered badly with Bakurov and Vetoshkin, and Sidorin got his share too. Only God knows what will happen to us near Wyglanduwka. I haven't received the reconnaissance information yet. Who knows how it will be?

We shook hands tightly. Dvornikov told me, 'Well, stand fast. Good luck!'

Assigning my deputy of technical services Zhurbenko to check the readiness of the battery and to instruct the infantrymen, I found time to read the letters. At home everything was going the same way as before. As for Ishkin, I had received the last letter from him just before I'd been discharged from the hospital – a whole four months had elapsed since then. With some trepidation, I opened the envelope bearing the stamp 'Passed military censorship'. Judging from the fact that the letter had travelled only two days, Mel'nikov's regiment was somewhere nearby, also in Poland.

The first news relayed by Vasiliy Vasilyevich was the following: The platoon commander from our battery, Petya Fomichev, had been bestowed the title Hero of the Soviet Union. I had mixed emotions over this piece of news – this highest honour was great, but it had been awarded posthumously. I thought back to when he'd been laying behind the self-propelled gun's superstructure, unconscious, with his head totally wrapped by bandage; only his closed eyes were visible through an opening. So, it had been a mortal wound. I was in bitter grief, even though I had understood back then that it would have been a miracle for him to survive. I also learned from the letter that our 1454th Regiment had been awarded with another Order – the Order of Suvorov 3rd Degree.

However, there was more bitter news. Guys on my old crew had been killed: the gunlayer Valeriy Korolev, the driver Vanya Gerasimov, and the gunloader Kolya Sviridov. Some of the vehicle commanders had died too: among them Sasha Minin, Nikolay Samoilov, and Vanya Tomin, who had died of wounds in a hospital. 'In general,' Vasiliy Vasilyevich wrote, 'very few of those who were with us back at the Kursk Bulge have survived.' He had written something else, but the censors had blotted out nearly a third of the letter. Maybe, knowing the cohesion of our crew, he had given details of the action in which Korolev had been killed?

How heavily did I take this news! Oh, Korolev, Korolev ... He was my best gunlayer. I wasn't to find out much more until after the war. Valeriy died on 26 July 1944. The brigade was in a fierce battle on the approaches to Przemysl, near Orly-Malkovice, but first they had to capture the town of Zurawice. It was taken in a night attack. Korolev, Gerasimov and Sviridov had all been killed in this night action. Their self-propelled gun had been set ablaze after stumbling into an ambush set by two German self-propelled guns. But how, why did it happen? Who was nearby?

While the column was stretching out in preparation for the march I called upon the chief of reconnaissance Captain Marchenko. He told me that Siedlce was not far away from Warsaw and warned me that the Germans would fight fiercely on this axis:

> Wyglanduwka is a large settlement, and the Germans have dug in over there pretty thoroughly, so you're going to have a tough time. Try to approach the town unnoticed – it's your only chance. You'll accomplish the mission only through surprise and the resoluteness of your assault. Most important – keep in mind that you'll be facing Vlasovites[3] from Russian and Ukrainian units. You know yourself what it means; you won't get off lightly against them ...

The Vlasovites

Our forward detachment left the landlord's estate precisely at 02.00. Revutsky's tank destroyer with infantry on board rolled out in front of the rest of the column as the point. My machine followed his at the head of the column; behind me were the other self-propelled guns and a Studebaker truck for the infantry who could find no room on the armoured vehicles. The emergency repair vehicle with a team of mechanics headed by Shpota brought up the end of the column. I had wanted Senior Technician Zhurbenko to be with us too – he would have come in handy during the march to ensure the smooth running of the vehicles, and in battle, to make the quickest repairs to damaged vehicles. However, Zhurbenko had disappeared just before our departure, as always.

The column was rolling at a low speed almost noiselessly; all lights were off except the rear lights to prevent rear-end collisions. In this quiet situation I collected my thoughts about the Vlasovites. The upcoming combat would necessarily be to the death, for they had no choice: either win or face a firing squad should they be captured. The Germans had been using the Vlasovite units to lead assaults and as rearguard units lately, distrusting their own demoralized troops. We had not come across any Vlasovites so far but had heard enough about them and had no warm feelings towards them. Unsurprisingly! They fought against us! However, their fate was unenviable. Most of them were shot after being taken prisoner, although no one had issued any kind of order in this regard. To be honest I was critical of these executions, though never openly. I opposed the execution of any prisoners. Some of our guys shot them to show off their gallantry, but they should have shown it in combat! The counter-intelligence officers would sort out who was who and how he'd come to be among the Vlasovites. There were filtration camps where such checks were conducted.

The distance between the regiment command post and Wyglanduwka, including all the detours and searchings for a ford, comprised 40 kilometres. We drove it in two and a half hours. We bypassed enemy-occupied villages without engaging them. Just before dawn, we assembled in the bushes 1 kilometre south of the village and immediately deployed in an attack formation. Silence, broken only by dogs barking and the sounds of a gramophone, hung over Wyglanduwka – apparently German officers had stayed up very late and were playing the same lyrical song *'Im eine Sommer Naucht'* ('On a Summer Night') over and over again. It was opportune that they were playing it, for the sounds masked our approach. If we started the attack at dawn, we still had about forty minutes to go. Inside the fighting compartment, the major and I took another look at the map of the area with the help of a pocket torch, discussed the situation, and decided to attack now, before it grew light.

We fell on the Germans like a bolt from the blue! Our riflemen and submachine-gunners slaughtered many of the enemy troops while they were still in bed. Our hand grenades were exploding in foxholes and trenches all over the place, and short bursts of submachine-guns were audible. Then our shells began to explode and our engines began to rumble! The village caught fire. In the light of the flames, we saw five enemy tanks standing in column in the middle of the village. Tankers were scurrying around near them. They were medium Panzer IV tanks. I ordered all the crews at once, 'Battery! At the tanks, fire!'

We managed to fire only three shots each and set two of the tanks ablaze. The rest managed to disappear, taking advantage of the smoke engulfing the village. When we skirted around the village and reached the northern outskirts, where we took up a line of defence, we had a chance to look around and saw a terrible scene! The frenzied locals were running about the village with buckets, trying to extinguish burning houses and sheds. They were opening cattle barns, stalls and poultry houses in order to save the animals. Animals leaping out of the inferno were burning alive: cows, sheep, goats, hens, turkeys and geese, often with hair or feathers on fire, bellowing, bleating, cackling or honking harrowingly. Crazed, rushing pigs were squealing unbearably. Our soldiers were helping to extinguish fires as far as possible, and freeing other animals.

The fire burned throughout the day and began to die down only after nightfall, having reduced half of the village to ashes. Only the blackened skeletons of incompletely burned-out houses and charred chimneys rose above the ground. However, that didn't seem to be enough for the Germans. At dawn they opened artillery and mortar fire on the burned-out village. People began to abandon the houses that had been spared, managing to collect only the most necessary items. They ran to the east to a shelter, counting upon our protection.

An enemy counter-attack was expected; surely the Germans would want to take back the abandoned positions. So while it was not yet fully light, Mozalevsky and I made a run for the shelter and advised the scared and grief-stricken locals to get as far as possible to the rear, explaining that we expected more fighting and that the Germans would try to reclaim the village. If they succeeded, out of malice they wouldn't spare the shelter or its inhabitants. Thank God, the people listened to us and left the village. We felt easier: there would be fewer needless losses.

A chain of low heights, which formed the second line of the German defence, stretched about a kilometre and a half from us. To the left of us, on the edge of a forest about 2 kilometres north of the village, they had artillery positions, from which they were periodically shelling Wyglanduwka and our positions. At dawn, I began to zero in on one gun on their positions situated on the nearest hill. We had high-explosive shells in our ammunition stock. This kind of shell required setting a time fuse so that the shell would explode just above a foxhole or a trench. Only then would a bursting shell shower splinters down on the concealed enemy troops. Each adjustment of the time fuse was equivalent to 50 metres, but we would have to hit a 1-metre-wide trench! This was high-precision work and we didn't have a lot of experience with these shells. Having set the aim, I ordered Bykov: 'H-E shell! Fuse 5! Fire!' – and off towards the target it went! How, though, can you calculate a distance within a metre using 50-metre increments?! After the first two shots over the target, we could suddenly clearly hear yelling from the enemy trenches in pure Russian, accompanied with gestures of shaking fists: 'Communists! Swine! You're pitiful shots!'

The scout chief had been right: there were either Vlasovites or some of Bandera's men here. I adjusted the distance and the third shell exploded right above the enemy trench! We had the target zeroed in. Now the whole battery fired with identical settings on the gunsights. The taunting ceased immediately. As we reloaded our guns, we could hear the screaming of wounded men coming from the enemy trenches. The battery fired several more salvoes with the high-explosive shells, and a deathly silence hung over the enemy defence line.

The defenders in the trenches had been silenced, but their snipers kept firing from their remote positions. Soon the enemy artillery opened fire on the battery. Artillery and mortar shells were exploding all around us, and the harassing sniper fire wouldn't let me stick my head out of the hatch. On several occasions, bullets whistled past my ear – what kind of chance did I have to observe? I had to lower the hatch cover and keep my eye on the action through a narrow crack between the hatch cover and the top armour of the super-structure. The exchange of fire had already been continuing for more than two hours, and over this period of time we had become accustomed to the enemy's manner of firing, taking cover from their next salvo of fire, before returning fire ourselves.

During one of the intervals between the artillery salvos, a female medic from the rifle company leaped out of a foxhole to render assistance to a wounded man, but she was immediately killed by a sniper's bullet. I didn't even have time to shout 'Get down!' to her, when she was hit and fell; a red blotch appeared on her blouse. In a second Mozalevsky and I were beside her body – the sniper didn't even manage to fire another shot, before we had carried her to the nearest foxhole. We checked for a pulse, but there was none. Mozalevsky pulled out her *Komsomol* membership card from a blouse pocket: it had a bullet hole in it; the sniper's bullet had hit her directly in the heart. The company commander came running up and Sergey handed her membership card to him. It was painful to see this cute girl, who was only about 18 years of age, and my heart was breaking over the injustice of what had just happened – having had no time to live her own life fully, she had sacrificed it to liberate the land of other people. It is especially offensive now, when we learn that the ungrateful Poles are vandalizing the graves and demolishing the monuments to our fallen soldiers, who gave their lives for the future of Poland and to free the Poles from Nazi occupation.

The Recklessness of the Battalion Commander

We were expecting an enemy counter-attack any minute. However, time passed and the Germans refused to attack. On the other hand, they continued to shell our positions relentlessly from the forest edge, inflicting heavy casualties on our infantry. The rifle battalion commander, plainly intoxicated, decided to attack and sent his chief of staff to me, who told me: 'The commander has ordered an attack! It will begin at 13.00!'

Attack across a two-kilometre, wide-open field?! In the middle of the day?! I considered this to be foolhardy in the extreme and fraught with the potential for enormous losses. I said as much to the senior lieutenant with the request to convey it to the rifle battalion commander. I then added, 'Tell the major that I am not his subordinate and the self-propelled guns will not attack!'

I was hoping that the major would take my opinion into account, but nevertheless decided to summon my platoon and vehicle commanders. They could only reach my self-propelled gun by belly-crawling. I had to give them a few words about the attack: 'A red flare from my vehicle will be the signal to attack. After that, everyone fires five shots at the Germans' artillery positions, and then goes on the attack at maximum speed with zigzags.'

Despite my admonitions, the commander hurled his rifle battalion into the attack. I was also compelled to advance to support the infantry. I sent up a red flare. All the battery's guns began to roar, and then the self-propelled guns moved out. As we moved to catch up with the lines of the attacking rifle battalion, we could see that the entire field was strewn with corpses: the infantry had begun to incur terrible losses from the very first minutes of the attack. They had been simply mowed down in the open field by explosions, shell fragments and machine-gun bursts.

Peering into the shady edge of the forest in front of us, I understood how dangerous the barrels of the enemy guns hiding there were to us. No lesser threat was posed by the enemy on the right, since our flank was unprotected. I signalled by flag to Revutsky, 'En echelon to the right!', and he dropped back a bit to cover the battery's flank. The self-propelled guns were flying at full speed, zigzagging across the field to throw off the enemy gunners' aim. This was perhaps the hundredth time over the course of the war that I had to attack while zigzagging and without firing, and so far I had somehow remained unpunished, though each time my vehicle received many glancing hits.

This time, though, the field was completely clear, with not a single tree or shrub for concealment, and there was still some distance to go to reach the forest! These 2 kilometres seemed to stretch like a rubber band the further we advanced. No one knew if his self-propelled gun was going to reach the enemy guns or burst into flames from a penetrating shell on the way. Most of all I feared that even if one vehicle stopped, it would become a sitting duck. Several motionless seconds would mean death for its crew.

Swivelling the commander's panoramic sight I saw that all the SU-85s were keeping pace with us, resolutely racing towards the enemy. Our engine groaned and roared as the vehicle flew towards the forest, obedient to the driver's will. I wasn't giving Yakov any commands so as not to distract him and not to disrupt the pace of the attack. I could see ricocheting hits appearing on one vehicle after another, but they continued to race without slowing down. My crew was shaken several times by glancing hits on the hull too, which was dangerous – due to the high speed the vehicle's tracks had the lightest grip on the ground.

Our attack was purely psychological, relying on the hope that the enemy gunners would lose their nerve seeing the Russian armour rushing towards them – we had no other way to dislodge the enemy under these circumstances. The infantrymen were increasingly lagging behind, for they could advance only with short rushes because of the heavy mortar and machine-gun fire.

There were no more than 400 metres between us and the enemy now! Obviously this was the final stretch. Who would have the upper hand?! With about 300 metres left to the edge of the forest, the flashes of the enemy anti-tank guns became less frequent, and then at about 200 metres they stopped completely. However, we kept closing with the guns without slowing down, guessing that possibly not all the gun crews had scattered.

'Sergey-1! From the machine gun, at the running gun crewmen! Fire!' I ordered Mozalevsky, who was already holding the machine gun ready.

The self-propelled guns overran the guns straight off and moved on towards the horse-drawn carts, which the Germans used to transport their shells. I managed to issue a warning not to kill the horses and immediately sent the signal: 'Follow me!' We quickly turned around and rushed towards the location where Revutsky's platoon was engaged – over there, judging from the explosions, our crews were battling enemy tanks. We encountered a difficult situation: Revutsky's vehicle was on fire, and a Panther was belching smoke about 100 metres away from it. Two other Panthers were pressing hard on Vetoshkin's self-propelled gun, the crew of which was firing using the panoramic sight, because the telescopic gunsight had been disabled.

'Battery! Fire at the lead Panther!' I ordered all the crews.

A salvo roared. The target Panther's turret was blown off! The second one quickly pulled back and managed to disappear behind the crest of the hill. Revutsky's self-propelled gun was now burning brightly, and hand grenades inside it were exploding. Crewmen – the driver-mechanic Vanya Pyataev, the gunloader Lesha [Russian diminutive form of Aleksey] Bessonov and the commander himself were standing nearby – all had their eyes fixed on the tragic fire as if waiting for something. Unable to bear all that was happening, Vanya and Aleksey were openly sobbing without restraint. I ran up to Pasha [Russian diminutive of Pavel]. Other crews of our battery ran up too. Barely able to control himself, Pasha pointed at the burning machine and we understood that the gunlayer Fedya Belyashkin and the submachine-gun platoon commander Ivan Zhurov, who had been inside the self-propelled gun with the crew – had been trapped inside the machine and had burned alive. We silently removed our helmets …

Later, staff clerks would write a death notice to the family of the latter: 'On 29 July 1944 your son, Guards Lieutenant Ivan Nikiforovich Zhurov died a hero's death in combat against the fascists one kilometre north of the village of Wyglanduwka, Siedlce *Uezd* [District] of Warsaw *Wojewodstwo* [Province].' They would also send a notice to Ivan's mother, Ulyana Fedorovna in Kharkov. Vanya's broken-hearted mother would never believe this notice and would wait for her son's return until her dying day.

The same notice would be written on the death of Senior Sergeant Fedor Alexandrovich Belyashkin – it would be sent to his brother Petr in Gorkiy Oblast's village of Kaverino; poor Fedor had no parents – he and his brother had grown up in an orphanage.

However, back in July 1944, we stood there silently for some time; then I told Pavel to walk to the rear with his surviving crewmen. By that time, the infantry had arrived – at best, only half of them. We pointed our self-propelled guns towards the north and resumed the advance.

The Tank Attack near Siedlce

We moved through some woods, past two-horse carts harnessed to powerful draught horses and now tethered to trees near stockpiles of ammunition crates. Soon the Germans opened a heavy concentration of artillery and mortar fire on our combat formations. Explosions of heavy shells toppled whole trees onto the self-propelled guns. They were obstructing the gunsights and observation devices, causing the fighting compartment to darken until the vehicle's movement shed the branches. However, more shells would burst again, shattering the short-lived calm of the woodland, and more trees and branches would fall on the vehicle again, clattering against the armour and plunging the crew into darkness. During these moments I commiserated with the riflemen and submachine-gunners following the self-propelled guns, who had no protection from the terrible wood splinters and shell fragments. The crews had managed to seat only some of the foot soldiers inside their fighting compartments.

At last we emerged from the beaten zone and falling trees, and found ourselves on the northern edge of the forest, overlooking the town of Siedlce. An overwhelming scene spread before us! Only a kilometre away from us there was a large formation of enemy tanks concealed in a grove.[4] They were standing in combat formation, defending with their line nearly half the town with its factory buildings and smoking chimneys. Before our eyes, suddenly about twenty tanks detached from the formation and moved towards the forest, seemingly unaware of our presence.

'All stop! Open fire only after a shot from my vehicle!' I ordered the crews in the clear.

At this moment, horse-mounted scouts appeared in the forest. It turned out that General Yushuk's 11th Tank Corps and General Kryukov's 2nd Cavalry Corps were approaching.[5] The situation was becoming complicated. The Germans had not yet detected our self-propelled guns, which were well-disguised in the green bushes, and I decided not to disclose our presence prematurely, before our tankers had an opportunity to come up and deploy into a combat formation. We could hear the engines of the German tanks rumbling to the north, and the engines of our friendly tanks advancing from the south. So we lurked and waited. The armoured enemy armada was quickly approaching. We allowed them to approach to within about 500 metres – there was no more time for hesitation! 'At the enemy tanks! Fire!' I ordered the crews and the entire battery.

Sergey Bykov's shot thundered. Immediately after it came three more loud reports from the other three guns. Four enemy tanks started to smoke or burn! The rest halted because of the surprise, but then came back to their senses and fired a reciprocal salvo. I managed to see Vetoshkin's self-propelled gun set ablaze one more tank, but then our vehicle was strongly jolted and enveloped in flames. I sensed a strong blow to my head and lost consciousness ...

I regained consciousness for the first time on the outskirts of Wyglanduwka. They were shifting me from a horse-drawn cart into an ambulance. I remember seeing Shuliko, the surgeon Grigorov, the medic Nadya Naumova, and then I passed out again. I only fully regained consciousness the following morning. Someone touched me, and I opened my eyes: I was lying on thatch in some shack, surrounded by wounded men, and Pavlik [another Russian diminutive of Pavel] Revutsky was sitting next to me and smiling. It was he who had touched me. We shook hands, but I couldn't say anything, because I couldn't open my mouth.

'I'm in this hospital too, but couldn't find you,' Pasha began to say. 'I located you on the lists only with the help of a nurse, who knew your number. Thank God, the crew managed to pull you out in time. I'm very happy you're alive!'

I pulled a mirror out of my pocket and took a look. A splinter had penetrated my lower jaw and smashed some of my teeth, and I was badly bruised. Because of this, my face was badly swollen; the whites of my eyes were red from haemorrhage. It became clear why Pavlik couldn't find me – indeed it would have been hard to recognize such a man!

Pavlik, who had received several wounds from shell fragments himself, continued angrily:

> That battalion commander is either a petty tyrant or he was simply
> drunk when he committed his battalion to that ruinous attack! A

brand new major! Two of our self-propelled guns were burned out because of him. If it hadn't been the first time with him, they would have sent him in front of a tribunal.

My friend's outrage agitated me and I began to mumble through badly damaged teeth, making my interlocutor strain to hear: 'Just so, Pavlik, just so! If the battery hadn't been there, he would have lost the whole battalion. Then they would have put him on trial ... and us too at the same time, saying we hadn't supported the attack properly.'

About an hour later we parted, having first exchanged addresses. Soon I was evacuated further into the rear. I was to meet Pavel Danilovich again exactly twenty years later. Even now I would say the same thing: the terrible losses in the battalion, the death of Fedya Belyashkin, and Pavel's burned-out self-propelled gun is on the conscience of the rifle battalion commander. It's a pity I don't remember his name. Did we really even think about it back then?!

Just as after my first wound I didn't return to my former regiment. That is why I'm going to relate several words about its further combat history and the fate of my comrades in it.

As I collected data for my book, I worked in the Ministry of Defence's Central Archive, but I found almost no documents in it related to the 1295th Kovel Red Banner Self-propelled Artillery Regiment. Primarily, only financial documents and a few reports had been preserved. The documents that I happened to read raised my doubts about the validity of the data presented in them. In a summary of the combat operations of the 1295th Self-propelled Artillery Regiment [SAP], operating as part of the 47th Army's 129th Rifle Corps, the following was written:

> ... Over the period of operations between 16 July and 6 September 1944, the 1295th SAP inflicted the following losses on the enemy: destroyed 20 enemy tanks, 14 assault guns, 45 guns of various calibre, 12 152mm (the Germans actually had 150mm) and 87mm guns (the Germans had 88mm guns), 61 machine guns, 8 mortars, up to 800 Hitlerite troops, 74 loaded vehicles, 50 loaded carts, 10 motorcycles. Apart from that 14 German soldiers and one officer were taken prisoner.
>
> Commander of the 129th Rifle Corps Guards
Major General Anashkin
Chief of Staff Colonel Gorshenin

Enemy losses have been exaggerated here several times over, especially in tanks and assault guns, in order to inflate their own combat successes and thus increase the number of awards and promotions. After all, why would those who compiled the dispatches while hiding in bunkers covered by three layers of logs need valid data? While the regiment received the honorific title of 'Kovel' and was awarded with the Order of the Red Banner for its actions in the ranks of the 129th Rifle Corps, it received only official gratitude for its fighting together with the 9th Mechanized Corps, although the men of the regiment had served gallantly and the regiment had suffered heavy losses with that latter corps.

The legendary driver of my crew Yakov Petrovich Mikhailov didn't survive the war. He was killed in action, fighting for the city of Paslek. By that time he had already been awarded four combat Orders! The gunloader of our crew Sergeant Major Sergey Mozalevsky was very badly wounded and apparently died soon thereafter, for he was never heard from again. The gunlayer Sergeant Major Sergey Bykov was also badly wounded, but survived. After demobilization from the Army, he worked for many years as a diesel locomotive machinist. I would never have the opportunity to see him again. In 1990 we buried Sergey Grigorievich Bykov at the Shalya Station of Sverdlovsk Oblast to the whistle of steam engines.

Chapter 15

In East Prussia

New Appointment

The wounded men were evacuated from Wyglanduwka a little farther to the rear and soon we found ourselves again in an improvised hospital in some landlord's manor. Buildings of all kinds were being used as hospitals back then, but here we were now sleeping on spring beds, not thatch. There was a large orchard around the place and those who could do it happily ate apples, pears and cherries; all I could do was watch them and good-naturedly envy them. Here, in this provisional hospital they made another, more successful attempt to feed me and I began to recover from the shellshock. Things were worse with the wound caused by the splinter.

Then I found myself in Gomel, where they began to feed me broth from a feeding bottle and my strength began to return to me gradually. After Gomel was Moscow, Evacuation Hospital No. 4641 on Usachev Street

My wound was serious, but the consequences of the shellshock were even worse, as I became temperamental for a time. My surgeon was Maria Semenovna. One day she made some sort of remark to me that my temperature was jumping around, implying that I was tampering with the thermometer in order to stay away from the front a little longer. I was indignant and said: 'Maria Semenovna, excuse me, but I'm no coward! Maybe you're judging me by your own subjective standards?!'

'You're insulting me! We'll discharge you tomorrow!'

'Fine! Have my dentures ready tomorrow and discharge me tomorrow!'

The very next day, indeed my dentures were ready and they discharged me. Everyone was supposed to receive a one-month leave after a severe wound, but I wasn't given one. If only I had kept my mouth shut! I wanted so much to see my family – of course I would have gone home.

So off to the front I went again. In the beginning of October 1944 after my discharge from the hospital I was sent to the 3rd Belorussian Front and assigned to the 1435th Self-propelled Artillery Regiment of the *Stavka* Reserve. I had to reach my destination little by little: first by train, riding for quite some time on running-boards clinging to handrails – there were no seats available, in the boxcars or on the platform cars either. I reached the *front* headquarters from

Kaunas, and then hitched rides to the regiment aboard passing vehicles. I still vividly recall a large sign alongside one of the front-line roads:

> GLORY TO THE INFANTRY – THE QUEEN OF BATTLE!
> GLORY TO STALIN'S FALCONS!
> GLORY TO THE ARTILLERY – THE GOD OF WAR!
> GLORY TO THE VALIANT TANKERS!
> FOR AN ACCIDENT – TO A TRIBUNAL!

The regiment was stationed in a forest near Wilkowiszki, resting and refitting after heavy fighting. The personnel lived in dugouts and those replacements who hadn't managed yet to get their gear or assignments lived in tents, which sheltered them from the cold autumn rains. The whole area was well-camouflaged from aerial and ground observation.

I reported for duty on my arrival to the regiment commander. Colonel Khatchev was about 40 years of age, a slender man, taller than average, with hair just beginning to turn grey. He looked quite intelligent. He was a native of Moscow, but army service had moved him around the country for quite a few years. The colonel told me about the regiment in detail and appointed me to command of the 3rd Battery of SU-85 self-propelled guns. There were only three SU-85s in the battery, and in the entire regiment only a total of thirteen instead of the authorized twenty.

In the command dugout, I introduced myself to the chief of staff Major Krasnogir', to his deputy Major Lebedev and to the assistant chief of staff Captain Taras Romanovich Raksha. From the headquarters, I went to get acquainted with the men in my new battery. A Muscovite Tolya Novikov and a guy from Saratov Fedor Klimov were the platoon commanders. After the recent fighting they had only one vehicle in each of the platoons. My driver was Sergeant Major Mamaev, gunlayer – Senior Sergeant Zakiy Gityatullin, gun-loader – Pavel Seregin of the same rank. I quickly introduced myself to the officers of the regiment. Captain Mariev was in charge of the 1st Battery, Captain Nikolaev commanded the 2nd Battery, and Senior Lieutenant Misha Grin' – the 4th Battery. The 1st and 2nd Battery commanders were closer to 30 years of age.

The repair teams and self-propelled gun crews were working feverishly. The repair teams were welding up cracks and holes received during the most recent action; the crews were putting weapons, devices, and the radio back into working order, and tuning the transmission system. As I was told, they had managed to find some time for gunnery training. I immediately joined them in their efforts. We remained in the forest near Wilkowiszki for about three weeks, until 20 October 1944.

From Endkunden to Stalluponen

At dawn on 20 October our regiment went on the advance together with units of the 28th Army. We had been ordered to capture a large Lithuanian settlement called Endkunden from the march and continue the advance towards the town of Kibartay on the border with Germany. Having heard the order everyone became agitated – of course, because soon we'd be crossing the East Prussian border!

Our artillery preparation began to thunder while it was still dark. Tanks, self-propelled guns and infantry moved into the attack behind a creeping barrage. I was troubled by the possibility of encountering panzerfausts. I warned the crews to keep vigilant watch on the roadside bushes, and on any other kind of obstacle behind which a *faustnik* could lurk, while for myself I was wondering how we could get hold of an MG-42 machine gun from the Germans sooner rather than later. I had become used to having one and always made good use of them on other fronts: they were good for combing the terrain and for wiping out infantry and *faustniki*. The fighting for Endkunden was brief: the German gun crews, shocked by the surprise, had no time to open aimed fire and we crushed the guns beneath our tracks. Our battery also captured four MG-42 machine guns. We gave a machine gun to each crew and handed one over to Misha Grin's 4th Battery.

We failed to capture Kibartay from the march and had to pull back to the start line. For a whole hour our Il-2 ground-attack planes pounded the enemy defences with bombs and delivered air strikes against pillboxes and weapons emplacements. A salvo from BM-31 heavy rocket-launchers (called *Andryusha*) completed the preparations for another attack: the rocket artillery battalion blanketed the enemy with 384 300mm rockets, each weighing 91.5 kilograms. The demoralized enemy couldn't withstand such a blow and we took the town.

The self-propelled guns rolled past a large two-storey brick building on the western outskirts of Kibartay. I thought that most likely before the war, this had been the post of a border guards detachment, and again I was agitated and excited, just as I had felt near the Western Bug before; for the second time we were about to cross a national border, but this time it was the German border. As if to confirm it, soon we saw a heavily leaning steel frontier marker, with its black and white stripes faded but visible, and a board bearing the inscription: 'FRONTIER. USSR – GERMANY'.

The advance was suspended for the night, and our self-propelled guns moved into emplacements that we had dug. The Germans were only about 800 metres away. On that night, being the regiment's officer on watch I had to have an unpleasant conversation with a regimental officer – the newly-promoted Lieutenant Colonel Arkhip Arkhipovich Vasilyev. I went to check the outposts and found Senior Sergeant Monin reclining. He was relaxing on sentry duty –

and at what a post! He'd been entrusted with guarding the regimental banner, and other colours and documents – the whole lot! I sternly warned him: 'Watch out or I'll have you punished!'

I came around a bit later for a second time to check on him, and found him smoking on duty, so I gave him a second warning. Just before dawn, I checked on him for a third time – and found Monin helping to unload bread from a commissary vehicle that had just pulled up. Typically, bread was received by the cooks, and he had nothing to do with it! I removed him from his post, ordered the sentry commander to replace the guard and warned, 'Senior Sergeant Monin is not to be placed on duty as a sentry.' I ordered Monin to be locked away in an improvised guardroom established in a shack.

Vasilyev summoned me in the morning. He was some kind of political officer! Vasilyev was an illiterate man, a drinker, a labourer from Leningrad by background. Somehow, though, he had contrived a way to climb the ladder of ranks, and recently he'd been promoted to lieutenant colonel. So, he summoned me and asked, 'Did you place Monin under arrest?'

'I did.'

'Why?'

I explained it to him: 'You know yourself that regulations ban sitting and smoking while on sentry duty.' He immediately pounced on me:

> Don't you know that he's the battery's Party secretary?! Don't you know that the battery's Party cell is subordinate to the regiment's Party organization? That the regimental Party committee is subordinate to the corps', the corps' – to the army's Party commitee? And the army committee is subordinate to the Central Committee itself! Don't you know that Comrade Stalin is the General Secretary of the Central Committee and the VKP(b) [*Vsesoyuznaya Kommunisticheskaya Partiya (Bolshevikov)* – All-Union Communist Party (Bolsheviks) – the official name of the Communist Party prior to 1952]?!!

In general, he recounted the entire Party hierarchy for me. I replied, 'I know all that, but if you consider it a disgrace for a Party secretary to be a sentry and to observe the regulations, don't put him on sentry duty. I can't let the Germans surprise and wipe out the regiment.'

He exploded: 'Release Monin immediately! I order you to free him!' I replied with a certain satisfaction, 'I will not carry out your order. I am not your subordinate today. As the officer on watch, I report only to the regiment commander and will not release the prisoner.'

That was not the end of the story. The deputy political commander went directly to the regiment commander to complain about me. The attack was going to begin at any moment, but Khatchev summoned me. Vasilyev was present too. I reported on the essence of the matter. Khatchev agreed with me: 'You've done everything properly. However, you must release Monin. I sincerely request that you unlock him and let him out.'

So I released him. Such matters had to make you laugh to keep from crying. Vasilyev swallowed the bitter pill and to his credit, let it be said that he didn't hold a grudge against me. Generally, though, he was a good-for-nothing and a drunkard. He couldn't live an hour without booze.

Once I was riding with him in a Willys and he suddenly blurted out: 'Nevertheless, it has played a major role!'

'What?'

'The Party!'

At the same time, he would often stop the car, walk behind a bush, take a gulp from a flask, climb back into the car, drive on, and resume praising the Party again.

On the whole during the war, there were more political officers that were simply hard to figure out. For example, one of them would give a speech, calling upon the men to do the right thing – he seems to be making sense and understands people. When he would compile a recommendation letter for awards, though, he wouldn't fail to remember that Party members and *Komsomol* members were first in line for them – not those who had acted more bravely. Party status and spirit for these people were everything! Who actually did the fighting, whose blood was being spilled, whose sinews were tearing – none of that mattered to them.

The commanders? All three self-propelled artillery regiment commanders I fought under drank like hell. Khatchev's regiment was inspected at the end of the war. Seventeen daily vodka allotments for the entire regiment were missing! Fellow officers from adjacent regiments, from the brigade and from the division used to visit him, and he never failed to entertain any of them. I really don't think he'd been stealing the vodka rations, but somehow he always seemd to have a 'reserve'. Fortunately for Khatchev when the deficit was discovered, there was a German distillery nearby. The shortfall was quickly replenished, and he got away with it.

As soon as he got drunk, Khatchev liked to call for Masha the cook: 'Kharitonov, bring Masha to me!' Kharitonov – his freckled adjutant, also a Muscovite, would find her and start dragging her back, but she never wanted to go and would shout: 'Major Mateborsky, they're dragging me off to Khatchev!' Mateborsky was the chief of the rear services and wouldn't give a damn about it – this cook meant nothing to him. The deputy political commander also wouldn't stand up for her – he was a drunkard too.

However, I have digressed. On that morning of 23 October, we resumed the offensive with no let-up. All the armour rushed forward – of course, the first

German city was looming ahead of us! We captured Stalluponen [present-day Nesterov] on the same day! After that, the 28th Army and our 1435th Regiment stood on the defence until 13 January 1945.

The Final Offensive

On 13 January 1945 the East Prussian offensive began and our regiment went on the attack in the ranks of the 128th Rifle Corps.[1] On 20 January we captured the city of Gumbinnen [present-day Gusev] with a powerful attack. Over these six days of fierce fighting my battery supported the infantry of the 55th Guards Rifle Division. Lieutenant Novikov's crew destroyed three cannons and two tanks; the commander himself was wounded, but refused to leave the battlefield until a German armoured counter-attack aimed at the division's flank was repulsed. Lieutenant Klimov's crew wiped out a group of *faustniki* concealed in some bushes with their captured MG-42. My crew knocked out two enemy tanks and disabled an entire anti-aircraft battery that had been deployed for direct fire. We found out about it from a flak-gunner we'd taken prisoner. Nevertheless, all three self-propelled guns of the battery were badly damaged.

As soon as the action ceased the regiment deputy commander for technical services Major Suma rode up to the battery with a repair team. They repaired all the vehicles in about four hours. The major directed all the welding work himself. He was quite a chubby man, but he acted with surprising energy and speed! He demanded the same from his subordinates and considered it as a matter of honour for the maintenance and repair men to have every armoured vehicle ready for action.

The advance of our troops continued. On 22 January the city of Insterburg [present-day Chernyakhovsk] was taken. Our regiment became involved in the fighting for Insterburg too, but now with Lieutenant General Galitsky's 11th Guards Army, the 3rd Belorussian Front's second-echelon formation which had been committed to develop the attack towards Königsberg.[2] The Nazis were not only defending tenaciously, but also launched two counter-attacks. Having good positions, our regiment together with the Guards repulsed both counter-attacks without losing a single vehicle.

Without any pause in the operation we continued the advance the next day and captured the village of Gross Ottenhagen after a brief, but hard fight. During this action the regiment lost one SU-85; Kolya Polyakov's self-propelled gun burned out together with its entire crew. Two more self-propelled guns were knocked out, but were recovered and repaired during the night.

On 29 January, fierce fighting erupted for Tarau, a major railway station. Enemy anti-tank guns and Nashorn tank destroyers blocked the advance of our troops. My battery was advancing on the left flank of the shock grouping. A large wooden house was burning in front of us, creating a dense cloud of smoke. I ordered the commanders, 'Follow me!' and plunged through the wall of smoke with my battery. Once on the other side, I led the battery behind the brick station house, putting us on the enemy's flank.

From here we opened heavy fire on the defending enemy. The experienced German gunners quickly began to pivot the gun barrels towards us. They managed to knock out Fedya Klimov's vehicle, but realizing they'd been out-flanked and were now receiving heavy fire from two directions, they withdrew, leaving two smashed anti-tank guns and a badly damaged tank destroyer behind. We captured Tarau Station, but there were now only eight operational self-propelled guns left in the regiment. The army commander ordered the regiment to remain on this line and wait for replacements. The 11th Guards Army continued the advance along the Pregel River, but now without us.

That evening the regiment commander summoned his subordinate officers to a spacious building of the rail depot and gave us our orders:

> We will have to stay here at Tarau Station until we receive more self-propelled guns. Everyone is to exercise utmost vigilance! Encounters with German units escaping from pockets are not excluded. The chief of staff will organize reconnaissance in neighbouring areas and patrols both within and outside the regiment's location. Remember, and explain to your troops: these are not Nazis, but civilians. In this regard, deputy political commander Vasilyev is to conduct educational work with the personnel and the local population.

Back to Tanks from the Self-propelled Guns
We had to wait about a month for the replacement vehicles to arrive and were pretty much surprised when two steam engines pulled into the station with T-34/85 tanks on open platform cars. Twenty-one tanks instead of the expected self-propelled guns! It soon turned out that the regiment commander had already received an order from the *front* commander Marshal Vasilevsky to hand the arrived equipment over to the 1435th Self-propelled Artillery Regiment. Essentially our self-propelled gun regiment was being converted into a mixed tank/self-propelled gun regiment, since we still had eight SU-85s. The staff's intense work on forming crews and units began with the stipulation that at least one or two seasoned veterans would be present in each crew. The remaining self-propelled guns were combined into two batteries with four vehicles apiece. The battery commanders remained the same. Grin' and I – now without vehicles – were appointed as commanders of the 1st and the 3rd Tank Companies. Senior Lieutenant Nugin Muflikhanov became my tank commander. The driver was Sergeant Aleksandr Nesterov from Orel Oblast, the

gunlayer Ananiy Markov was from the Nenetskiy National District. Sergeant Fedor Tardenov from Omsk Oblast was the gunloader, and the radio operator – machine-gunner Corporal Ivan Lesovoy, was from Sumy Oblast.

Königsberg

Somewhere in the middle of March, our regiment arrived in the area of the 11th Guards Army's 16th Guards Rifle Corps and was attached to Major General Maksimov's 11th Guards Rifle Division. We spent the rest of the month advancing towards our ultimate objective Ponart, an ancient East Prussian town located just south of Königsberg. We had to break through five separate lines of pillboxes. The walls of those pillboxes were so thick that the shells of the tanks and self-propelled guns had little effect on them. We were forced to adopt the following tactics: interpreters and demolition teams would carefully approach the pillboxes, while our tanks bypassed and encircled them. Once surrounded, the defending occupants would be given a chance to surrender through the interpreter. Those who refused would be blown up together with the pillbox by emplaced demolition charges. The tactic proved to be slow but effective, without allowing enemy counter-attacks. Of course we were fortunate that we encountered neither tanks nor assault guns in these fortified districts.

At the end of March we captured the city of Godrinen and continued our advance, approaching Königsberg. Bloody fighting began. We would have to overcome two powerful defence lines, reinforced by tanks, assault guns and large numbers of artillery pieces. The regiment commander summoned the officers:

> Push your way through and don't turn! If you expose your flanks to fire, you're going to get burned! According to intelligence information, somewhere around here there are two Tigers – they may be concealed in shacks or even inside buildings. That's why you must destroy both shacks and houses. The main thing, though: don't let the *faustniki* get close! Rake every suspicious place with machine-gun fire from a safe distance.

Having heard the regiment commander's advice, I summoned the crews and informed them about the hidden Tigers and the combat tactics we should employ, and then added recommendations based on my own experience:

> Do not fire on the move; there's little chance of hitting your target and we have to conserve ammunition. We'll fire from short pauses and halts made at the gunlayer's order whenever he catches a target in his gunsight. Forget about using the scale on the turret ring: a

target might shift away before a gunlayer can take a reading and get back to his gunsight. If we spot a tank or anti-tank gun, we're going to race towards it at full speed, with zigzags. The speed affects the gunners – they get unnerved; the manoeuvres will throw off the aim of an enemy gunlayer, and glancing hits are not dangerous for a tank.

On the morning of 5 April, the preparatory artillery barrage began, in which the famous *Katyusha* and *Andryusha* rocket-launchers took part. Then a funny thing happened. A battalion of *Andryushas* fired one salvo, and a launch frame flew out together with a missile! The Germans shouted over the radio: 'Russians – you've gone crazy. You're hurling shacks at us!'

After a most intense artillery preparation, we went on the attack. The regiment commander's tank followed the combat formation of tanks and self-propelled guns, and from time to time issued orders to the units in the clear: it was simply impossible to use the code tables during combat.

My company was moving on the left flank. The tanks raced at high speed across a field, slightly weaving. Shells were exploding all around us. Glancing hits kept shaking the tank time and again, making us cringe. Thank God, though, that I didn't notice any panic among my comrades – and this was the main thing for success in combat!

Having leaped across the enemy trench line, we were now flying towards the artillery positions. Our infantry behind us was already engaging the enemy in fierce hand-to-hand fighting – those who had rifles worked with bayonet and rifle butt; others tossed hand grenades, while submachine-gunners who had run out of ammunition slashed at enemy heads with their submachine-gun barrels. The Germans began to pull back via communication trenches, unable to withstand such a fierce onslaught. The smoky haze from burning houses screened the tanks from anti-tank fire, and I ordered: 'Company! From a stop by the fence! At the shack, by salvo! Fire!'

The shack began to burn immediately, and the tank hidden inside it caught fire too. It jerked backwards, but stopped, engulfed in flames. However, it wasn't a Tiger – it was a Nashorn! None of its six crew members leaped out of it. The enemy guns were gradually neutralized as a result of the six-hour combat, although the enemy managed to knock out three of our tanks and a self-propelled gun. However, we had captured the first line of defence!

Incidentally, I had the opportunity to fight in SU-122 self-propelled guns for a long period of time, then in the SU-85. This may be controversial, but I can say that I preferred the self-propelled gun to the T-34/85, for it was 30 centimetres lower and lighter by one ton.

The tanks and the infantry took up favourable combat positions on the line attained and stopped. About two hours after the fighting stopped, our maintenance and repair team came around in two emergency repair vehicles – as always Major Suma with his deputy Captain Kulomzin was with them. All the damaged machines were put back into combat-readiness overnight, while the crews worked through the night to dig emplacements for the tanks. It was hellish work! The rocky ground refused to yield to the shovels and we had to move dozens of cubic metres of earth, or there would be no shelter for the machine from artillery and aviation. My new crew proved their worth superbly, though. In retrospect, I can say that the hands of tankers and self-propelled gunners were blistered throughout the war from all the constant digging.

Only by dawn did we have our vehicles emplaced, and it was just in time! Junker bombers came over almost as soon as we had finished. The regiment's positions were pounded from the air, but there was not a single direct hit.

The next day, the 11th Guards Rifle Division and our 1435th Self-propelled Artillery Regiment resumed the advance on Ponart. We had to break through a second, even more formidable defence line. The aviation and artillery preparation lasted for an hour and a half; we felt the earth shake even in our jumping-off positions. Battling our way through the defence line, we emerged on the southern outskirts of Ponart. Heavy street-fighting broke out – we were opposed by tanks and assault guns, and our infantry fired intensely from submachine-guns and machine guns at garrets, cellars and ground-floor windows, where tank hunters could be lurking with their panzerfausts.

The infantry division operating on the main axis received reinforcements in the form of ten JS-2 heavy tanks, which successfully engaged some Tigers in a meeting clash, while we, using our tanks and self-propelled guns, covered their flanks and tried to develop the success by driving into the depths of Ponart. The enemy artillery and tanks were firing fiercely, and our tank company came to a stop, returning fire from behind shelter. The advance stalled. I decided to emerge on the flank of the German tank formation by advancing my tank along a ravine and through some bushes. I thought by knocking out a few German tanks from this flank position, I could get the company moving again. However, my crew had managed to destroy only one German tank when two Panzer IV tanks turned up from somewhere behind us and set my tank ablaze.

'Abandon the vehicle!' I ordered the rest of the crew, and immediately tossed out a smoke grenade. As we were leaping from the burning machine, a German machine gun opened up, and although it was firing blindly, a bullet clipped my left shoulder. We started belly-crawling back to our friendlies, stopped in the ravine and Sasha Nesterov, my driver-mechanic, quickly bandaged my wound. By nightfall, when the fighting had ceased, I found Irina Krasnogir' – the regiment's senior surgeon, and now it was her turn to treat the wound and apply a thick bandage. I begged her not to tell her husband – chief of staff

Krasnogir' – or the regiment commander about my wound, so I could stay with my men. They never found out about it.

We continued fighting on the southern outskirts of Ponart for three days! The whole city was on fire, multi-storeyed buildings were collapsing, trees were falling, but the Germans kept resisting tenaciously and rejected our offered ultimatum. However, on the afternoon of 8 April, a large group emerged from a casemate in our sector. When they came closer to us, I began to talk to them in German, but they turned out to be French. They told me: 'We're from Alsace and Lorraine.' We took them prisoner. I told them about the current situation and they rejoiced to hear that we would take Berlin soon. Of course they'd been fighting on the German side, but they'd been conscripted, and they didn't want to fight for the Germans or especially to die for them. They sympathized with us, but couldn't do much about it. The Germans were brutal and might have shot them had something gone not to their liking.

On 9 April, the garrison of the fortress city of Königsberg capitulated. After the capture of Königsberg, our regiment was relocated to the vicinity of Pillkallen [present-day Dobrovol'sk] and stationed on an urban estate. We had to be at full combat-readiness, for entire enemy regiments and battalions were trying to break out of encirclement towards the Baltic shore, hoping to be evacuated by sea. In addition, the Germans were bringing in fresh troops by sea to try to open an escape route for surrounded units. In general we had to keep a sharp lookout and be ready for any contingency!

According to intelligence the enemy was planning a landing near the city of Rauschen [present-day Svetlogorsk] on the Baltic coast. On 7 May, when this information arrived, the regiment commander ordered me to move out with a rifle battalion and to occupy the city.

That night we slipped over to Rauschen. The city was being defended by a garrison, and from the sea it was being guarded by gunboats and apparently coastal pickets. The coastline here was quite high – perhaps about 100 metres. We dug emplacements for the main and reserve positions – generally speaking, we made ourselves ready.

We launched the attack suddenly, with no artillery preparation. The garrison put up fierce resistance. The action lasted for two hours, and three of our tanks were irrevocably destroyed before the Germans finally withdrew. There were many dead enemy troops and we took 200 soldiers and officers prisoner. We emerged on the coastline and the enemy's naval forces engaged us. We had to repulse the gunboats' attack. We sank two of them; the others withdrew and disappeared out to sea.

The town seemed to be desolated – not a single citizen! A dead place! Apparently all the civilian population had been evacuated by sea.

It was the same in other towns. The population was badly frightened. Initially, when we entered East Prussia, we saw German leaflets and posters that said: 'Death or Siberia!' They were afraid of Siberia and its extreme colds. Later, as we approached the Oder and the Germans were conducting total mobilization, their propaganda shifted to other slogans – everywhere there were posters with a Red Army soldier drawn from the waist up, wearing a helmet with a star on it. Below the figure were crossed bones and the slogan, 'Victory or death!' As a result, most of the population fled as we approached, and rarely would someone stay.

We strolled along the streets of Rauschen and did some sightseeing. It was purely a resort town, well-furnished for leisure. Asphalt roads snaked down the slope to the sea. In the centre of the city there was – I remember it well even now – a large, rectangular pond; perhaps it is still there.

We returned to Pillkallen on the evening of 8 May. The next morning, 9 May 1945, we woke up early from excited shouts. Chief of staff Major Krasnogir' ran into the officers' quarters and shouted: 'Guys! That's it! The war is over! That's all! It's the end!'

We rushed outside, and it is hard to describe all that was going on out there! Everyone was firing into the air from all sorts of weapons. There was dancing, leaping, and accordions were playing! The regiment commander ordered the preparation of a celebratory dinner. Our commissaries displayed a lot of zeal, and our two regimental cooks, Masha from Michurinsk and Fedor Yashmanov from the Vyatska region managed to prepare a lavish feast. Masha, who was respected by all of us, did her best and prepared a splendid Ukrainian borsch and some cold appetizers. Using whatever we had available – meat, potatoes and American Spam – Fedor even managed to prepare two second courses! Our comedian Sergeant Shokhin from Moscow Oblast parodied Fedor's unusual accent to everyone's delight: 'Felloos! Come oon, get your stoof, goo away and don't be ooffended!

The chief of rear services Mateborsky and his deputy Gulev supplied drinks, and everyone was given not the usual front-line ration of 100 grams of vodka, but a full glass. Only later did I realize that we had fired our regiment's final shot on 8 May 1945 back in Rauschen.

The Days of Peace ...

Peacetime finally arrived, but there were troubles and incidents. We received an order to forage locally for food, so vehicles began to roam all over East Prussia picking up hens, geese, piglets, calves, grain, peas; in general, anything and everything edible. Only just recently, we had been warned not to eat anything obtained locally, which had supposedly all been poisoned. Of course we cleaned out all the local sources of food very quickly. So, we had to contrive something.

We began to form fishing crews and switched to eating flounder quite willingly. The most difficult was the situation with the bread supply, especially when the breadpans at the bakeries were greased with motor oil because of a lack of butter.

Then 'ChP' [Russian initials for 'extraordinary occurrences', which can mean any sort of accident, disaster, or unfortunate event] incidents began to intrude. Three of our sergeants raped a 12-year-old German girl called Kristal.

I must acknowledge that rapes did take place. It was so disgraceful that I don't even want to talk about it now. There was a Muscovite among us called Zhora Kirichev, a self-propelled gun commander. Back when we had entered Gross Ottenhagen, the infantry had continued on ahead, but we had to stop to refuel and replenish our ammunition. While there, some sergeant major was escorting about 300 German females down the street. Zhora was ogling the women. The sergeant major called out to him, 'Go ahead and take the cutest one!'

Zhora didn't hesitate and picked one out. He took her away, and several days later came down with a case of the clap. At the time there was a standing order: once you caught VD, you would be sent into a penal battalion. A doctor treated Zhora and recorded that his case was an exacerbation of an old illness. Otherwise he wouldn't have escaped being sent to a penal battalion. He was teased over this for quite some time later: 'You're a fool! You should have chosen the ugliest one – you would have gotten away with it!'

So, it was unsafe to go for the German women. I refused to rape because of moral principles. When three of our sergeants perpetrated the rape, Khatchev summoned me and ordered me to conduct an investigation. How could I do it?! I didn't even have a dictionary!

I arrived at the girl's house, and became acquainted with her mother, Anna. Then I conversed mostly with her. Rather I should say that I spent about three days trying to question her; it was difficult to communicate without a dictionary. If I didn't know the right word, I had to find some way to express it. It was like trying to get to Berlin via Vladivostok.

I conducted the investigation after a fashion and took an interest in their traditions. Anna told me that people there met each other the same way as in our country – say, at a party. Then they'd go out together, and eventually get married. However, if a husband determined that he wanted a divorce, he had no right to do so until he had found another husband for his wife.

Anna was smoking cigarettes, so I asked her: '*Warum Sie rauchen?*' [Why are you smoking?] She explained that she had begun to smoke after her husband's death, and now she couldn't give it up.

They showed me a vestry book [*Kirschbuch*] – a large, thick book filled with the genealogy of the people's lineal lines recorded over several centuries: birth dates, marriages, death dates. A huge church seal was on every sheet, verifying the validity of the records.

Unlike townsfolk, who had fled as we approached, the peasants had remained – how can one abandon his farm, his animals? So we socialized with the farmers. On the whole, what can I say? They were more civilized. First of all, how responsible and orderly they were, and all this in the countryside! Everywhere it was neat and clean, everything was in its proper place, so unlike our corner of the world, where everything is always so messy that it is embarrassing to walk through it, even in the city, not to mention the village. I checked out a cattle shed once – all the cattle were thoroughly groomed. Every farmstead had a diesel engine, and it did all the work: threshing, milling the flour, and producing fodder for the cattle. Everything was mechanized! A farmer just had to switch various attachments – and all would go swimmingly! Secondly, they made our Michurin out almost to be a god of some sort.[3] Their every peasant was a follower of Michurin. Their wheat was so bountiful. You'd climb up into a garret and find an enormous pile of grain. Simple peasants were hybridizing cherries with currants! One more thing – fine asphalt roads ran everywhere. You could drive to any village, town or city, from the smallest to the largest, on asphalt roads.

Our soldiers said nothing about the local life, preferring to hold their tongues, because it was forbidden to praise anything German. I kept silent, too.

I wrote out a report on the results of my investigation for the regiment commander and presented them verbally. Khatchev placed those three sergeants under arrest for five days – and that was it! Apparently, he spared them because he knew that the Germans used to rape our women and girls too.

On one September day we posed for photographs for keepsakes, and handed our tanks and self-propelled guns over to the units which would be staying behind in East Prussia. Then the self-propelled gun crews left for Nikolaev, the tankers – to Slutsk, and I was sent to Leningrad, to the Higher School for Officers ...

Time goes by. Already sixty years have elapsed since the last salvoes of the Great Patriotic War, and a lot has changed in the country and in the life of all of us over this time. Fate scattered the brothers-in-arms to different corners of our immense country. It's been sad to find out at each reunion that someone else has passed away. However, every reunion was an exciting event, full of discovering new details about past battles, revealing new facts and events of which we were not only unaware, but couldn't even imagine. The final day of each reunion always wound up with a farewell party, featuring the unforgettable 'front-line 100 grams'. By now our joint trips to the battlefields have slipped into the past, and about fifteen years ago our reunions in Moscow also ended. It is sad that twenty years ago I used to send more than a hundred Victory Day greeting postcards, and now I send only ten of them ...

However, all those who have passed on are still alive for me. They live in my heart and in my memory, and this book was written mostly on the basis of memories that still recall the way my combat comrades looked back in those 'fateful forties'. They have also preserved their military valour and their indescribable front-line bonds. Even now, with a stirring in my heart, I can see my brothers-in-arms on the attack, just as if it happened yesterday – and I bow my head before the living and the dead.

Notes

Chapter One: My Journey to the Front
1. The inside of the turret ring within the tank was marked with a scale, which guided the gunlayer to point the gun in a particular direction.

Chapter Two: Stalingrad
1. This was the *X let Oktyabrya* [Tenth Year of October] State Farm, located approximately 12 kilometres (or 7.2 miles) north-east of Kalach-on-the-Don.
2. The 1st Tank Army's counter-attack blunted the southward drive of the German XIV Panzer Corps towards Kalach. The State Farm and Lozhki were likely being defended by the 60th Motorized Division.

Chapter Three: Kursk 1943
1. It was not uncommon for Red Army tank crew members, particularly the gunloader, to pass out during heavy combat from the fumes from the gun and the ejected shell casing.
2. While it is true that the Germans had Tigers, Panthers and Ferdinands at Kursk, the Panthers were all with Army Group South on the other side of the Kursk salient.
3. On the morning of 7 July 1943, the 307th Rifle Division's positions screened Ponyri Station and ran east through 1st of May State Farm and Hill 257.1 to Nikol'skoye 2. The area around 1st of May State Farm and Hill 257.1 was attacked by the 86th Infantry Division with armoured support and support from the Ferdinands of the 656th Heavy Panzerjäger Regiment. The 129th Tank Brigade, to which the 1454th Self-propelled Artillery Regiment was attached, was in the second echelon, supporting the first echelon with fire and prepared to launch counter-attacks.
4. This is a reference to the German remotely-controlled demolition vehicle, the *Sd.Kfz. 302/303 [Sonderkraftfahrzug* – Special Purpose Vehicle], known as the Goliath. Packing 75 to 100 kilograms of high explosives, this miniature caterpillar-tracked vehicle was steered to the target by a controller via a telephone cable attached to the rear of the vehicle.
5. Known familiarly as 'limonka' [lemon] because of its shape, the F-1 was an anti-personnel fragmentation grenade.

Chapter Five: To the Dnieper River, August-September 1943
1. Krysov is describing the German 7.92mm *Panzerbüsche* 39, which fired high-velocity, steel-core cartridges, capable of penetrating almost 36mm of face-hardened armour plate at 100 yards.

2. Bogdan Khmel'nitsky (1595–1657) was a Cossack hetman who led an uprising against Polish-Lithuanian magnates with the aim of establishing an independent Ukraine, and later agreed to the Ukraine's incorporation into the Russian Empire.
3. Central Archive of the Ministry of Defence, Russian Federation [TsAMO], f. 420, op. 54236, d. 5, l. 28.

Chapter Eight: The Pursuit to Fastov

1. After the liberation of Kiev, the 1st Ukrainian Front's forces were pushed aggressively in diverging directions towards the south-west and west, dispersing its strength and creating an exposed salient – an inviting target for von Manstein. As Krysov continues his account, we can see how fluid and confusing the situation was in the immediate aftermath of Kiev's recapture.
2. Elements of the 1st SS Panzer Division *Leibstandarte Adolf Hitler* reported clearing the town of Popel'nya of Russian forces by 10.00 on 14 November 1943. See Rudolf Lehmann, *The Leibstandarte III: 1st SS Panzer Division Leibstandarte Adolf Hitler* (Winnipeg, Canada: J.J. Fedorowicz Publishing, 1990), p. 317.

Chapter Nine: Von Manstein Attempts Another 'Backhand Blow'

1. XXXXVIII Panzer Corps' 1st SS Panzer Division *Leibstandarte Adolf Hitler* had been ordered to attack Krakovshchina and to capture the town of Brusilov on the night leading to 20 November 1943.
2. This is undoubtedly Hill 185.6, described as being 3 kilometres south-west of Brusilov in Lehmann, *Leibstandarte III*, p. 330.
3. The 1st SS Panzer Division *Leibstandarte Adolf Hitler*'s 2nd SS Panzer Grenadier Regiment attacked Brusilov on 20 November from the direction of Morozovka with Tiger support. Evidence to support Krysov's claim of knocking out eight Tigers with his platoon here is sparse. The SU-85's main gun was certainly capable of penetrating the Tiger's side armour, especially from close range. If these were all Tigers, then this was a significant blow to the 1st SS Panzer Division *Leibstandarte Adolf Hitler*. In November 1943, the 1st SS Panzer Division had on paper ninety-five Panzer IVs, ninety-six Panzer V Panthers and twenty-seven Panzer VI tanks (see Thomas L. Jentz (ed.), *Panzer Truppen 2: The Complete Guide to the Creation & Combat Employment of Germany's Tank Force, 1943–1945* (Arglen, PA: Schiffer Military History, 1996)), p. 117. Lehmann's history of the 1st SS Panzer Division doesn't mention the loss of eight Tigers on 20 November 1943 south of Brusilov, though it does mention armoured losses, some of which were recovered and successfully put back into operation. However, 1st SS Panzer Division was clearly suffering significant attrition in its complement of Tigers, since by 23 November 1943 it was reporting only four serviceable Tigers (see Lehmann, *Leibstandarte III*, p. 333). As for the non-lethal penetration of an armour-piercing round fired by a Tiger at long range, in war anything is possible.
4. In fact, the 1st SS Panzer Division's orders for 22 November 1943 were to leave a thin defensive screen south of Brusilov and move the bulk of 2nd SS Panzer Grenadier Regiment to Divin for a subsequent thrust towards Yastreben'ka. So

again, Krysov's self-propelled artillery regiment would be facing an attack from the same opponent it had confronted in front of Brusilov on 20–21 November. See Lehmann, *Leibstandarte III*, p. 331.

5. According to the 1st SS Panzer Division's records, the reinforced 2nd SS Panzer Grenadier Regiment set out for its attack on Yastreben'ka at 05.55, with the support of three Tigers. It reported heavy contact and strong anti-tank fire from its front and flank between 08.15 and 10.05 hours, when 'the attack got stuck in the enemy's overwhelming fire from weapons of all calibres'. See Lehmann, *Leibstandarte III*, p. 332.

6. The SU-85 tank destroyer was built on the chassis of the T-34 tank.

7. At 11.30 hours, *Leibstandarte*'s 1st SS Panzer Regiment reported that it had twenty-five Panzer IV tanks of its II Battalion in Divin ready for action. These were subordinated to *Obersturmführer* Kraas' 2nd Panzer Grenadier Regiment. The 2nd Panzer Grenadier Regiment launched a second attack at 13.05, which succeeded in breaking into Yastreben'ka at 16.15. Clearly, this is the 'avalanche of advancing armour' witnessed by Krysov, and the 1st SS Panzer Division's records match Krysov's account rather closely at this point. See Lehmann, *Leibstandarte III*, p. 332.

Chapter Thirteen: The July 1944 Offensive on the Kovel Axis

1. While most of the Army Group North Ukraine's panzer divisions had moved wholesale northward to try to plug the gaping holes torn into Army Group Centre by Operation Bagration launched two weeks previously, a cursory examination of German daily situational maps conducted by David Glantz shows that the 5th SS Panzer Division *Wiking* left behind a *kampfgruppe* [combat group] in the sector of the 129th Rifle Corps. Kampfgruppe Muehlenkamp was equipped with up to twenty Panthers and a few Tigers at the time, though it received additional Panthers and Tigers over the next three weeks, bringing its total strength to forty-two Panthers and two Tigers by 1 August 1944. The presence of Kampfgruppe Muehlenkamp accounts for the tanks and assault guns encountered by Krysov's 1454th Self-propelled Artillery Regiment on Hill 197.2. I want to thank David Glantz for this information.

2. SMERSH is the Russian contraction of *Smert' shpionam* [Death to spies], and was the Russian counter-intelligence branch within the Red Army. It had a presence in all Red Army units at this point in the war.

Chapter Fourteen: From the Western Bug to Siedlce, Poland

1. Again, this was most likely the 5th SS Panzer Division *Wiking*'s *kampfgruppe*, which had evidently conducted a fighting withdrawal from the Kovel area.

2. It is unclear what Krysov claims to have encountered on the Lukow–Brest road; the situation was extremely fluid, but it appears as if there might be some under-standable exaggeration present here. One possibility is that Krysov's platoon stumbled upon the rear echelon, artillery and command vehicles of SS *Totenkopf*'s Panzer *Abteilung* 3, which attacked southward east of Siedlce on 28 July, just as the

165th Rifle Division's forward elements were reaching the Lukow–Brest road. The panzer *abteilung*, a reinforced battalion-sized unit, ran into the 1st Ukrainian Front's advancing 11th Tank Corps, 2nd Guards Cavalry Corps and forward elements of the 165th Rifle Division, before disappearing from the German daily situational maps thereafter. Again, I want to thank David Glantz for this information.

3. This is the short-hand reference used by Red Army soldiers to apply to any Soviet turncoats fighting for the German side, even though many were not actually members of former Red Army General A.A. Vlasov's Russian Liberation Army.

4. These were undoubtedly panzers of the 3rd SS Panzer Division *Totenkopf*, which had been rushed to Siedlce to try to blunt the 1st Ukrainian Front's northward thrust from the Western Bug to isolate the 'fortress city' of Brest.

5. Actually, the 11th Tank Corps and the 2nd Guards Cavalry Corps were already in this area when the forward elements of the 47th Army's 129th Rifle Corps arrived. Krysov was simply unaware of that.

Chapter Fifteen: In East Prussia

1. The 128th Rifle Corps' adversary for the offensive towards Gumbinnen was the Hermann Goering Panzer Corps, although its Hermann Goering Panzer Division deployed near Insterburg was withdrawn and sent elsewhere, primarily to Poland, soon after the operation began. The Gumbinnen–Insterburg–Königsberg axis was unquestionably the most heavily defended sector in East Prussia, and the 28th Army would have to punch through dense fortifications manned initially by the 61st Infantry Division. The 5th Panzer Division and 56th Infantry Divisions would shift to the Gumbinnen–Insterburg axis as soon as it became clear that this was the major Soviet thrust on the northern sector. For a good discussion of this operation, see David M. Glantz, ed., *The 1986 Art of War Symposium: From the Vistula to the Oder: Soviet Offensive Operations, October 1944–March 1945, A Transcript of Proceedings* (Carlisle, PA: Center for Land Warfare, U.S. Army War College, 1986), pp. 302–337.

2. Stymied by forests, fortifications and tenacious defensive resistance on the direct Gumbinnen–Insterburg route, 3rd Belorussian Front commander Chernyakhovsky directed Galitsky's 11th Guards Army to a bridgehead over the Inster River north of Insterburg, which outflanked German defenders on the Gumbinnen–Insterburg axis. 11th Guards Army then became the main shock force for the subsequent advance on Königsberg. Its primary adversary during this advance continued to be the 5th Panzer Division.

3. Ivan Vladimirovich Michurin (1855–1935) was a noted Russian botanist and practitioner of selection, famous for his work on hybridization and cultivation methods.

Index